Ethereum™

by Michael G. Solomon

for
dummies®
A Wiley Brand

Ethereum™ For Dummies®

Published by: **John Wiley & Sons, Inc.,** 111 River Street, Hoboken, NJ 07030-5774, www.wiley.com

Copyright © 2019 by John Wiley & Sons, Inc., Hoboken, New Jersey

Published simultaneously in Canada

For general information on our other products and services, please contact our Customer Care Department within the U.S. at 877-762-2974, outside the U.S. at 317-572-3993, or fax 317-572-4002. For technical support, please visit https://hub.wiley.com/community/support/dummies.

Wiley publishes in a variety of print and electronic formats and by print-on-demand. Some material included with standard print versions of this book may not be included in e-books or in print-on-demand. If this book refers to media such as a CD or DVD that is not included in the version you purchased, you may download this material at http://booksupport.wiley.com. For more information about Wiley products, visit www.wiley.com.

Library of Congress Control Number: 2019936125

ISBN 978-1-119-47412-8 (pbk); ISBN 978-1-119-47411-1 (ebk); ISBN 978-1-119-47406-7 (ebk)

Manufactured in the United States of America

C10008978_032119

Contents at a Glance

Table of Contents

Introduction

Blockchain technology is one of the most talked about disruptive technologies of the decade, and Ethereum is the most popular blockchain implementation. Blockchain technology holds the promise of making business interactions faster, cheaper, and more trustworthy.

Ethereum For Dummies introduces blockchain and Ethereum, covers their effect on today's ways of doing business, and teaches you how to design and develop your own Ethereum decentralized applications. You learn how to set up a development environment and write smart contracts that create and control transactions on the Ethereum blockchain.

About This Book

Blockchain technology has the potential to change how business operates. The unprecedented opportunities blockchain promises to provide include easy data sharing among large groups, transparency, trusted transactions, and complete historical audit trails. Today, most organizations protect transaction data as a valued asset, but sharable data could change everything. Sharing trusted data with many participants in a business process has the potential of revolutionizing how organizations interact with one another, reducing the need and cost of middlemen and providing unprecedented transparency to business processes.

Staying current and pertinent means becoming part of this emerging blockchain business model. *Ethereum For Dummies* gives you the foundation of blockchain and Ethereum, and teaches you, in clear language, how to design and write your own software for the Ethereum blockchain environment.

Foolish Assumptions

I don't make many assumptions about your experience with blockchain technology, application programming, or cryptography, but I do assume the following:

>> You have a computer and access to the Internet.

>> You know the basics of using your computer and the Internet, and how to download and install programs.

>> You know how to find files on your computer's disk and how to create folders.

>> You're new to blockchain and you aren't an experienced software developer. If you already know how to write software applications, you can skip the sections on programming basics.

Icons Used in This Book

TIP

The Tip icon marks tips (duh!) and shortcuts that you can use to make learning and using Ethereum and Solidity easier.

REMEMBER

Remember icons mark the information that's especially important to know. To siphon off the most important information in each chapter, just skim through these icons.

TECHNICAL STUFF

The Technical Stuff icon marks information of a highly technical nature that you can normally skip over.

WARNING

The Warning icon tells you to watch out! It marks important information that may save you headaches when writing your own blockchain applications.

Beyond the Book

In addition to the material in the print or e-book you're reading right now, this product also comes with some access-anywhere goodies on the web. Check out the free cheat sheet for more on Ethereum and Solidity at www.dummies.com/cheatsheet/ethereumfd.

You'll find summary information on Ethereum and Solidity tools as well as tips on how to use them effectively. The cheat sheet is a reference to use over and over as you gain experience in developing Ethereum decentralize applications.

In addition, if you'd rather download the code you see in this book instead of typing it, go to `www.dummies.com/go/ethereumfd`. You can download zip files for each of the projects you'll create to develop and test smart contracts.

Where to Go from Here

The *Dummies* series tells you what you need to know and how to do the things you need to do to get the results you want. Readers don't have to read the entire book to just learn about some topics. For example, if you just want to learn about smart contracts, you can jump right to Chapters 8 and 9. On the other hand, if you need to set up your own development environment, read Part 2, which tells you how to do that with clear, step-by-step instructions.

1
Getting to Know Blockchain and Ethereum

Get a big-picture overview of the Ethereum blockchain and how it works.

Discover how blockchain technology addresses distributed application problems.

Explore use cases that are good fits for blockchain technology.

Chapter **1**

Introducing Ethereum

B lockchain technology is the most disruptive technology introduced in our generation, and Ethereum is by far the most popular blockchain implementation in use today. You can't read many technology articles or blogs without seeing something about how blockchain changes everything. Although some claims seem to be a little far-fetched, blockchain technology really is a game-changer.

Blockchain, which first burst on the scene in 2008, has gained global notoriety for what it has already changed and what is coming. At first, blockchain was all about a new type of electronic currency. But now, partially thanks to Ethereum, blockchain is so much more than a new way to pay for things. It's a new way to think about things. It enables people and businesses to conduct business without many of the obstacles that have existed in trade relations for centuries.

In this book you learn about what blockchain is and why it is viewed as so radical. You discover how powerful Ethereum is in diverse domains and how you can harness its promise and power in your own organizations. If you want to learn what Ethereum is and how it can work for you without having to trudge through hundreds of pages of theory and background, this is the book for you.

Describing Blockchain Technology

You learn a lot more about blockchain technology in Chapter 2, but before you meet Ethereum, you need to know a little of Ethereum's backstory.

TIP

If you already know what blockchain is, this section will be like watching yet another depiction of why Bruce Wayne became Batman. Feel free to skim it and move on to the next section. There are only so many ways you can kill Thomas and Martha Wayne.

Blockchain technology was introduced to support a new type of digital currency that you can trade in a trustless environment. Traditional currency exchanges require a trusted third party between the parties. Even if a buyer provides coins or bills to a seller at the point of transaction, some government provides the guarantee of the currency's value. There is always a middleman. If the exchange involves a payment card or check, other financial institutions participate to handle the transfer of funds between parties.

In 2008, Satoshi Nakamoto published a paper that changed everything. Nakamoto's paper described a new way to store and distribute data with verifiable integrity among a group of nodes that don't trust one another. You learn more about how Nakamoto's proposal works, and about bitcoin, the cryptocurrency proposed in the paper, in Chapter 2. At this point, the most important takeaway is that this paper showed how to take the requirement for a trusted (and omnipotent) central authority out of the mix. Using this new technology, called blockchain, application developers can create environments in which nodes that do not trust one another can share data that they can trust.

The idea is based on several concepts that are simple to consider but difficult to put into practice. First, data is logically presented as a ledger. The data isn't really stored that way; you can just think of it as a ledger. A ledger is a way of recording data as transactions occur. One interesting feature of this ledger is that you can only add data to it. You can't change anything after you've added it. So, the only two operations you can perform on this ledger are add and read. We refer to the "add only" property as the *immutability property*. In short, blockchains are immutable. As you'll see, immutability is crucial for the technique to work.

Another feature is that data is added to this ledger in blocks. *Blocks* are collections of transactions, each with an owner's address. *Addresses* are the unique IDs of accounts in our ledger system. When there are enough transactions to make a new block, some of the blockchain participants begin a process of adding a new block to the ledger. Each new block is linked to the previous block, making a chain. That's where the term blockchain comes from. A *blockchain* is basically a bunch of blocks where each block is connected to its predecessor.

Then, the entire set of blocks, or the entire blockchain, is shared with other participants. These participants are called *nodes.* These nodes communicate with one another and each stores an exact copy of the blockchain. Many blockchain networks are made up of thousands of nodes, and keeping all of the copies of the blockchain in *sync* (that is, ensuring that every copy is the same) is another revolutionary feature of blockchain technology.

Blockchain technology is built on a *democracy governance mode.* Before any new block is added to the blockchain, a majority of nodes must agree that the new block is valid. All nodes agree to accept the majority decision. That's how the blockchain stays in sync. Nodes essentially vote on all new blocks. Different blockchains use different voting methods, but one of the more common ones requires nodes to solve very hard mathematical puzzles to earn the right to add a new block to the blockchain. As an incentive for doing the hard work, the node that solves the puzzle first gets a reward. The reward encourages nodes to pitch in and help do the hard work of solving verification puzzles.

Part of the puzzle solution involves creating a mathematical hash of the previous block. By storing the previous block's hash in the current block, every node can quickly determine if any block has changed. Each node periodically scans the blockchain to ensure that nothing has changed. This is how nodes can be sure that the blockchain is the same across the entire network. And, because no block can change after it is added to the blockchain, you never have to worry about overwriting data.

Putting it all together, a blockchain makes it possible to share a set of data with many nodes that you don't trust. You can trust the democracy of the network, though. As long as you can trust that more than half of the nodes on the blockchain network are going to be honest, you can trust the blockchain.

The last big advantage to blockchain technology is that you can put rules of operation in blocks on the blockchain as well. These rules are called *smart contracts.* A smart contract is just a program that lives in a blockchain block and governs how data is added to the blockchain. Because all blockchain data is immutable, even the smart contract code is immune from changes. That's how you can exchange currency without a bank. As long as there are rules that dictate how a currency exchange is carried out, transaction data can be recorded on the blockchain and be part of the permanent ledger.

For example, suppose you want to buy a car. You have enough digital currency in your blockchain account to buy the car, and the car owner has the car's title stored in the blockchain. You can offer to buy the car and if the seller accepts your offer, a smart contract handles the transaction. The smart contract would verify that the title is owned by the seller and that you have enough money in your account to make the purchase. If those two requirements are met, the smart contract would transfer the sales amount into the seller's account and transfer the title to your account. Without any middleman, you have purchased a car and paid for it without carrying a wad of cash around.

TIP

Of course, you really purchased a title to a car. Blockchain handles digital assets. You still have to physically get the keys and the car from the seller.

Introducing Ethereum

Bitcoin was the first blockchain technology application. It was revolutionary and defined the first widely used digital currency, called *cryptocurrency*. The *crypto* part of the name refers to the use of cryptographic hashes to ensure the integrity of the blockchain. The shared ledger literally keeps a copy of every cryptocurrency transaction that gets verified by all nodes. Using this approach, bitcoin created a permanent record of every exchange of their cryptocurrency. And, because account owners are identified only by an address, bitcoin has always enjoyed a measure of anonymity.

TECHNICAL STUFF

Although bitcoin addresses aren't linked directly to people, many exchanges have records of identities that are related to addresses. At some point, you have to exchange your cryptocurrency for real currency. That switchover point is where many law enforcement officials focus when they're trying to track down criminals using cryptocurrency.

As bitcoin became more and more popular, researchers began to see more applications for blockchain technology beyond cryptocurrency. In 2013, Vitalik Buterin, the cofounder of *Bitcoin Magazine,* published a whitepaper that proposed a new, more functional blockchain implementation. This new proposal was for the Ethereum blockchain. After gaining interest and attracting technical and financial support, the Ethereum Foundation, a Swiss non-profit organization, was founded and became the developer of Ethereum.

Ethereum wasn't created just to exchange cryptocurrency. In fact, it was designed from the beginning to be different. The core features of Ethereum are the smart contract and ether. *Ether* is the native cryptocurrency that Ethereum supports, although you can create your own tokens to exchange value in many other forms. Smart contracts provide an execution environment that ensures integrity across all nodes. Any code that executes on one node executes the same way on all nodes. This guarantee makes it possible to deploy a wide range of applications across untrusted environments.

The foundational guarantees Ethereum provides support many types of value exchanges without the concern about fraud, censorship, or any involvement by a third party. When you interact with an Ethereum application, you don't have to rely on any intermediary to broker your transactions. You don't need a bank, wholesaler, or transaction broker to provide trust. As a result of Ethereum's *disintermediation,* you can often complete transactions faster, with far lower service fees and without requiring approval from external authorities.

Ethereum is a comprehensive, decentralized application platform that expands the range of capabilities beyond what was possible before blockchain technology. Whereas legacy solutions to data and process sharing required third-party authorities to enforce integrity, Ethereum provides process and data integrity, along with disintermediation. The possibilities are just beginning to be explored.

Exploring Ethereum's Consensus, Mining, and Smart Contracts

Ethereum provides integrity in the way it implements immutability and smart contracts. Immutability isn't actually a blockchain guarantee. You can change data in any block — even after other blocks are added to the blockchain. However, as soon as you change a block, that block and all subsequent blocks fail integrity checks and your node is out of sync. Instead of saying that the blockchain is immutable, it is more accurate to say that any changes (mutations) to the blockchain are easily and immediately detected.

Ethereum is based on democracy. Each node gets an equal vote. Every time nodes get a new block to add to the blockchain, they validate the block and its transactions, and then vote whether to accept or reject the block. If several different blocks are submitted by different nodes, only one of the blocks can receive votes from a majority. The block that gets more than half of the network node's votes gets to join the blockchain as its newest block.

One of the first problems is to determine when a new block is ready for the blockchain. When too many conflicting blocks are submitted, the voting process slows down. Ethereum makes it hard to add new blocks to keep the number of new block collisions low and to make voting faster. Ethereum uses a consensus protocol called *Proof of Work (PoW)*, which sets the rules for validating and adding new blocks. PoW makes add blocks to the blockchain difficult but profitable.

Ethereum defines ether as its cryptocurrency. You can transfer ether between accounts or earn it by doing the hard work of adding blocks to the Ethereum blockchain. The Ethereum PoW mechanism requires that nodes find a number that, when combined with the block's header data, produces a cryptographic hash value that matches the current target, which is a value that is adjusted to keep new block production at a steady rate. Finding a hash value that matches the current target is hard. You have to try on average more than a quadrillion values to find the right one. That's the point. Using a PoW mechanism makes it so hard to submit a block that fewer blocks are submitted, which reduces the number of collisions. The node that finds the right value gets a small ether payment for the effort. This process is called *mining,* and the node that wins the prize is that block's *miner.*

Mining regulates the speed at which new blocks get submitted as candidate blocks, and results in a number that is easy to validate. Finding the right number to solve the puzzle is difficult, but verifying the number is fast and easy. Another interesting aspect of mining is that each block's header contains a hash from the previous block. Ethereum nodes use the hash to easily detect unauthorized block changes. If a block changes, the hash result doesn't match and the block becomes invalid.

Mining is also a way to make money using blockchain technology. Mining has become competitive, and most of today's miners invest in high-performance hardware with multiple GPUs to carry out the complex operations. To keep the mining process fair, Ethereum uses a complexity value that makes the mining process even harder as miners get faster. Adjusting the complexity allows Ethereum to regulate the new block frequency to an average of one new block every 14 seconds.

The glue that holds the Ethereum environment together is the smart contract. Ethereum is much more than just a financial ledger, and smart contracts provide much of its rich functionality. Each Ethereum node runs a copy of the *Ethereum virtual machine (EVM).* The EVM runs smart contract code in a way that guarantees that smart contracts execute the same way on all nodes and produce the same output. Running smart contract code is not optional. Smart contracts execute based on specific rules and cannot be subverted or halted. The EVM smart contract guarantees provide a stable platform for automated transaction processing that you can trust. Smart contracts provide the primary power of the Ethereum environment.

One of the known weaknesses with software is that attackers can sometimes bypass its controls and carry out unintended actions. That type of attack is more difficult in Ethereum, primarily due to its smart contract implementation. Attackers can't directly attack the blockchain and make unauthorized changes because any such changes will be immediately detected. The next most likely attack vector is the smart contract interface to the blockchain data. Ethereum guarantees that smart contract code, which is translated into *bytecode* before it is written to the blockchain, executes on every EVM instance the same way. Also, the EVM determines when code executes and what code executes. Attackers have few opportunities to leverage smart contract code, which makes Ethereum an even more secure environment.

Buying, Spending, and Trading Ether

Ethereum runs on ether (ETH), its main cryptocurrency. The majority of all existing ether was pre-mined when Ethereum first went live on July 30, 2015. Miners continually create ether, but the amount of mined ether is less than 30 percent of all ether in existence. The lifecycle of Ethereum transactions requires that you first acquire ether to participate in Ethereum. Many exchanges support exchanging legal tender, also called *fiat currency,* for cryptocurrency, including ether. You can navigate to https://99bitcoins.com/best-ethereum-exchange-review-comparison for an independent comparison of several popular exchanges.

Before you can interact with the Ethereum blockchain, you need to create at least one account. Creating an Ethereum account is essentially just creating a cryptographic private and public key pair, and generating the associated address, which is based on your public key. The software that handles this process is called an Ethereum *wallet.* You learn about different options for Ethereum wallets in Chapter 6. You can use a wallet provided by an exchange or a standalone wallet. After you create your Ethereum account, you'll need to select an exchange to purchase ether.

After you select an exchange, you set up an exchange account and provide a funding source. Your main funding source is generally a bank account. The most common way to buy ether is to withdraw funds from your bank account and use that money to exchange for ether. Figure 1-1 shows the purchase ether web page for the coinbase.com exchange. Note that the funding source for this account is a Bank of America account.

You can also purchase ether using cash. A growing number of cryptocurrency ATMs allow you to exchange cash for different types of cryptocurrency. All you need is the private key you generated using your Ethereum wallet and cash. However, you will pay for this convenience. Cryptocurrency ATMs often use exchange rates that are less favorable than more traditional exchanges. One current service, localcoin ATM, works just like a regular ATM. Navigate to https://localcoinatm.com to see where you can find ATMs and how to use them. Figure 1-2 shows several steps in the process of purchasing ether with cash from an ATM.

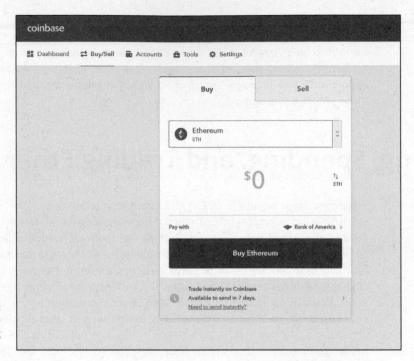

FIGURE 1-1:
Purchase
ether using
coinbase.com.

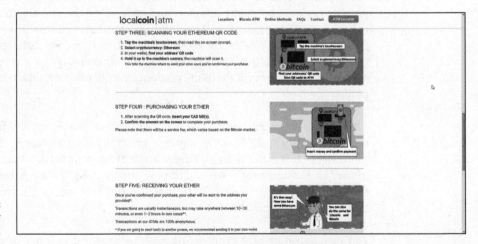

FIGURE 1-2:
Purchasing ether
with cash.

After you own ether, you can interact with other Ethereum accounts and send them some of your ether in exchange for good or services. Or you can simply hold on to your ether in hopes that is goes up in price. Ether, along with other cryptocurrencies, fluctuates in price continuously. Many investors buy and sell cryptocurrencies as investments, just like trading fiat currencies or commodities. Figure 1-3 shows the main coinbase.com dashboard with popular cryptocurrency prices.

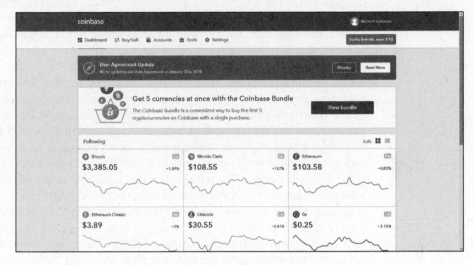

FIGURE 1-3:
Current
cryptocurrency
prices.

At its highest price, ether sold for around $1,400. At the time of this writing, it was down near $100. Whether cryptocurrency is a good investment depends on your appetite for risk and belief in its long-term value.

In addition to buying and trading ether, you can spend it just like any other currency. Of course, you generally have to buy from a vendor that accepts ether. Several service providers make it easy to accept payments with ether, such as Pay with Ether. This company provides the software and the services to make it easy for vendors of any size to accept ether as payment. Visit www.paywithether.com/ to find out more about this payment option.

TECHNICAL STUFF

There are ways to spend cryptocurrency at vendors that don't directly accept it. Several companies are planning to offer Visa cards that you fund with cryptocurrency. One company, Wirex, allows users to convert their cryptocurrency to USD, GPB, or EUR and use their card at any vendor that accepts Visa.

Cryptocurrency is growing rapidly, but only a small number of vendors accept it. If you really want to pay with ether or other cryptocurrencies, take a look at TenX. This company offers a popular Visa card funded by cryptocurrency. The card isn't available everywhere, but the company expects to increase its availability over time. Navigate to https://tenx.tech/en for more information on TenX and their cryptocurrency payment card.

Getting Started with DAO and ICO

Blockchain technology has given rise to new classes of organizations and opportunities. You'll often hear about *decentralized autonomous organization (DAO)* and *initial coin offering (ICO)*. These terms simply describe endeavors that Ethereum makes possible. You'll read a lot about these terms as you learn more about Ethereum, so it makes sense to cover them here.

A *DAO* is an organization that operates only on the rules set forth in its smart contracts. In reality, most DAOs require some human interaction, but the majority of the functionality is automated. For example, assume in just a few years that autonomous vehicles (driverless cars) are more common. A DAO would be like a driverless Uber or Lyft car. The car waits for a passenger, and then drives to the pickup location when someone needs a ride. The autonomous car completes the trip and the passenger pays with cryptocurrency. The car just earned some money. However, the car's maintenance smart contract detects that the brakes need replacing. So the car drives itself to a mechanic and pays for new brakes, using the profits of previous rides. The autonomous vehicle does not need human interaction to carry out its primary business function or to get necessary service. The autonomous vehicle is the same idea as a DAO.

A DAO conducts business and engages in transactions without requiring human interaction. Today's DAOs are relatively simple, but it is expected that they will grow in complexity and eventually replace (or at least compete with) some existing human-based businesses.

Like all businesses, Ethereum-based or Ethereum-related businesses need funding to operate. Many traditional methods for raising funds exist, including soliciting private investors, securing loans, or selling shares in the company. In addition, Ethereum opens new options for funding businesses.

Businesses that use Ethereum often create their own tokens, also called coins, that represents value associated with the business ventures. Businesses sell these tokens to raise funds to launch the business. These *ICOs* essentially exchange one type of currency for a digital item of value. Tokens may represent an expected future value as ownership in a new venture or current value that entitles the holder to some benefit. Either way, tokens are similar in some ways to stock shares. An ICO is a popular method to fund a new blockchain-based business. If you want to learn more about the most popular ICOs, navigate to `www.coindesk.com/ico-tracker` to explore coindesk's ICO Tracker, shown in Figure 1-4.

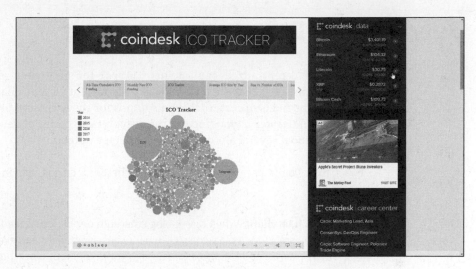

FIGURE 1-4:
coindesk ICO
Tracker.

Exploring the Ethereum Ecosystem

The *Ethereum environment*, or ecosystem, is made up of several different parts. You've already learned about most of these pieces, but it helps to put those pieces together in one place. Starting from the lowest level of the blockchain, Ethereum is made up of the following components:

>> **Blockchain:** The collection of data blocks that is the core of Ethereum. Each block contains data and smart contract code, and is cryptographically linked to its predecessor, creating a chain of blocks.

>> **EVM:** The Ethereum virtual machine, which runs smart contract bytecode. Each Ethereum node runs an instance of the EVM.

>> **Wallet:** Software, hardware, or physical paper that stores the public and private keys that correspond to an Ethereum account. The wallet stores the capability to access crypto-assets on the Ethereum blockchain.

>> **Exchange:** A service the allows its users to exchange fiat currency for cryptocurrency.

>> **Development environment:** The set of tools to write, compile, and perform unit tests on smart contract software.

>> **Testing environment:** A simulated Ethereum blockchain used to perform integration testing on smart contracts and complete decentralized applications (dApps).

>> **Client interface:** The client user interface's software and libraries used to interact with Ethereum smart contracts.

You learn much more about the details of each of these components in Chapter 4.

Delving into Development Tools

Developing decentralized applications (dApps) for Ethereum requires several types of tools. Each of these tools provides support for various phases of software development and is necessary to create dApps for the Ethereum blockchain environment. In Chapter 4, you find out the different categories of development tools and learn about several alternatives for each type of tool.

Tools that you'll use when developing Ethereum dApps are in the following categories:

>> **Blockchain client:** When developing Ethereum dApps, you'll need to implement a local EVM. A blockchain client launches a local EVM and executes your smart contract code. It also interacts with your Ethereum blockchain.

>> **Development and testing blockchain:** Deploying to the live Ethereum blockchain, also called *mainnet,* is the last step in the development process. Before deployment, you want to interact with a local version of an Ethereum blockchain. Because live blockchain access costs ether, you should carry out development and testing on a local blockchain to avoid costs and errors.

>> **Compiler and testing framework:** After you have a local EVM and local blockchain, you'll need a way to interact with your smart contract code and place it on your test blockchain for test execution. A development and testing framework provides the tools you need to carry out development and testing tasks.

>> **Source code editor/IDE:** Although you can use any text editor to write smart contract source code, an editor or integrated development environment (IDE) that is designed or extended to support Ethereum smart contract source code development will be very helpful. IDEs can increase developer efficiency and make it easier to create good smart contract code.

As you work through the exercises in this book, you'll learn more about each of these tools and install an example from each category.

Building Blockchain Apps

The process of building blockchain applications is not radically different from developing traditional applications. You have a few additional considerations and a few additional steps. As you work through the chapters in this book, you'll learn each of the tasks required to develop effective and efficient blockchain applications for the Ethereum environment.

The main differences between traditional applications and blockchain applications is the distributed, transparent nature of the data and the fact that writing data to the blockchain costs money. Distributed and transparent data means that you can't rely on the blockchain to provide any confidentiality. Anything you write to the blockchain is visible by users on any node. That should affect how you design your applications and data. Be careful when collecting data from users and storing it on the blockchain. Always assume that any blockchain data is available to the public.

The other main difference is that writing to the blockchain costs money. The development and testing processes normally occur with simulated blockchains that use only fake cryptocurrency, but live blockchain I/O has a real cost. Most developers aren't used to calculating computation and access costs. Because this is generally a new concept, many developers may put this consideration off until later in the development cycle. This decision is a mistake. It is always easier and cheaper to address blockchain access cost problems early in the development process. If you wait until the end, any changes will likely have cascading effects and costs.

As with any good development practices, do everything you can to fully understand what your users want and need. Design your software with the users in mind and always cater to their needs first. Then make you software meet their needs in ways that are the most effect and economical. Stick with good software design and development principles, while incorporating blockchain-specific considerations, and you'll be on your way to developing a good blockchain dApp.

IN THIS CHAPTER

» **Understanding distributed applications**

» **Examining Bitcoin's solution to the distributed dilemma**

» **Building blockchains**

» **Contrasting blockchains and databases**

» **Describing ways to use blockchain**

Chapter **2**

Learning about Blockchain

B*lockchain technology* is basically a distributed ledger that is shared between lots of computers and can run verifiable software to control how data is added. Blockchain technology depends on the capability to distribute data and software to many computers, using a technique called distributed processing. *Distributed processing* is the practice of spreading applications across multiple computers, and is a different way of looking at where data is stored and where application code is run from the more traditional centralized model.

Software applications have to run somewhere. Today's applications can run on endpoint computers and devices, or on servers you connect to through a network. Regardless of where software runs, the computer or device running it has limited capacity. Growth has always been a challenge for computing environments, and at some point, users will probably want services faster than the computer running an application can handle. That's where distributed processing comes into play.

In distributed processing, computers work together in teams to solve problems. If done well, distributed processing can help address the increasing demands that growth causes. However, it turns out that getting computers to work together in teams is hard.

Fortunately, a really smart researcher found a way to enable groups of computers that don't trust each other to work together in a manageable way. This new approach to distributed processing and data storage is called blockchain technology, and it has revolutionized the way people think about distributed processing and trust.

In this chapter you learn about how cool blockchains are, how they are built, why they are different from anything in the past, and most importantly, what you can do with them.

Exploring Distributed Applications

Way back in the early days of computing, it became clear that computers couldn't do everything. They could do some things really fast, such as solving math problems, but even when doing what they do best, computers would eventually run out of processing capability. The Apollo 11 moon landing almost didn't happen due to a computer overload. The navigation computer in the lunar module was getting radar data too fast and threw 1201 and 1202 alarms. Those alarms basically meant that the computer couldn't keep up with the data it was receiving. NASA engineers quickly determined that the error wasn't bad enough to abort the mission, so the landing attempt continued. But for a few seconds, a computer overload almost caused NASA to scrub the landing.

TECHNICAL STUFF

Rumor has it that a deviation from the official NASA checklist ended up causing the lunar module 1201 and 1020 program alarms. According to the checklist, the docking radar should have been turned off once the lunar module undocked from the command module. The astronauts turned on the landing radar and left the docking radar on as well in case anything bad happened and they had to return to the command module. The navigation computer couldn't handle input from two radars at once, so it triggered the program alarms.

Digging into distributed processing

One solution to application overload is to split up the computing load among multiple computers. What would have happened if the lunar module had been equipped with two computers? Maybe each one could have handled a different radar and no errors would have occurred. Of course, computers in 1969 were far larger and heavier than today's devices. Adding a second computer at that time was just too heavy and expensive.

Today things are quite different. Our smartphones are way more powerful than the computers the astronauts took with them to the moon. And they're far smaller and lighter too. Because computers are so small, fast, and affordable, we see distributed processing all the time in today's applications. And networks are faster and cheaper to access. Most applications that run in a web browser or on a mobile device are distributed. That means part of the program runs in the browser or on the mobile device, and another part runs on a server.

For instance, when you shop online, your web browser connects to a web server to fetch a list of products. The web server probably connects to an application server and a database server to get the data, and then returns it to your web browser. If you try to fetch more data from the same website, it is highly likely that you'd end up connecting to a different server. The entire process is transparent because it appears that you're running software on one big computer. That's the beauty of distributed processing.

Web applications are just one example of distributed processing. Other examples include specialized servers, such as graphics processing, and parallel processing, where multiple CPUs or computers split up data and work on each part of the data at the same time. The goal in each case is the same: allow more users to run an application than is possible when using a single computer.

TIP

Even though parallel processing really is a type of distributed processing, it's generally considered a separate type of computing. In traditional parallel processing, all processors have access to the same area of shared memory. Traditional distributed processing, however, uses multiple computers, each with its own separate memory.

Several popular architectures of distributed systems exist. The difference between architectures is in which components carry out different types of processing. The main distributed processing architectures follow:

>> **Client-server:** A capable client computer does much of the work, while relying on the server only to store and manage shared data. You'll find this architecture in small offices that run software on workstations connected to a central database server.

>> **Three-tier:** Simple websites use this approach, in which a client connects to a server, such as a web server, to get some content. The web server often needs to get data from a database server, which might also handle some of the processing.

>> **n-tier:** This architecture is an extension of the three-tier architecture, where jobs are clearly defined and multiple servers are used for specific tasks. Server types in an n-tier architecture can include web servers, application servers, database servers, and other servers that pervade specialized services. Most of today's websites, such as shopping sites, are web applications running on n-tier architecture.

>> **Peer-to-peer:** In this architecture, all *nodes,* or participating computing components, are considered equal. Storage and processing is shared among nodes. Examples of peer-to-peer networks include file-sharing networks and the Linux software and updates distribution network.

Figure 2-1 shows the main four distributed processing architectures.

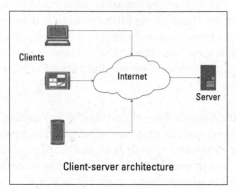

Client-server architecture

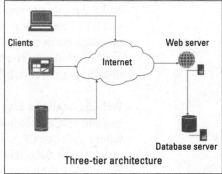

Three-tier architecture

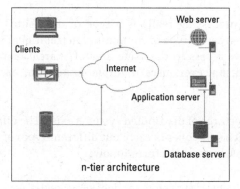

n-tier architecture

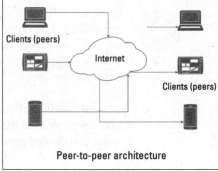

Peer-to-peer architecture

FIGURE 2-1:
Distributed processing architectures.

Exploring problems with distributed processing

Distributed processing all sounds good, but there are problems with distributing programs and data. First, all computing nodes (computers running parts of a distributed application) have to trust one another. That's not a problem if one company owns all of the computing nodes, but computers owned by competing companies simply do not trust one another. How can you trust that your competitor calculated that discount for your customer properly? Or even worse, suppose that your competitor saw a transaction for one of your customers and decided to cancel the transaction and then steal your customer? Lots of trust problems arise when attempting to distribute processing across multiple computing nodes that are not centrally controlled.

Scheduling and availability are other common problems. If you don't own and manage all of the computing nodes, how can you make sure that they are always available when you need them? Could they be tied up running someone else's applications? Or could one or more computing nodes be turned off or unavailable for some maintenance reason? These are just some of the problems with distributed processing.

Think of it this way: what if your family grew and you couldn't fit everyone into your car anymore? If you couldn't afford a bigger car, you'd have to do something to get your family from point A to point B. If your neighbor has no kids and a huge SUV, that could help solve your problem! All you have to do is get your neighbor to agree to share the SUV and coordinate your trips with your neighbor. But what if your neighbor doesn't want to go where you want to go? How do you solve that problem? And what if one of the vehicles breaks down? Or what if your neighbor wants to sleep late on Saturday but your kids have a 7 a.m. game? Coordinating computers is at least as hard as coordinating cars.

When it comes to distributed processing, four main problems must be solved (and all of these problems relate directly to trust):

>> **Launching remote processes:** How a process on one computer launches a process on another computer.

>> **Communicating between remote processes:** How processes running on different computers communicate and coordinate activities.

>> **Storing one version of data in multiple locations:** How to store and update data on different computers without running into confusing differences.

>> **Getting multiple computers to work together:** How different computers handle issues such as resolving conflicts between computers and handling system load and outages.

Launching remote processes

Distributed processing makes it possible for one computer to spread the computing load by running part of the application on other computers. That means computer A has to launch part of the application on computer B. Security immediately becomes a problem. Traditionally, an operating system authenticates users that log in to that computer and then authorizes those users to run some programs. When a program run request comes from a different computer, figuring out how to limit who can run which programs can be difficult.

Assuming that you resolve the security issues, you have to define a protocol for how one machine requests that some process runs on another machine. You have to define what type of message should be sent and what data has to be included so that the target computer understands what it is being asked to do.

Communicating between remote processes

After computers can remotely launch processes on other computers, distributed systems have to communicate to work together. That means some process on machine A has to talk to another process on machine B, formally called *inter-process communication (IPC)*, to get any work done between the two computers. The main problem with IPC is that all participating computers have to agree on the format of messages they want to exchange and the rules to communicate. Computer B may encounter problems or take longer than expected. In those cases, it has to be able to communicate back to computer A that things aren't going well. And if things do go well, computer B needs to know how to sends its results back to computer A.

Storing and synchronizing one version of data in multiple locations

One of the more difficult problems with distributing applications is storing data in multiple locations and keeping all the copies of data the same. Centralized data storage is a lot easier because there is only one copy of the data. Suppose Mary's checking account balance on computer A is decreased (she bought a large cappuccino at the local coffee shop). At the moment the data is changed, Mary's checking account balance stored on computer B is incorrect. If Mary then uses a mobile app to transfer money into her account and that mobile app happens to be running on computer B, her balance could be all messed up. If computer B's balance is considered to be correct, the cost of the cappuccino hasn't been deducted from Mary's account and she has more money in her account than she should have. If computer A's balance is considered correct, there is no record of the deposit and Mary has less money in her account than she should have.

Getting multiple computers to work together

The last remaining big problem is just getting computers to work together nicely. Computers work as independently quite well, but it takes effort to get them to work together. For instance, if two computers store copies of the same data and both run the same programs, users expect that both computers will keep their data the same. But if computer A crashes and users change data on computer B while computer A is down, the data will be different. When computer A boots, its data will be old and inaccurate, and it becomes difficult to get computers A and B to coordinate to get their data back in sync.

Even if one of the computers doesn't crash, anytime users try to change the same data but on different computers, the two computers must negotiate to see which change should be allowed. These types of problems happen frequently and make distributed processing more difficult as you add more computers and users.

Presenting some solutions to distributed processing problems

Computer scientists have been working on the problems with distributed processing for several decades. No one has completely solved all of the problems, but there are solutions to each problem you just learned about.

Launching remote processes

Remote Procedure Call (RPC) and *Remote Method Invocation (RMI)* are just two ways to define how computer A can launch a process on computer B. These two approaches simply set the communication rules and message formats for how two computers can run distributed processes. These aren't the only solutions to remote process launching, but they have been around for a while and lay the foundation for process distribution.

Communicating between remote processes

The capability for processes running on different computer to communicate with one another is formally called *inter-process communication (IPC)*. IPC is necessary to get any work done between the two computers. The main problem with IPC is that all participating computers have to agree on the format for exchanging messages and the rules for communication. Different standards, each with its pros and cons, exist. As with all distributed processing issues, all participating computing nodes must agree on how and when they communicate and what the messages look like.

Storing one version of data in multiple locations

Lots of approaches to synchronizing multiple copies of data exist. The biggest question is how to handle stale copies of data when one copy gets changed. One method is to mark the unchanged copies as "bad" or "stale" until the changed copy of data is written to the other copies. This approach raises all kinds of problems with timing and concurrency. Eventually, two users will update the same data on different computers at about the same time. A set of rules must be in place to govern which user wins.

Other methods for keeping data in sync are to apply locks to data before updates are allowed and to support merging multiple copies of data. Yet another approach is to place a timestamp on all data updates and resolve all conflicts by accepting the earliest change to the data. All existing approaches make developing and using distributed data applications more difficult, which is why computer scientists continue to search for a better way.

Getting multiple computers to work together

The last problem has perhaps the fewest standard solutions. In most cases, coordination among distributed computing nodes is based on one of two approaches: temporary dominance or consensus. *Temporary dominance* means that one computing node becomes a node with authority and decides a course of action. Some approaches arbitrarily assign nodes to have decision authority in a round-robin approach, and others have nodes vote for a leader when they have a conflict. Either way, this approach depends on granting one computing node the authority to decide.

The other main approach is to have all participating computing nodes engage in some game to come up with a decision. When a majority of nodes agree on some outcome, the group has reached consensus and accepts the majority decision. Many types of consensus "games" exist, and many are based on having computers solve puzzles. You learn more about consensus later in this chapter. Consensus is a major part of the "big solution."

Examining the Bitcoin Solution to the Distributed Dilemma

In 2008, Satoshi Nakamoto published "Bitcoin: A Peer-to-Peer Electronic Cash System." That paper contained a description of a new system of handling electronic currency. It described a data structure that consisted of a chain of special blocks, called a blockchain. This new approach makes it possible for many nodes that do not trust one another to exchange currency without a central authority.

Satoshi Nakamoto is a fictional name. Even today, we still don't know who wrote that paper. The author could be a single person or a group of people. Regardless, Nakamoto started a revolution in distributed computing.

Nakamoto proposed blockchain — now known as blockchain — technology to implement the new cryptocurrency called bitcoin. In a few short years, bitcoin has become a viable currency and blockchain has started changing the way we look at distributed processing.

REMEMBER

One common mistake when you're new to blockchain is to confuse bitcoin and blockchain. They were proposed at the same time in the same paper, but they aren't the same. *Bitcoin* is a cryptocurrency that is an implementation of block-chain technology. *Blockchain* can be implemented in many ways, not just to support bitcoin. The subject of this book, Ethereum, is another wildly popular implementation of blockchain.

Let's take a look at how blockchain provides a solution to each of the problems with distributed processing.

TECHNICAL STUFF

>> **Launching remote processes:** Blockchain technology is based on a collection of computing nodes connected in a peer-to-peer network. That means no node has more authority than any other node. Each blockchain node runs as a completely independent computing device and doesn't support launching remote processes on other nodes.

>> **Communicating between remote processes:** This one is easy. Remote processes don't communicate in blockchain technology because there are no remote processes.

It looks like we've just ignored the first two problems with distributed processing. That's because blockchain technology is out to solve only a few problems, not all of them. By ignoring remote processes, blockchain simplifies its approach to distributed processing and storage.

>> **Storing one version of data in multiple locations:** Perhaps the greatest contribution of blockchain is how its central data structure is constructed. A blockchain is an ever-growing chain of blocks, with the blocks linked into a chain structure. New blocks can be added only if a majority of the nodes agree to each addition. After a block has been added to the blockchain, it can't be modified. This feature solves the problem of keeping old data in sync. The only problem left to solve is coordinating how the blockchain expands.

>> **Getting multiple computers to work together:** The other large contribution of blockchain is in defining how *peers* — nodes that operate at the same authority — work together. They have to agree on when to add blocks and under what rules. The blockchain definition sets up these rules in a simple and straightforward way that makes it hard to break the rules and easy for everyone else to see if any node did so.

You'll see that blockchain uses distributed processing to handle data storage and trust issues, and doesn't focus on performance.

Describing Blockchains

At its core, a *blockchain* is pretty simple: It is a bunch of blocks of data linked into a chain. All blockchains start with a *genesis block*. The only thing that makes a genesis block special is that it isn't linked to a previous block. The genesis block contains header info and contents data. All other blocks also contain header and contents data, but they also contain a link to their predecessor block.

TIP

Each block's data can have different contents, in different formats. Blockchain block contents aren't constrained in the same way as database records are. The structure of data that you store in each block can be dynamic, to fit the data you're storing.

Examining blockchain details

You can think of a blockchain as being a big spreadsheet, except that each row may have different columns and a different number of columns. Instead of being identified by row number and column letter, each data value is identified by a key. That makes it easy to identify data in each block.

At a higher level, a blockchain can be viewed as a big spreadsheet that is shared with every node in the blockchain network. Every copy of the blockchain is identical, and all nodes must agree before any new blocks are added to the blockchain (think of adding new rows to the spreadsheet). That way, the blockchain always stays in sync.

All blocks, except the genesis block, include a previous block link. This link is a cryptographic hash of the previous block's header metadata. A *cryptographic hash* is a number that uniquely represents a block of data. It is the output of a mathematical function given the data of the block as input. Hash functions make is easy to calculate a fixed-length number that represents a large amount of input data. And even though a hash function returns a shorter number than the size of the input, the returned hash value is unique for data used as input.

Different blockchains use different hash functions. For example, Ethereum uses the Keccak-256 hash function to calculate the hash value on the previous block. Ethereum uses that hash value as the link to attach a block to the previous block on the chain. The link Ethereum uses is the result of the Keccak-256 calculation of the previous block's header information and a random number, called the *nonce value*. Ethereum nodes compete to be the first to find the right nonce that results in a hash value matching the current complexity target. Figure 2-2 shows the blockchain architecture.

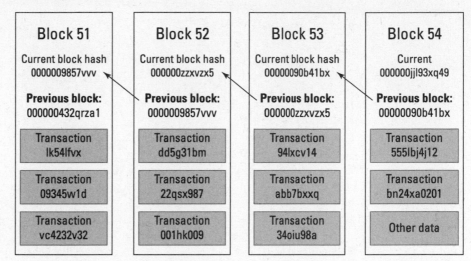

FIGURE 2-2:
Blockchain
architecture.

TECHNICAL
STUFF

Blockchain uses data from a block, along with a nonce, to calculate a hash value that represents the block. The word *nonce* means "a number that is used only once." A nonce is used to increase the uniqueness of a hash value for a block. Calculating a hash on a block using two different nonces will return two different hashes.

Each Ethereum block contains some header information, including a timestamp, a block number, a version number, and other descriptive information, and content data. The *content data* can be any data that makes up the contents of the block, which can be plaintext data, encrypted data, or even executable code. A blockchain, when described only in terms of the blocks, looks like a straightforward data structure. But the real power of blockchain is how the data structure is created, extended, and used in applications.

Current blockchain implementations define blockchains as *immutable* data structures, which means that after each block is added to the blockchain, it can never be changed. This immutability property helps to solve one of the more difficult problems of storing distributed data in multiple locations. If the blockchain cannot be changed after a block has been added to the chain, the only remaining problem with data synchronization is how to control when blocks are added to the chain. All blockchains have clear rules that control the process of adding blocks.

Protecting blockchain visibility

You can build two types of blockchain: public and private. Your choice depends on what you're trying to do with your blockchain. *Public blockchains* are available to pretty much anyone, but *private blockchains* are only available to users authorized by the blockchain owner, as shown in Figure 2-3.

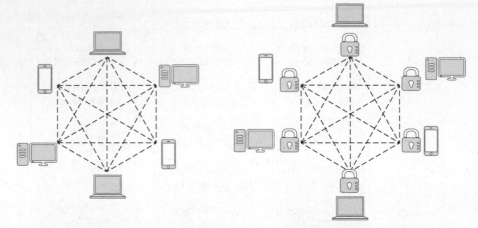

Public Blockchain
- Permissionless
- All nodes can freely access the blockchain without restriction.
- The blockchain is shared and available to all.

Private Blockchain
- Permissioned
- Only nodes authorized by the owner can freely access the blockchain.
- Data is shared and available only to authorized users.

FIGURE 2-3:
Public versus private blockchains.

Public blockchain

Anyone can interact with a public blockchain, also called a *permissionless blockchain*. All you need is a valid address, and you can read the blockchain and even submit transactions. This is the most popular type of blockchain, and one that most people think of when associating blockchain with cryptocurrency. Public blockchains ensure that no one organization controls the blockchain because any computer can become a node and each computer maintains a full copy of the blockchain.

TECHNICAL STUFF

Not all nodes store full copies of blockchain blocks. Full nodes do maintain complete copies of the blockchain, but lightweight nodes store just some blocks of the blockchain. Lightweight nodes often store recent blocks and provide transaction validation services for clients.

Private blockchain

Prior authorization is required before you can access a private blockchain, also called a *permissioned blockchain*. Private blockchains are almost always owned by a single organization or a small group. The blockchain owner requires that each blockchain user request authorization to interact with the blockchain data and provide access credentials with each access request. Private blockchains provide organizations the features of blockchain applications without having to expose all of their data to the general public.

Building Blockchains

You've already learned that blockchains are immutable and all nodes have to agree before new blocks can be added to the blockchain. Let's look at how those two requirements are enforced.

Agreeing to add blocks

The first rule blockchain nodes must agree to is how to allow new blocks to be added to the blockchain. Because no node has more authority than any other node, the nodes use consensus to agree to add new blocks. *Consensus* in this sense simply means that when enough nodes agree to take some action, that the action is approved and agreed upon by all nodes. Most consensus strategies use simple majorities to succeed. So, as long as more than half of nodes agree to take some action, the action is approved.

Several consensus approaches are in use or proposed:

>> **Proof of Work:** Proof of Work (PoW) is the most popular consensus protocol used today, and is used by both bitcoin and Ethereum. Proof of Work means that some nodes compete to try to be the first to solve a mathematical puzzle. The puzzle is to find a random value to combine with a block's header, such that the hash of the combined data matches a pattern. Solving the puzzle is hard, but verifying the solution to the puzzle is easy. The first node to solve the puzzle receives a reward for doing the work, and gets to add the new block to the blockchain. The block, along with the value the winning node found to solve the puzzle, is sent to all nodes. Each node quickly verifies the block and then adds it to their local blockchain. Although Proof of Work is the most popular consensus protocol and works well, it takes enormous computing power to complete. That means Proof of Work requires computers to use lots of energy, which produces a lot of heat.

>> **Proof of Stake:** The Proof of Stake (PoS) consensus protocol will likely replace Proof of Work. The developers of Ethereum already have plans to move to this protocol. The Proof of Stake protocol provides a similar level of consistency as the current Proof of Work protocol without using so much computing power (and wasting energy). Each node that wants to compete to add a new block locks some of its cryptocurrency and submits it as a bet. The "winning" node that gets to add the new block to the blockchain is chosen based on the size of the bet and other criteria intended to randomize the selection. The random part of the selection criteria keeps the richest node from always adding new blocks.

>> **Delegated Proof of Stake:** Delegated Proof of Stake (DPoS) is a modified PoS protocol. Most of the pool of candidate nodes are selected as in the PoS protocol, but a small number of additional nodes are added to the pool based on votes. All nodes in the network can vote for some nodes to be included in the selection pool. The nodes receiving the highest number of votes are added to the selection pool, and the winner is randomly selected from all nodes in the pool. DPoS makes PoS fairer and less likely to favor the richest nodes.

>> **Delegated Byzantine Fault Tolerance (dBFT):** The last consensus protocol is based on a dilemma encountered in all distributed systems: the Byzantine Generals' Problem. This problem is a hypothetical situation that makes it easy to see how hard it is to get a consensus. Suppose nine generals and their armies from the Byzantine Empire have surrounded Rome and are waiting to attack. The generals have agreed that they must all attack or retreat in unison. If any general breaks rank and doesn't do what the other generals do, they all will be defeated. In this case, consensus is necessary for survival. Because generals can communicate only through couriers, any courier could be bribed or even captured. Either of these actions would cause a message to be lost or changed. Any general could also be bribed to lie or just become scared and make the wrong decision. It is difficult for any general to trust that all other generals agree on any decision. The dBFT protocol ensures that all generals agree on a single course of action, even when some messages are changed or lost.

The dBFT protocol is based on groups of nodes electing a delegate to represent them. Each time a new block is proposed for the blockchain, a speaker is randomly selected from the delegates. The speaker calculates the block's hash and sends that to all other delegates. If at least two-thirds of the delegates agree with the calculated hash, the block is added to the blockchain. Otherwise, the block is discarded and the process starts over with new delegates and a new speaker being selected.

Making blocks immutable

The reason why so much effort is put into ensuring consensus is that after a block is added to the blockchain, it never changes. Well, that's the goal. Technically, it is possible to change blockchain data, but it is very, very hard to do and very easy for anyone to detect the change. Using POW consensus protocol, the level of effort alone makes changing blocks pretty close to impossible. Let's see why.

Before you add a block to the blockchain, you must calculate a cryptographic hash of the previous block. That is the link to the previous block and the guarantee that it will never change. When you calculate the hash value of the previous block, that block's header (which is part of the data used to calculate the hash value) includes the hash of its predecessor block. So if anyone ever changes any block, all blocks in the blockchain after that one are invalid. They're invalid because the hash values for all subsequent blocks don't match up.

It is easy to validate a blockchain. All you have to do is step through the blockchain, block by block, and make sure that the hash value stored in each block is the correct hash of the previous block header. As long as all the hashes match, the blockchain is valid. That's why blockchains are called immutable. You can change blockchain data, but doing so immediately invalidates that copy of the blockchain.

Reviewing the building process

Now that you know about consensus and immutability, let's look at the steps used to build a blockchain:

1. Users submit requests to a blockchain node. Requests can be financial transactions, code to run, documents, or really any data.

2. When a node has enough data to create a new blockchain block, it organizes the data and adds header information, including block number, timestamp, and other descriptive details.

3. The complete block is submitted for a consensus decision. Blockchain nodes carry out the steps in the consensus protocol to determine whether the new block should be added.

4. Each node validates that the block adheres to all requirements, and then adds it to their local copy of the blockchain.

Keeping all blockchains consistent

After following these steps, every copy of the blockchain should contain the same blocks, but it doesn't always work out that way. Although I've said that a blockchain is just a linked chain of blocks, there is more to it. The blocks in a blockchain are stored in a tree structure for efficient processing. The actual list of blocks on the blockchain are stored in the linked (or chained) list called the *active chain*. If two separate nodes solve puzzles for two different blocks at about the same time, they both would transmit their blocks to the entire set of blockchain nodes. Some nodes would add block A and others would add block B. Now we have a situation where the blockchain is not the same across the network.

This can happen in real life but it lasts only for a short while. Within minutes, a new block is added to the blockchain. The node that solved the puzzle solved it for its own copy of the blockchain. That means the winning node either depends on the previous block being block A or block B. Let's assume this new block is based on the blockchain that previously ended with block B. When the winning node sends its block to all other nodes, those nodes with A as the last block will fail to verify this new block (because the hash was calculated for block B). That block will be rejected and now there are blockchains of different lengths. Although digging into the details of blockchain construction is interesting, the topic is beyond the scope of this book.

Ethereum defines a consistency rule that states when blockchains of different lengths exist on different nodes, the longest blockchain is the correct block-chain. So everyone discards the blockchain that ends with block A and uses the longer blockchain. Block A may go away, but all of its transactions are put back into the pool to be placed into the next block on the blockchain. So even though block A didn't make it on the stable blockchain, its contents may still be in an upcoming block.

Understanding How Blockchains and Databases Store Data Differently

Up to now, it may seem that storing data in a blockchain is pretty much the same as storing it in a database. While the data is at rest (no one is accessing it), that may be the case. However, big differences exist in how data on a blockchain and data in a database are stored and used.

Storing data in a traditional database

Traditional databases store data in a central location. Clients connect to that central location to read and write data. Regardless of the architecture of the database, you can generally do four things with data: Create, Read, Update, and Delete. These are called the CRUD operations:

» **Create:** Add a new record to a database, possibly with some generated identifying data.

» **Read:** Locate an existing database record, generally through a search of key or index data, and then copy the record into a memory buffer for local access.

» **Update:** Copy local changes to data back into the original record in the database. The update operation saves updated data in the database.

» **Delete:** Locate an existing database record, much like with the read operation, but then remove the record from the database. A deleted record no longer exists; you can't access the previous contents of a deleted record.

Because data in a traditional database is stored in a central location, it is possible for multiple clients to read data, modify that data locally, and then write the data back to the database in an update operation. If client A and client B access the same data at the same time, and both modify that data, only one client can save his or her changes. For example, if client A saves changes first, then when client B saves his changes, they will overwrite client A's changes.

This process illustrates a classic concurrency problem. Database management systems (DBMSs) have long struggled with this issue. Today's databases generally use one of three techniques to avoid having clients overwriting other valid changes:

» **Locking:** The DBMS lock a record, or group of records, as the client reads them. While that client keeps local copies of records, no other clients can access those records for updating. The client releases locks when he or she is finished with those records, which allows another client to apply their own locks. This approach is safe, but makes it hard for many clients to share common data because it forces clients to wait in line for data to update.

» **Timestamp ordering:** Each time a client wants to read a record, the DBMS records the time and compares it to the transaction timestamp and the record write timestamp. The DBMS compares these timestamps to determine when it is safe to read the record, and only allows reads when they are safe from data collisions. In this scenario, trying to read a *dirty record* (one that is being updated by another client) could cause your transaction to terminate. That makes it harder to write user-friendly applications.

» **Optimistic concurrency control:** The previous two options assume that collisions will occur. Optimistic concurrency control assumes that collisions will not occur frequently. Clients can read records any time without restriction. When a client attempts to write a record, the DBMS compares the previously read record with the current record in the database. If these differ, another client has updated the record, and the write fails. If the record has not been changed, the write succeeds. This concurrency control technique generally supports the most scalable application design.

Traditional databases make it easy for applications to share data, carry out CRUD operations, and maintain data consistency in high-throughput environments. They don't do such a good job at maintaining audit trails of data changes. They also require substantial effort to avoid having a database failure crash the entire application.

A distinct advantage to storing data in a database is access performance. DBMSs take advantage of features such as indexes to decrease the time it takes to locate or sort records. Record access is often one of the critical indicators of overall database application performance. Because DBMSs are optimized for performance, this storage option works well where users demand quick response and high throughput.

Storing data in a blockchain

A blockchain handles data differently than a traditional database. One of the biggest differences is that a blockchain does not support CRUD operations. The only database operations are Write, which is the same as Create, followed by populating data before writing, and Read. After data has been placed in a block and added to the blockchain, that data cannot change. A blockchain does not have Update and Delete operations.

The other big difference between blockchain data storage and databases is their location. A complete copy of the blockchain is stored on every full blockchain node. Much of the difficulty in maintaining a blockchain network is ensuring that all blockchain nodes store the same data. Each blockchain implementation has strict rules for maintaining a synchronized blockchain across the network, and those rules make detecting differences between nodes easy (and quick).

This distributed storage property of a blockchain makes it extremely resilient, because the failure of any node or nodes will have a negligible effect on the rest of the blockchain network.

Blockchain storage was never designed for high-performance situations. The storage method does support fast traversals through the block tree, but accessing individual data items within blocks takes some time. Remember that blocks can contain data in different formats, which must be filtered for searching.

Table 2-1 summarizes the differences between storing data in a database and on a blockchain.

TABLE 2-1
Differences between Databases and Blockchain

Feature	Traditional Database	Blockchain
Location	One central database copy	Each node stores a complete copy of the blockchain
Operations supported	Create, Read, Update, Delete (CRUD)	Read, Write
Performance	Optimized for short response time and high-throughput	Not optimized for performance
Integrity	Dependent on DBMS and application	Consensus and immutability provide integrity
Transparency	As allowed by central DBMS	Each node stores a complete copy of the blockchain
Control	Centralized	Decentralized

Effectively Using Blockchains

Blockchain offers some interesting features, but it might not be a good technology for every situation. Before jumping in and trying to design a blockchain application, think about how blockchain may meet some of your design goals but may not meet others. In this section, we look at some features that blockchain offers.

Transferring value without trust

One of the unique strengths of blockchain technology is that is supports transferring items of value between entities that do not trust one another. In fact, that's the big pull for blockchain. You have to trust only the consensus protocol, not any other user. Your transactions are carried out in a verifiable and stable manner, so you can trust that they are being handled properly and securely.

Reducing transaction costs by eliminating middlemen

Whether you're considering transferring money from one party to another or providing a product for payment, nearly all transactions need a middleman, such as a banker, an importer, a wholesaler, or even a media publisher. Because blockchain allows entities that don't trust each other to interact directly, it eliminates most middlemen. Blockchain makes it possible for producers to interact directly with consumers. For instance, artists can offer their art directly to buyers, without needing a broker or a publisher, and these savings can be passed directly to the consumer. Although blockchain transaction handling does incur a small cost, it is generally much less than what middlemen charge. That's good for producers and consumers.

Increasing efficiency through direct interaction

Lower fees aren't the only benefit of eliminating middlemen. Any time you can remove one or more steps in a process, you increase efficiency. Greater efficiency generally means reduced time required for a process to complete. For example, suppose a musician decides to release her latest single directly to her fans by using a blockchain delivery model. Her fans can consume the new single the moment it drops. With a publisher, there is some delay while the content is delivered, approved, packaged, and then finally released.

Although the delay for digital media may be minimal, blockchain can eliminate any delays introduced by middlemen. The contrast becomes even clearer when looking at managing the process of delivering physical goods by using blockchain. If you buy strawberries from California, have you ever thought about how many processors stand between you and the grower? Blockchain can reduce the number of people who participate in the supply chain for pretty much anything.

Maintaining complete transaction history

Another design feature of blockchain is its immutability. Because you can't change the data, anything written to the blockchain stays there always. "What happens in blockchain, stays in blockchain." That's good news for any application that would benefit from a readily available transaction history. Let's revisit the strawberries example. You may go to the grocery store today and buy strawberries with a label that says "Fresh from CA." You really have no way of knowing whether the strawberries came directly from CA or first from, say, Spain (the second leading exporter of strawberries.) But with blockchain, you could trace a pint of strawberries all the way back to the grower. You'd know exactly where your strawberries came from and when they were picked. This level of transaction history exists for every transaction in blockchain. You can always find any transaction's complete history.

Increasing resilience through replication

Every full node in any blockchain network must maintain a copy of the entire blockchain. Therefore, all data on the blockchain is replicated to every full node, and no node depends on data that another node stores. This feature is a big deal for resilience. In a blockchain application, several nodes could crash or otherwise be unavailable without affecting the other users of the application. Fault tolerance is built into the blockchain architecture. In addition, distributing the entire blockchain to many nodes owned by many different organizations practically eliminates the possibility of any organization controlling the data.

Any application that benefits from high availability and freedom of ownership may be a good fit for blockchain. Many database applications go to great lengths to replicate their data to provide fault tolerance, and blockchain has it built right in!

Providing transparency

The last main category of blockchain features is directly related to the fact that the entire blockchain is replicated to every full blockchain node. Every full node can see the entire blockchain, which provides unparalleled transparency.

The data stored in blocks may be encrypted, although the data itself is available to any user of any node. To decrypt the data, a user needs the proper decryption key(s). (If the data is unencrypted, anyone with access to a node or the blockchain itself can see it.) Blockchain transparency makes it possible to trust the integrity of the data. Nodes routinely verify the integrity of each block, and therefore, the whole blockchain. Any modifications to the "immutable" blockchain data become immediately evident and easy to fix.

IN THIS CHAPTER

» **Exploring uses for Ethereum applications**

» **Describing financial services and ICOs**

» **Simplifying identity management**

» **Examining industry applications**

» **Empowering governance**

Chapter **3**

Exploring Use Cases for Ethereum

E thereum is a great implementation of blockchain technology, but unlike the current marketing hype, it doesn't solve all of the world's problems. However, it does solve some problems that have proved to be hard nuts to crack! The trick is in knowing where Ethereum shines and where is may not be the best choice. To ease into an understanding of when to use Ethereum, you examine some successful use cases. In general, blockchain is a good fit when you need to exchange something in an environment in which the players don't trust one another.

First, you need to look at what *exchange something* means. The traditional definition is to trade things of value. But in some cases, the exchange implies simply answering a question. For example, "who are you?" is a valid question. Today, most answers to that question involve an audible answer that is accompanied by additional proof, such as a picture ID. Blockchain technology in general, and Ethereum in particular, can handle many types of exchanges well.

In this chapter, you discover some of the ways in which Ethereum solves problems elegantly and provides a solution that just can't be addressed as cleanly using non-blockchain approaches. After reading this chapter, you should have a clearer picture of how Ethereum works as an effective tool in your problem-solving toolbox.

Diving Into Ethereum Applications

The first thing that comes to mind when you think of blockchain is probably cryptocurrency. Yes, blockchain does that, but it also does far more. Many personal and business interactions involve exchanging funds, products, and services. Entire industries exist to act as brokers that manage the exchanges and provide a level of mutual trust (that is, both parties of an exchange trust the broker.) The Ethereum implementation of blockchain can solve many types of problems with exchanges that involve some type of transfer or exchange among untrusting parties. And the beauty of Ethereum is that it removes the need for the broker, or middleman.

For example, suppose you want to buy a used car. You have several options that come with different costs. If you break down all the different options, most of the cost differences are based on trust. You probably have the highest level of trust for a dealer who primarily sells new cars and also offers certified pre-owned vehicles (the term *used car* has an air of questionable trust.) This trust and assurance make these types of car the most expensive. You pay a higher price to a dealer who has invested lots of time and money into building a reputation you can trust.

On the other hand, you could see a car with a "For Sale" sign parked at the grocery store. Although the car may look good, you have no idea about its owner, condition, or history. You would be taking on risk because of a lack of trust in the seller, which is why this kind of transaction is generally cheaper than buying the same used car from a dealer.

The used car example is one that could benefit from Ethereum. Suppose all car manufacturers, mechanics, and body shop workers were required to submit information to a public Ethereum blockchain whenever a car was serviced or repaired. Anyone could get the complete history of a car at any time. You wouldn't have to trust the seller. If you decide to buy the car, another Ethereum app could allow you to transfer the agreed-upon purchase price to the seller in exchange for the legal title. The app would ensure that the transaction is legal and safe, and adheres to all appropriate laws and regulations. And you don't have to pay a middlemen to handle your transaction. You do have to pay a small fee to record your transaction on the blockchain, but it would be a tiny fraction of a dealer upcharge.

The used car example highlights a small number of ways that Ethereum can help solve problems. In general, blockchain provides core features that solve four main problems with exchanges of any type:

>> **Transparent transactions:** No entity "owns" transactions. Anyone with access to the blockchain can view all transactions. You may not be able to see the contents of each encrypted transaction, but you can see the address and the fact that a transaction exists.

In this chapter, I am talking about public blockchains, to which anyone can add a transaction if they have the right software or pay the right fee. Private blockchains are not generally visible to the public, and only certain parties may add transactions to them. You read more about private blockchains elsewhere in the book.

>> **Traceable history of all data:** Because you can see all transactions, you can create a trace of every asset from its introduction to the blockchain through the current time. This feature makes tracing the history of anything recorded on the blockchain easy.

>> **Reduced overhead:** By eliminating middlemen and brokers, producers and consumers can interact directly. This direct interaction can greatly increase efficiency and speed up transaction processing times.

>> **Lower cost:** In addition to making transaction processing more efficient, Ethereum can lower transaction costs by removing extra processing steps and handlers. Instead of paying a broker or other middleman to process a transaction, you have to pay only a small transaction fee to the blockchain.

Ethereum really shines when applications benefit from its core features. In the next sections, you learn about some of the types of applications that are good fits for Ethereum. You see how problems that are hard to solve with other technologies are easy to solve in Ethereum. As you read through these use cases, think of how Ethereum can solve problems for your organization.

The rest of this chapter focuses on four groups of Ethereum use cases:

>> **Financial services:** Applications that manage financial transactions

>> **Digital identity management:** Applications that associate an identity with a person or device

>> **Specific industry vertical applications:** Applications that provide or support services that apply to specific industry vertical markets

>> **Governance services**: Applications that provide services related to government agencies

Exploring Financial Services

Financial services are interactions that involve some exchange of currency. The currency can be legal tender, also called *fiat currency*, or it can be cryptocurrency, such as Bitcoin or Ethereum's default currency, *ether (ETH)*. Ethereum apps do a great job of handling *pure currency exchanges,* or exchanging some currency for a product or service. Financial services may center on handling payments, but there are more nuances to the many transactions that involve money.

Banking

Historically, banks or other financial institutions were necessary to conduct trade. Although physical currency can change hands between individuals, the process gets more complex when the number of participants grows. For example, if you want to buy food at the grocery store, you have several options to pay at the register: cash, check, and card. All three options involve a bank.

TIP

One of the primary services banks provide is serving as an uninterested, trusted third party to broker transactions. If you trust the person or organization with whom you're doing business, you probably don't need a bank.

Although you don't have to get cash at a bank, there's a good chance that at least some of your cash came from cashing a check someone gave you or withdrawing money from one of your own accounts. Although banks make getting cash easy with ATMs and satellite branches, you still have to interact with bank employees or banking devices at some point.

If you pay with a check or card, you are asking the vendor to trust that your bank or card-issuing institution will provide money to pay what you owe. No money changes hands at that point — just a promise. The entire transaction is based on trust. Only a handful of cards are generally accepted because those are the ones vendors trust. They believe that the bank or payment card company will follow through and provide the payment to complete the transaction.

Financial transactions, except those that simply consist of one person handing cash to another person, involve some middleman to broker the transaction. Vendors generally pay a transaction fee to have the middleman move the money around. For example, paying with a credit card can add a 2 percent to 5 percent service charge to the vendor's cost. Even though you may not see the transaction fees, rest assured, they are built into the price of goods and services!

Cryptocurrency

Blockchain was initially proposed as a vehicle to implement a cryptocurrency, Bitcoin. Ethereum also implements cryptocurrencies. The default currency for Ethereum is ether (ETH), but Ethereum supports many other types of tokens. *Cryptocurrency* is currency that is stored exclusively on a blockchain. Users can access their currency through their blockchain accounts and can transfer units of cryptocurrency to and from other accounts.

Although this sounds a lot like depositing and withdrawing money from an account at a bank, there is a huge difference: There is no bank! That's the beauty of Ethereum. You establish an Ethereum account, and then add funds in the form of ETH or any supported token. To do this, you generally have to send fiat currency to an exchange that will allow you to buy cryptocurrency and then transfer it to your account.

TIP

Exchanges aren't banks, but it is common to link a traditional bank account to an exchange account. You have to transfer money from the "outside world" to your Ethereum account at some point. Linking to a bank isn't technically required — some exchanges operate like ATMs. You can deposit cash to purchase ETH or other tokens directly.

After you have cryptocurrency in your account, you can use it to buy goods and services from any vendor that accepts it. Let's say your local grocery store decides to accept ETH. When you check out, all you have to do is transfer an amount of ETH from your account to the grocery store's Ethereum address. You don't have to involve a bank at all. The ETH goes directly from your account to the grocery store's account. And because you have conducted the transfer using Ethereum, you don't have to trust the grocer and the grocer doesn't have to trust you.

This model cuts out processing middlemen such as the bank or payment card companies. The cryptocurrency is transferred in real time and you pay a small transaction fee, currently less than $0.01 USD for a standard transfer, which is far less than the fees traditional processors charge. The transaction works like a person-to-person cash transfer, but you don't have to carry a wad of cash around with you all the time.

Real estate

Another rich field for Ethereum in the financial services domain is real estate transactions. As with banking transactions, Ethereum makes it possible to conduct transactions without a broker. Buyers and sellers can exchange currency for legal title directly.

Ethereum's smart contracts can validate all aspects of the transaction as it occurs. The steps that normally require an attorney or a loan processor can happen automatically. A buyer can transfer funds to purchase a property after legal requirements are met, such as validating the title's availability and filing required government documents. The seller receive payment for the property at the same time the title transfers to the buyer.

Ethereum can also go far beyond real estate purchases. Maintaining property commonly requires many documents and records. Property history is required for many decisions and can be a prerequisite for satisfying insurance claims.

Ethereum provides a framework for storing the complete history of a property's title as well as its physical history. Ethereum real estate management apps can keep a transparent log of all property maintenance and ownership details. Ethereum makes it easy to search through a property's history to see if there has ever been a fire, flooding, or a termite infestation. It can be used also to predict upcoming maintenance needs.

Rental property owners often have to spend substantial effort keeping track of upcoming reservations, past renter information, maintenance needs and history, and profitability assessment over time. Ethereum can help meet all these needs by storing rental information in a blockchain that is immutable and available to anyone.

Creating Ethereum escrow applications

Many transactions aren't as immediate as shopping at the grocery store. In that situation, you have the groceries with you, you pay for them, and then you leave with them. Other transactions take some time to resolve. Suppose you order a hardcopy of this book from your favorite online bookseller. When you complete your transaction, you've paid for the book but you won't have a physical copy of the book for at least a day.

Paying for a book up front and then waiting for the delivery isn't a big deal, but what about buying something more expensive, such as a diamond ring? You might be less willing to pay a lot of money up front and then wait for the product. *Escrow accounts* provide a way of holding money while a transaction completes. The buyer places money in an escrow account, and after the seller validates that the money is in the account, the seller ships the product. When the buyer receives the product, the money is released to the seller.

Ethereum's smart contracts can automate escrow accounts and remove the need for an account manager. The seller and the buyer each interact with the Ethereum escrow account directly to provide a trusted way of processing payment for transactions that aren't immediate.

Examining ICOs

Bitcoin provided the first workable alternative currency in the digital realm. It has been wildly popular and has become more than just an alternative to fiat currency. Instead of having to constantly exchange fiat currency for cryptocurrency and vice versa, cryptocurrencies have matured to a point that conversion to another currency isn't always necessary.

Many new business ventures have been created that are entirely funded by cryptocurrency. Such initiatives are commonly funded through an *initial coin offering (ICO)*, which allows investors to purchase tokens specific to a project (the ICO). ICOs aren't specific to Ethereum, but many new Ethereum-based ventures start funding drives through ICOs. The most common Ethereum token standard, and the one most ICOs use, is *ERC-20*, which supports core functions that govern how tokens are created, exchanged, and valued.

The ICO process is similar to an IPO (initial public offering) in more traditional financial environments. An ICO is a way to state a business venture intention and invite investors to invest in the new organization through crowdfunding. In turn, investors own tokens that represent an ownership stake in the new venture. ICOs are largely unregulated and can be risky. But they also can provide opportunities to get in on the ground floor of new and exciting opportunities.

Establishing Digital Identity Management

Asserting one's identity has always been challenging, but doing so in the digital world has proved to be extremely difficult. The process of asserting an identity is fairly simple, but executing it well is the problem. Some entity, normally a person, submits a claim to be the owner of an identity by providing a unique identifier for the identity. In simple applications, you type your user name to claim to be a certain user. This is called the *identification* step.

But you can't just provide any identity. You have to prove that you own that identity by providing additional information. In other words, you have to make additional claims against the identity, The most common way to do this in many applications is to provide a password. This is the *authentication* step. You are asking the application to authenticate that you are who you claim to be.

The application then compares the information you provided (password) with stored information to see whether you provided the correct password. If you did enter the password that matches, the authentication system accepts your claim that you own the identity and authorizes you to access the application. More secure applications use techniques other than, or in addition to, passwords, such as smart cards, tokens, or biometrics. Regardless of the techniques used, a trusted authority has to intervene to determine whether an identity claim is valid.

Ethereum apps provide a unique opportunity to help manage identities. Each Ethereum user account has a unique address and is associated with a unique pair of keys. These keys allow the owner to access any blockchain resources associated with the account. A unique identity can be one of the resources associated with an account and is identified by the account's address.

Establishing an identity would require some interaction with a governing authority to verify that you are, in the physical world, who you claim to be. This step is similar to providing a picture ID and is necessary to keep people from creating multiple false IDs. After you establish an identity, you can make additional claims against that identity and provide additional information, such as name, address, and biometric information. These claims are stored as part of your identity and provide authentication in a similar way that passwords do. But using Ethereum is far safer. You don't have to trust any entity to protect your private information and only you can access your blockchain data because you control the keys.

Managing individual and device identities

Identities don't have to be limited to people. Each Ethereum account can represent an identity, and that identity can refer to a device. If you're wondering why your toaster needs an identity, think of all the smart devices on the market today. If you have the budget, it isn't hard to have your house lights, refrigerator, stove, heating, air conditioner, entertainment center, and many other electronic devices on your home network. Getting all these devices to talk to one another and play nice can be challenging.

Giving each device a unique identity is a great first step. Just like people, devices have descriptive attributes that describe their state. Devices have names, functional categories, locations, and permissions. As a simple example, your printer could detect that it needs more ink and automatically order more. The printer's identity would be robust enough to tell the vendor where to send the ink and how the order will be paid. A real person would have to install the ink cartridges, but that might be changing as well.

The explosion of Internet-connected devices, called the *Internet of Things (IoT)*, has raised many questions about securing and managing these devices. Although no comprehensive solution exists, proposing a straightforward way to manage these devices as individuals is a good start. And as more and more IoT devices become more autonomous, having a verifiable identity allows them to operate with minimal oversight or human interaction.

Reducing fraud and identity theft

Ethereum solutions for managing digital identity can help dramatically reduce fraud and identity theft. The offline world has a few globally accepted identifications standards. Most people have a driver's license and many have a passport.

These two forms of ID are issued by government agencies and are accepted as proof of identity in most situations.

However, these forms of ID do not have a digital counterpart. If an Ethereum standard for identity management were to be globally accepted, you would be able to present your digital identity upon demand. Having your identification information stored in a blockchain is much more secure. You are the only one that has access to your identification attributes because you control your own keys. You wouldn't have to re-enter identification information and a separate user account for every website and remote system you access.

In addition to the reduction in data duplication, any changes to your identity claims would be stored in an immutable block. That makes it virtually impossible to use someone else's identity without leaving a clear audit trail leading right to the attacker.

Examining the ERC-725 standard and beyond

Fabian Vogelsteller, the creator of the ERC-20 Ethereum token standard, has proposed ERC-725, an Ethereum identity standard. ERC-725 is a smart contract interface that defines how to define, configure, and use identities in Ethereum. Developers can implement the interface in their own smart contracts to manage digital identities in Ethereum. Defining the standard as a smart contract interface allows competing implementations to share the same core functionality and ultimately be compatible with one another. Therefore, an ERC-725 identity should be usable in a wide range of applications.

ERC-725 isn't the only effort to standardize digital identity management in Ethereum. The uPort initiative defines multiple simple layers, as opposed to the monolithic approach embraced in ERC-725. The developers of uPort state that their protocol is more granular and easier to customize due to its layered functional approach. The layered approach makes it easier to customize specific aspects of the uPort implementation to suit an organization's specific needs.

Examining Industry Applications

Ethereum use cases don't have to be generic and apply to multiple domains. Many vertical markets have specific needs that Ethereum applications can address. In this section, you learn about three vertical markets that benefit from Ethereum solutions.

Healthcare

Healthcare has become one of the most popular topics of conversations ranging from politics to research to spending. It seems that everyone is interested in increasing the quality of healthcare while reducing its cost. The availability of large amounts of digital data have made advances in healthcare possible.

Researchers can analyze large amounts of data to explore new treatment plans, increase the overall effectiveness of existing drugs and procedures, and identify cost-saving opportunities. This type of analysis is possible only with access to vast amounts of patient medical histories. The main problem for researchers is that a patient's *electronic health record (EHR)* is likely stored as fragments across multiple practices and databases. Although efforts to combine these records are ongoing, privacy is a growing concern (we're back to the trust problem) and progress is slow.

EHR management is a good fit for an Ethereum app. Storing a patient's EHR in an Ethereum blockchain can remove the silos of fragmented data without having to trust each entity that provides or modified parts of the EHR. Storing the EHR in this way also helps clarify medical services billing and payment. With comprehensive medical procedure history all in one place, medical services providers and insurance companies can see the same view of a patient's treatment. A full history makes it easier to figure out what should be billed.

Another advantage that Ethereum apps can provide in the healthcare domain is in managing pharmaceuticals. Blockchain EHRs provide the information for medical practitioners to see a full history and a current snapshot of a patient's prescription medications. It also allows researchers, auditors, and even pharmaceutical manufacturers to examine the effect and possible side effects of their products. Having EMRs available but protected can provide valuable information to increase the quality of healthcare services.

Energy

Another vertical market with interesting blockchain opportunities is in energy management. Smart city planners realize that energy management is a core requirement for using technology to enhance inhabitants' quality of life. Just collecting data isn't enough. Smart meters provide real-time information on energy use and allow energy providers to restrict energy distribution at peak times. For instance, summertime demands for electricity in hot climates can push the limits of electricity providers. Smart meters can limit the energy used in single homes to cumulatively lower the overall energy demand.

Ethereum apps make it easy to give each smart meter an identity and allow it to autonomously manage the energy it requires to power devices in its home. When the electricity provider needs to limit overall output, it can contact smart meters identified in the blockchain and request that each one reduce its electricity use. The blockchain provides an up-to-date list of participating smart meters and automatically keeps an audit trail of how well each one manages its energy use. Storing energy usage data by using a blockchain makes it possible for energy suppliers, manufacturers, and service providers to access the data to identify new business opportunities. Using a blockchain takes the data out of the silo.

Smart meters aren't only consumers. As home solar panel installations increase and the panels become more efficient, the likelihood that a home will produce more electricity than it uses increases. In addition to autonomously monitoring energy use, a smart meter with a blockchain identity can also manage energy produced and delivered to the energy grid. The blockchain history of energy production would keep a detailed list of billing offsets that may substantially reduce a homeowner's energy bill.

Supply chain

One of the earliest large-scale Ethereum use cases is the management of supply chains. The process of managing products from the original producer to the consumer is expensive and time consuming. With today's tracking of goods, consumers have difficulty knowing much about the products they consume. Some products, such as electronics and appliances, might have descriptive tags that identify places and times of manufacture, but most of the products we consume don't provide that type of information.

Suppose you buy Alaskan salmon at your grocery store. Aside from the trust you place in your grocer, there isn't any way to know that the fish really came from Alaska. Ethereum supply-chain apps can provide consumers with complete information that lets them trace their product all the way back to its origin. In the case of the salmon, the fisherman who caught the fish would create the first entry in the blockchain. Every transfer of ownership from that point until the salmon ends up in the grocery store display would be tracked and recorded. A user-friendly Ethereum app could provide a trace all the way back to the day your fish was caught. Or, if you become ill after eating a Caesar salad, you could use blockchain data to find out what farm provided the romaine lettuce.

Implementing supply chain management provides multiple benefits. The first is transparency. Producers, consumers, and anyone in-between can see how each fish traveled from the place it was caught to where it was finally purchased. Anyone can trace its path and the time it took to get there. Inspectors and regulatory auditors can ensure that each participant in the supply chain met required standards. This increased transparency occurs while eliminating unnecessary middlemen. Each transfer in the process occurs between active participants, not brokers. With Ethereum supply-chain apps, you can track a product all the way back to its origin and verify the product's authenticity claims.

TIP

Proper tracking of physical products in the blockchain depends on accurately associating the physical product with the digital identifier. For example, I recently checked my bag when I flew on a commercial airline. The agent was busily engaged in a conversation with another agent, and swapped tags with another traveler. His tag was attached to my bag and vice versa. When I arrived, my bag was nowhere to be found. After investigating, we found that my tag arrived on the same flight as me, but it was attached to the wrong bag. My bag had flown to Mexico with the other gentleman's tag attached. It took four days to get my bag back. Always remember that the blockchain only represents the physical world — it isn't really the physical world.

Enabling Effective Governance

The last category of potential good use cases for Ethereum apps is in governance. Governing bodies should be responsible and accountable to the people they govern. Although this is not always the case, it is the ideal. Equitability, transparency, and auditability are three characteristics that should describe all government functions. Ethereum apps can help approach these goals by using foundational blockchain features to manage governance functions.

Tax payment

Governments fund their operation through taxes. Taxes are crucial to every governmental function and of vital interest to every taxpayer. Blockchain technology allows governments and taxpayers to interact in a way that provides both parties the transparency and auditability to assess taxes fairly. Taxpayers can record income and expenses in the blockchain ledger, and governing agencies can use that information to assess taxes. Taxpayers can also submit payment, or even accept refunds, through an Ethereum cryptocurrency transfer.

Ethereum-based tax payment maintenance could effectively eliminate the need to keep detailed records and receipts. Audits would take less time and effort because all supporting information would already be recorded in the blockchain. Although the outcome of the audit might not be any more desirable, at least Ethereum might make the process proceed more smoothly. And because audits would be simpler and faster, auditing agencies could carry out more audits using blockchain data.

Government spending

Currently, only some details about how governments spend money is made public. If all government spending were funded by cryptocurrency and recorded on a blockchain, all transactions would be available for review and audit. Any person with blockchain access could track payments. Transaction sources and recipients would either be divulged by the agency creating the payment or noticeably "secret." You may not be able to find out who owns a blockchain account that receives government funds, but you could still see how much cryptocurrency is transferred to the address. This new level of transparency would encourage politicians to reduce or (one hopes) eliminate secret payments.

Voting

A vote is a classic transfer of choice or approval from one person to another. Blockchain technology has the potential to greatly simplify the voting process. You've seen how Ethereum apps and standards can help manage digital identities. In much the same way, Ethereum can support identities in casting votes during an election. Because casting a vote is a transaction, each vote would be associated with a unique Ethereum address. The only piece of the puzzle left to address is to validate the registration of each account as an authorized voter.

Each voter's identification claims would contain descriptive attributes that identify the voter's eligibility and voting district. Any vote cast would be recorded on the blockchain and become part of the voting record. Calculating election results would be greatly simplified and the complete immutable record would reduce the many criticisms encountered in today's elections.

Policy development

Public policy development in many ways is an extension of the voting issue. The policy development process generally includes identifying a problem, collecting input from the community, developing a policy to address the problem, and then implementing the policy. Ethereum apps to manage interaction with the public can have multiple beneficial effects. Using blockchain to interact with the public would make governance functions more transparent and auditable by providing members of the public with a full record of the input and actions leading up to a policy change. It should also provide a mechanism for feedback to monitor the results of new or modified policy.

Notary

The last governance function that represents a good Ethereum use case is the notary function. In the real world, a notary provides assurance that a signature on a document is authentic. In the digital world, an Ethereum account can sign a document in a way that associates the digital identity with that document. If an Ethereum account appends a hash of the document with the author's private key, anyone can verify the signature by decrypting the hash with the account's public key and then comparing the decrypted value with the hash of the document. If the two match, that means the account really did sign the document AND it has not been altered. In this way, an Ethereum app can provide notary services.

Setting Up Your Ethereum Development Environment

IN THIS CHAPTER

» **Examining the Ethereum blockchain structure**

» **Understanding smart contracts and Solidity**

» **Paying for blockchain access**

» **Surveying Ethereum development tools**

» **Exploring the Ethereum application development lifecycle**

Chapter **4**

Examining the Ethereum Ecosystem and Development Lifecycle

The Ethereum blockchain implementation provides a rich environment for developing decentralized blockchain applications. These decentralized applications, or *dApps,* are unique in that the code and data are stored in the blockchain. Each node executes the code in the same way and guarantees that the results are the same.

The capability to deploy application code and data across an entire network ensures that the shared ledger remains the same for all nodes and that changes are allowed only in specific circumstances. The blockchain doesn't need an external authority to determine whether data is valid — the rules that govern the blockchain itself determine whether new data is valid and can be added to the blockchain.

In this chapter, you discover the components of an Ethereum dApp. You find out how code modifies the blockchain, and how to pay for the ability to add data. And finally, you learn about the Ethereum dApp development process, what tools you need to develop dApps, and how the pieces fit together.

Exploring the Ethereum Blockchain Block Structure

Ethereum dApps primarily populate blocks, add them to the blockchain, and query existing blocks. That sounds pretty simple, right? However, lots and lots of details are hidden in those simple goals. Before you can start to build blocks and add them to the blockchain, you need to know a little bit more about the contents of an Ethereum block and how the chain is built.

TECHNICAL STUFF

I describe only basic block and chain details. The authoritative reference for Ethereum internals is the Ethereum yellow paper, at `https://ethereum.github.io/yellowpaper/paper.pdf`. You can also find a pretty good third-party detailed discussion of Ethereum block structure internals at `https://ethereum.stackexchange.com/questions/268/ethereum-block-architecture`.

A *block* is a data structure that contains two main sections: a header and a body. Transactions are added to the body and then submitted to the blockchain network. *Miners* take the blocks and try to solve a mathematical puzzle to win a prize. Miners are just nodes, or pools of nodes, with enough computational power to calculate block hashes many times to solve the puzzle. In Ethereum, the mining process uses the submitted block header and an arbitrary number called a *nonce (number used once)*. The miner picks a value for the nonce, which is part of the block header, and calculates a Keccak-256 hash on the block header. The result has to match an agreed-upon pattern, which gets more difficult over time as miners gets faster at mining blocks. If the first mining result doesn't match the pattern, the miner picks another nonce and calculates a hash on the new block header. This process continues until a miner finds a nonce that results in a hash that matches the pattern.

The miner that finds the solution broadcasts that solution to the rest of the network. That miner collects a reward, in ETH, for doing the hard work to validate the block. Because many miners work on blocks at the same time, it's common for several miners to solve the hash puzzle at almost the same time. In other blockchains, these blocks are discarded as orphans. In Ethereum, these blocks are called uncles. An *uncle block* is any successfully mined block that arrives after that block has already been accepted. Ethereum accepts uncle blocks and even provides a reward to the miner, but the reward is smaller than the one for the accepted block.

TECHNICAL STUFF

Ethereum rewards miners of uncle blocks to reduce mining centralization and to increase the security of the blockchain. Uncle rewards provide an incentive for smaller miners to participate. Otherwise, mining would be profitable for only large pools, which could eventually take over all mining. Encouraging more miners to participate also increases security by increasing the overall work carried out on the entire blockchain.

The *header* of a block contains data that describes the block, and the *body* contains all the transactions stored in a block. Figure 4-1 shows the contents of an Ethereum block header.

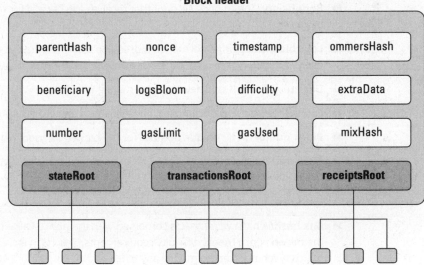

FIGURE 4-1:
Ethereum block header.

Each Ethereum block header contains information that defines and describes the block, and records its place in the blockchain. The block header contains these fields:

>> **Previous hash:** The hash value of the previous block's header, where the previous block is the last block on the blockchain to which the current block gets added.

Ethereum uses the Keccak-256 algorithm to produce all hash values. The National Institute of Standards and Technology (NIST) Secure Hashing Algorithm 3 (SHA3) is a subset of the Keccak algorithm. Ethereum was introduced before the SHA-3 standard was finalized, and Keccak-256 does not follow the SHA-3 official standard.

» **Nonce:** A number selected that causes the hash value of the current block's header to adhere to a specific pattern. If you change this value (or any header value), the hash of the header changes. You learn more about how Ethereum uses the nonce value shortly.

» **Timestamp:** The date and time the current block was created.

» **Uncles hash:** The hash value of the current block's list of uncle blocks, which are stale blocks that were successfully mined but arrived just after the accepted block was added to the blockchain.

» **Beneficiary:** The miner's account that receives the reward for mining the block.

» **Logs bloom:** Logging information stored in a *Bloom filter* (a data structure useful for quickly finding out if some element is a member of a set).

» **Difficulty:** The difficulty level used in mining the block.

» **Extra data:** As the name implies, any extra data used to describe the block.

» **Block number:** The unique number for the block (assigned sequentially).

» **Gas limit:** The limit of gas for the block. (You learn about gas later in this chapter.)

» **Gas used:** The amount of gas used by transactions in the block.

» **Mix hash:** A hash value that is combined with the nonce value to show that the mined nonce meets difficulty requirements. This hash increases the difficulty for attackers to modify any block.

» **State root:** The hash value of the root node of the block's state trie. A *trie* is a data structure that efficiently stores data for quick retrieval. The *state trie* is used to express information about the state of transactions in the block without having to look at the transactions.

» **Transaction root:** The hash value of the root node of the trie that stores all transactions for the block.

» **Receipt root:** The hash of the root node of the trie that stores all transaction receipts for the block.

The body of an Ethereum block is just a list of transactions. Unlike other block-chain implementations, the number of transactions — and as a result the size of blocks — isn't fixed. Every transaction has a processing cost associated with it, and each block has a limited budget. Ethereum blocks can contain lots of inexpensive transactions or just a few expensive ones or anything in between. Ethereum designed a lot of flexibility into what blocks can contain. Figure 4-2 shows the content of an Ethereum transaction.

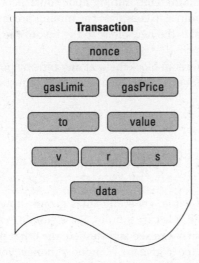

FIGURE 4-2: Contents of an Ethereum transaction.

Ethereum transactions contain the following fields:

>> **Nonce:** Each Ethereum account keeps track of the number of transactions it executes. This field is the latest transaction, based on the account's counter. The network uses the transaction nonce to ensure that transactions for that particular account are executed in the proper order.

>> **Signature:** The digital signature of the account owner, proving the identity of the account requesting this transaction.

>> **Gas price:** Unit price that the account is willing to pay to execute this transaction.

>> **Gas limit:** Maximum total amount you are willing to pay to execute this transaction.

>> **To:** The address that is the recipient of this transaction. For transfers, the address is the account that will receive the transfer. For calling functions, the address is the address of the smart contract.

>> **Value:** The total amount of ether you want to send to the recipient.

>> **Data:** The actual data submitted as the transaction body. Each type of transaction may have different data based on its functionality. For calling functions, the data may contain parameters.

As users submit transaction requests to nodes, the nodes create transactions and submit them to the transaction pool. Miners then pick transactions from the pool and build new blocks. After an Ethereum mining node constructs a block, it starts the mining process. The first miner to complete the mining process adds the block to the blockchain and broadcasts the new block to the rest of the network.

TIP

You can look at the public Ethereum blockchain at any time by going to Etherscan at https://etherscan.io/. Etherscan lets you see blockchain statistics as well as block and transaction details.

Describing Smart Contracts

When you exchange items of value, generally rules govern how the transaction takes place. In many cases, the rules are simple. For example, you me $1.89, and I give you a soft drink. Each party can see and validate the other party's contribution to the transaction. If you try to give me Monopoly money, you won't get your soft drink. Even though this transaction seems simple, there's more to it than meets the eye. In most cases, if a soft drink costs $1.89, you'll have to tender more than that for it. You'll have to pay taxes as well. So there's another participant in the transaction: the government. Instead of keeping all the money, I have to send some of it to the government for taxes.

Moving even simple transactions like the soft drink example into the digital world takes some careful thought. You can't just send money to people and trust that they'll do their part. You need some way to enforce rules and compliance to make sure that all parties are treated fairly.

Smart contracts help you enforce rules when you exchange anything of value in Ethereum. The simplest way to describe smart contracts is that they are programs that execute when certain transactions occur. For example, if you create a soft-drink-purchase smart contract, that software code will run every time someone buys a soft drink. The smart contract code is stored in the blockchain, so all nodes have a copy of it. Also, it doesn't matter where the software runs: All nodes are guaranteed to run it the same and get the same results as every other node.

TECHNICAL STUFF

Ethereum smart contracts are *Turing complete,* which means they can compute anything that is computable with enough resources. Turing completeness is important because Ethereum smart contracts aren't limited in the types of actions they can carry out. They can carry out any complex algorithms you can design.

The soft-drink smart contract starts with the buyer. Here's how the exchange might happen:

>> The buyer creates a transaction that sends money to the seller in exchange for the soft drink.

>> The buyer sends the seller's address as input to the smart contract's address.

>> The smart contract runs to carry out the transaction. It verifies that you have enough money in your account to pay for the soft drink.

>> The smart contract verifies that the seller has the soft drink you want in stock.

>> The smart contract deducts funds from the buyer, sends the funds to the seller, and tells the seller to send the soft drink to the buyer. In the same step, the smart contract sends the required tax to the tax authority account and sends the remaining amount to the seller's account.

The process may seem tedious, but it is straightforward and makes sure each transaction occurs in the same way. This example is too simple for real-life exchanges, and I left out some important details. For starters, we assume that the seller will send the soft drink to the buyer. Real-life exchanges require an extra layer of protection for both sides. Smart contracts use escrow accounts (see Chapter 3) all the time to hold a buyer's money until the seller delivers the goods or services.

Smart contracts provide the governance and predictability of Ethereum. Without them, Ethereum would just be a cool distributed storage technique. But with them, Ethereum is a stable decentralized platform that supports interactions and exchanges between untrusting users, including extremely complex transactions. It is easy to see the steps necessary to buy a soft drink. Other transactions, such as real estate transactions, are far more complex, have many dependencies and requirements, and generally involve several people and organizations. Ethereum smart contracts can help developers create software that eliminates middlemen, streamlines complex processes, and reduces the overall cost and time required to complete even the most complex exchanges.

Introducing Solidity, the Language of Smart Contracts

Smart contracts are software programs. With enough resources, smart contracts can do anything any other software can do. You can write Ethereum smart contracts in several languages:

>> **Mutan:** An older smart contract language that was deprecated in 2015.

>> **LLL:** A Lisp-like language, obviously developed to look like the language Lisp. Although LLL is still supported, it's not used for many current smart contract projects.

>> **Serpent:** A language that looks like the Python language. As of September 2017, Serpent is not recommended for current development.

>> **Bamboo:** A relatively new language that focuses on making blockchain state transitions explicit and avoiding code reentrant issues.

>> **Viper:** Another relatively new language that focuses on security and simplicity.

>> **Solidity:** Currently the most popular smart contract development language. Solidity looks like the JavaScript language and provides a full-featured language for developing general-purpose smart contracts.

TIP

Solidity is the most popular language for smart contracts, and the one you're most likely to encounter. For that reason, I chose to focus on Solidity in this book.

If you're comfortable with JavaScript, picking up Solidity will be a little easier. If you don't know much JavaScript, that's okay. You're going to learn the basics of Solidity from the ground floor. In fact, I start with a program that may look familiar: the ubiquitous "Hello world" program.

You'll see this code again in Chapter 7, where you dig deeper into each part of this simple program. For now, take a look at this very simple smart contract code:

```
pragma solidity ^0.4.25;

contract helloWorld {
  function printHelloWorld () public constant returns (string) {
    return 'Hello world!';
  }
}
```

That's what a Solidity smart contract looks like! After the heading, you define your contract, and then any functions that make up the inner workings of the program. After you write and test a smart contract, you can deploy it to a blockchain (more about this in Chapter 7), and then execute it. When you get everything right, your smart contract will show you the iconic "Hello world!" message.

As you learn more about Solidity, you'll see that it does look a lot like JavaScript but also feels a bit like C++ and Python. The developers of Solidity based the language on all three languages. It supports inheritance, libraries, and user-defined types that can be quite complex. It is also a statically typed language, which means you have to provide explicit datatypes for the variables you create and use.

Above all, Solidity is a smart contract development language. Even though it looks like other languages, it includes primitives and an orientation designed to interact with the Ethereum blockchain. In Chapters 8 and 9 you learn a lot more about how to write to and read from the Ethereum blockchain by using Solidity.

Working with the Ethereum Virtual Machine

You write smart contract code in Solidity, but it won't run in its source form. Almost all programs written in any language have to be translated into a runnable format. Some languages, such as C++, are compiled languages. When you write a C++ program, you have to use a compiler to compile the program into an executable that an operating system can run. Other languages, such as Python, are interpreted. You run a program that provides a runtime environment, which interprets your code and executes the commands.

Other languages, such as Java and Solidity, exist in-between compiled and interpreted languages. You compile the programs you write in both of these languages, but you compile your source code to opcode, also called bytecode. *Opcode* is an optimized sequence of operations that your language's runtime environment can understand. The runtime environment is often referred to as the language's *virtual machine.* In Java, programs run in the Java virtual machine (JVM). All Solidity smart contracts run in the *Ethereum virtual machine (EVM).*

The EVM is present on all nodes. When you install Ethereum, you get the EVM, and it runs whenever you run Ethereum. That means any time a smart contract runs, it runs on all EVMs across the Ethereum network. Ethereum ensures that smart contracts run the same way on all nodes and get the same results. That's how the blockchain remains consistent across all nodes.

The EVM uses a stack-based architecture, and has its own area in memory for the code it runs and the data it stores in addition to each smart contract's local storage. Although the EVM is a Turing complete virtual machine, its execution is limited by the amount of gas allowed by each smart contract run. That limitation avoids using excessive computing power for nodes across the Ethereum network (or bankrupting an account with a programming error or malicious code that tries to run forever.).

As you can see, running every smart contract on every node in the Ethereum network is a lot of work. Every additional instruction in a smart contract causes thousands of nodes to do more work. To reduce the computation waste on so many machines, Ethereum includes incentives for using computation resources conservatively and sets upper limits on just how much work a smart contract can carry out. In the next section you learn about how Ethereum sets these limits.

Fueling Your Code with Gas

A couple of the fields in the block header include the word *gas*. Those fields refer to the cryptocurrency cost of accessing the blockchain and executing code. Because Ethereum storage and processing is distributed across many nodes, individuals and organizations need an incentive to commit their computing resources to blockchain operation. Gas is that incentive.

Gas refers to the fee that transaction initiators pay to process their operations. Ethereum users use ether to pay miners. To keep costs manageable, each transaction has a maximum amount of gas you're willing to pay. If you set this limit too low, many miners may pass up your transaction and you may have to wait to get your transaction into a block. After your transaction is selected by a miner, you have to pay a small amount of gas for every computational step required to complete the transaction. The good news is that you don't have to pay the maximum each time you start a transaction and you get a refund for any gas that isn't used in the transaction.

Gas serves several purposes in the Ethereum ecosystem. First, it encourages developers to create efficient smart contracts, which require less computational resources than sloppy or unoptimized smart contracts. Any savings of computational resources are magnified by the thousands of nodes on the Ethereum network. Being conservative lowers costs all around.

Second, gas limits make it harder for malicious users to write code to consume available network resources. Denial of service (DoS) attacks on Ethereum networks could tie up all nodes if unrestrained smart contracts were allowed to run. Gas allows upper limits to be established that stop DoS attacks in their tracks.

And finally, charging gas for accessing data stored on the blockchain discourages blockchain growth because it makes developers think through the justification for putting data on the blockchain. This approach also encourages developers to be creative when determining how to store context data. Although in many cases it would be easier to store data in a block, gas cost often leads to other designs that leverage local storage.

Two main variables are used to calculate the total cost of a transaction:

» **Gas used:** The total amount of gas that a transaction uses. Each computation in a smart contract has an associated computation price.

» **Gas price:** The price, in Ether, of one unit of gas used in the transaction.

The formula for calculating the cost of gas for a transaction is

Total gas cost = Gas used * Gas price

TECHNICAL STUFF

If you're interested in calculating your own gas usage, every Ethereum operation and its associated cost (in gas) is listed in the spreadsheet at http://ethereum. stackexchange.com/q/52/42.

Gas price is expressed in wei units. *Wei* is a denomination of ether cryptocurrency. One ether (ETH) equals 1e18 wei (that's 1,000,000,000,000,000,000 wei). The current gas price fluctuates, but at the time of this writing, it's somewhere around 2 Gwei (2,000,000,000 wei).

Ethereum gives both miners and transaction requesters substantial flexibility. If you request a transaction, you get to set a maximum gas price and total amount of gas you're willing to pay. That gives you the ability to limit your cost. Of course, if your limits are too low, your transaction may never make it to the blockchain. From the miner perspective, you can cherry-pick the transactions you want to put into blocks. When cash flow is high, you can choose only the best paying transactions. On the other hand, when things are slower, you have the option to take lower paying transactions. Regardless, Ethereum lets you choose.

Surveying Tools for Developing, Testing, and Deploying Ethereum Apps

You use different tools for every phase of the process of developing and deploying Ethereum dApps. Many tools are available; this section covers a few of the more popular ones.

You need multiple tools to address the requirements of the multiple levels involved in developing Ethereum dApps: source code development, testing, compiling, and deploying your smart contract code. In this section, I briefly describe some of the more popular development tools in each of the following categories:

>> **Ethereum blockchain client:** This software runs the Ethereum blockchain and EVM, making a computer a blockchain node.

>> **Development and testing blockchain:** This tool sets up a local, or non-live, blockchain to use before deploying code to the live blockchain.

>> **Compiler and testing framework:** A compiler translates source code into bytecode for the EVM, and testing tools help to identify and fix bugs.

>> **Source code editor and integrated development environment (IDE):** These tools include editors and suites of tools designed to help developers write code.

Ethereum blockchain client

The Ethereum blockchain client establishes an Ethereum node, downloads part, or all, of an Ethereum blockchain, and launches the EVM. Ethereum client software makes a computer or device an Ethereum node in the blockchain network.

Ethereum clients nodes can be full nodes or light nodes. *Full nodes* store the entire Ethereum blockchain, which at the time of this writing is 182.5 GB. You can go to `https://bitinfocharts.com/` to see the current Ethereum blockchain size, along with lots of other stats for popular blockchains. That's a lot of storage to dedicate just to keeping a copy of a blockchain. An alternative to full nodes is to connect to the blockchain network as a light node. *Light nodes* store only a portion of the blockchain. Either way, you need to install Ethereum client software to connect to the network.

REMEMBER

Remember the root hash fields in the Ethereum block header layout shown earlier in the chapter? Light nodes download and store block headers but don't fetch all of the block contents. That reduces the blockchain storage requirement to a point that small devices, even Raspberry Pi, can become light nodes. The light node fetches block contents only when to user needs it to complete some task, such as checking a balance or submitting a new transaction.

All Ethereum clients support the Ethereum standard and implement the EVM. The main difference between clients is the programming language in which each one is written. Because all clients provide the same core functionality, the choice is largely based on your language preference. Table 4-1 lists several Ethereum blockchain clients.

TABLE 4-1   ### Ethereum Clients

Name	Language	Where to Get It
Cpp-ethereum	C++	`http://ethdocs.org/en/latest/ethereum-clients/cpp-ethereum`
Ethereumjs-lib	JavaScript	`http://ethdocs.org/en/latest/ethereum-clients/ethereumjs-lib`
Geth (go-ethereum)	Go	`htpps://ethereum.github.io/go-ethereum`
Parity	Rust	`https://www.parity.io/`
Pyethapp	Python	`http://ethdocs.org/en/latest/ethereum-clients/pyethapp`

Development and testing blockchain

One of the strongest features of blockchain technology is that the blockchain is immutable. Although that's great for integrity, it makes developing smart contract code more difficult. Software rarely works correctly the first time its written. The development process is made up of multiple snapshots of software as it matures to become the final product.

Putting your code on the live Ethereum public blockchain is the last step in the development process. Before you're ready to do that, you need a local or non-live blockchain environment to use while developing and testing. That way, you put only the final, bug-free (you hope) version of your code on the live blockchain.

TECHNICAL STUFF

You don't have to use separate tools to create a private blockchain. You can set one up yourself and configure your Ethereum client to use it instead of the live Ethereum network. If you want to build your own private blockchain from scratch, check out the resource at `souptacular.gitbooks.io/ethereum-tutorials-and-tips-by-hudson/content/private-chain.html`.

Tools in this category provide a development and testing blockchain that you can use while you add features to your code. Table 4-2 lists the four main Ethereum development and testing blockchains.

TABLE 4-2 **Ethereum Development and Testing Blockchains**

Name	Description	Where to Get It
Ganache	Most popular tool with developers for easily creating a private network	truffleframework.com/ganache
Truffle	A suite of development tools that includes its own private network	truffleframework.com
Cliquebait	Uses docker instances to simulate a real blockchain network	github.com/f-o-a-m/cliquebait
Local Ethereum Network	Easy-to-use scripts to set up private blockchain networks	github.com/ConsenSys/local_ethereum_network

Compiler and testing framework

The EVM runs bytecode, so you'll need a compiler to translate your source code into bytecode. Tools in this category also provide the functionality for monitoring how your smart contracts execute and identifying bugs. Table 4–3 lists several Ethereum compilers and testing frameworks.

TABLE 4-3 **Ethereum Compilers and Testing Frameworks**

Name	Description	Where to Get It
Truffle	Popular suite of tools to manage smart contract development, testing, and deployment	truffleframework.com
Solidity compiler (solc)	Solidity software includes a command-line compiler that can be called from IDEs	github.com/ethereum/solidity
Solidity compile (solcjs)	Solidity compiler written in JavaScript	github.com/ethereum/solc-js
Remix	Web-based suite of Ethereum development tools that includes a Solidity compiler	remix.ethereum.org
Populus	Web-based IDE for smart contract development	github.com/ethereum/populus
Embark	Framework for developing dApps for multiple blockchains	github.com/embark-framework/embark

Source code editor/IDE

You can use any text editor to write smart contract sources code, but several editor environments are designed to help developers write and manage code. These tools help you to develop code efficiently. Table 4–4 lists several source code editors and IDEs that help you develop Ethereum smart contracts in Solidity.

TABLE 4-4 ## Source Code Editors/IDEs

Name	Language	Where to Get It
Atom	Popular IDE with Solidity extensions	atom.io
Visual Studio Code	Microsoft's IDE with Solidity extensions	marketplace.visualstudio.com/items?itemName=JuanBlanco.solidity
Vim Solidity	Solidity extensions for Vim (a vi-like editor)	github.com/tomlion/vim-solidity
Remix	Web-based IDE popular with new Solidity developers	remix.ethereum.org
EthFiddle	Web-based IDE focused on simplicity	ethfiddle.com
Superblocks Lab	Web-based IDE with many built-in blockchain integration features	lab.superblocks.com
Pragma	Simple web-based IDE that offers auto-generated code segments	www.withpragma.com

Describing the Ethereum Development Lifecycle

Smart contract development generally follows the same process as the traditional software development lifecycle, but with a few nuances. The basic steps in the software development lifecycle are as follows:

» **Planning:** This phase includes gathering specifications and designing the solution.

» **Coding/development:** After planning is complete, developers start writing code to implement the planned solution.

» **Testing:** Unit testing should occur throughout the coding phase, but after all coding is complete, the entire software product undergoes testing to ensure that all the pieces work together as designed. If testers find flaws, you have to go back at least to the coding phase, and perhaps even to the planning phase, to make changes to fix the flaws.

» **Deployment:** After fixing any remaining flaws, the properly functioning software is released to the production environment. This phase also includes maintenance activities, which monitor the software and respond to newly identified flaws or requests for enhancements.

Although the main phases of the software development lifecycle are the same for smart contract development, the design of blockchain technology raises a few issues. First, remember that the blockchain data is immutable. Also, smart contracts are deployed to blocks in the blockchain. After you deploy a smart contract, it can never change. That's good if you want it to stick around forever, but it can be bad if you find out later that you deployed a smart contract with a bug. Figure 4-3 shows the smart contract software development life cycle.

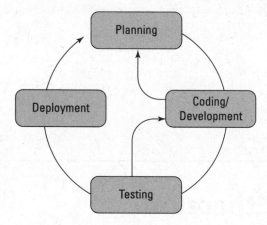

FIGURE 4-3:
Smart contract
software
development
lifecycle.

Testing is more important when dealing with blockchain technology because updating smart contracts is awkward and can be difficult. Each new smart contract deployment gets a new address, so you have to ensure that all references to the old smart contract are updated to refer to the new smart contract. Also, you have to be careful about how the updated smart contract handles data. If the changes you made in the smart contract change how it handles data, you'll have to figure out how to deal with the data already in the blockchain. Another issue is that until you deploy a smart contract, you'll be testing it on a local, or private, blockchain. Your test environment may not reflect how the real blockchain operates.

These are just a few issues you'll encounter when developing for a blockchain. Pay attention to the quality of your testing activities. Thorough testing takes time, but it can save a lot more.

Introducing Smart Contract Development Tools

In the following chapters, you learn how to set up a development environment and develop smart contracts by using the Solidity language. As you learned in this chapter, multiple tools are available for each stage of development. Instead of covering all the tools, I chose one from each category so you can focus on learning Solidity. You can use a different tool if you want — all of the ones listed are good choices.

Here is what you will use:

>> **Ethereum blockchain client:** You'll use Geth, which is easy to install. Many tutorials use Geth as their client.

>> **Development and testing blockchain:** Ganache-cli is the chosen development and testing blockchain. Ganache-cli makes it easy to set up new blockchains to test your smart contracts.

>> **Compiler and testing framework:** I chose the Truffle suite, which provides an effective and easy-to-use collection of tools for compiling and testing your new smart contracts.

>> **Source code editor/integrated development environment (IDE):** This choice was the hardest. From so many good options, I chose the Atom IDE. For your development, try a few alternative editors/IDEs as well to see which one is your favorite.

In the next chapter, you learn how to download, install, and configure these tools. Then you'll be ready to learn how to develop your own smart contracts.

Chapter **5**

Getting and Configuring Ethereum Development Tools

The most popular language for developing decentralized applications (dApps) for the Ethereum blockchain is Solidity. Before you can learn how to develop dApps in Solidity, however, you need to have all the tools installed and available. Depending on your needs, you can designate a computer to be your development workstation, or you can use web-based tools to develop code from any web browser.

For the examples in this book, I chose to use software that installs locally on a PC. Installing all these tools will give you the ability to write smart contract software, compile it, deploy it to a test environment, test it, and finally deploy it to the real blockchain.

In this chapter you build your own Ethereum development environment. By the end of the chapter, you'll be ready to get started developing your own smart contracts and dApps.

Examining Why Multiple Ethereum Development Tools Are Available

The first thing you might notice when building an Ethereum development environment is that you have a lot of choices. Overall, many choices are a good thing, but they make getting started a little more confusing. Remember that Ethereum is a complete blockchain environment. Running the blockchain is one thing — developing code for the blockchain is a bigger endeavor and requires more tools.

The Ethereum Foundation is the Swiss non-profit organization that introduced, and now promotes and supports, the Ethereum platform. Their website, `https://ethereum.org/`, is a treasure trove of great information about all facets of Ethereum. Ethereum is an open-source project, which means that the source code for the Ethereum blockchain environment is available to anyone who wants it. Ethereum can theoretically run on any computing device.

The runtime environment for Ethereum smart contracts, EVM (Ethereum virtual machine), is implemented in many different languages. Each implementation allows Ethereum to run on different platforms, giving anyone setting up a new node choices in how to run the EVM. For example, if performance is the highest priority, a C++ implementation might be the best choice. But if the capability to integrate additional functionality with the EVM is a goal, a JavaScript or Python implementation might be a better choice.

The open-source community is a worldwide group of users and developers who contribute to projects in which they have a stake. Ethereum users and developers often engage in rigorous debates about how to best advance the product. These debates commonly result in different opinions about the best way to meet goals. One of the more common debates is over which user interface is better. One school of thought is that a *command-line interface (CLI)* is the most flexible and the easiest to script. This type of user interface tends to work best for lower-level utility-type tools. On the other hand, an integrated *graphical user interface (GUI)* is more user friendly and makes tasks such as software development easier. That's just one example of why you may see both CLI and GUI versions of tools.

As a result of diverse people contributing to the community, you'll find multiple software products that address the needs of each step in the development process. Several different test network implementations exist because a group in the Ethereum community felt that making it easier to set up a test network would draw more developers to the Ethereum platform. Others focus on integrated testing tools. And others decided to extend their favorite editors and IDEs with extensions that support Solidity.

As you look at the available options in each tool category, remember that each one is there because a group of Ethereum enthusiasts saw an opportunity to fill a feature gap. Although it may take some time, it can be interesting to read through the features and benefits of some competing products to see how they differ.

TIP

If you want to get involved in the Ethereum community, check out the Ethereum website at `https://ethereum.org/`. At the bottom of the home page, you'll see a Community section with links to various ways to participate.

The tools you'll install and configure in this chapter are the ones you'll frequently see used by other Ethereum developers. You'll find lots of online tips, tricks, and tutorials for Ethereum development using these tools. The environment you build in this chapter will allow you to work through the examples in this book and learn from other online resources — without having to start over installing new tools.

Downloading, Installing, and Configuring All the Pieces

Now that you're ready to build your Ethereum development environment, let's dive right in. You'll learn how to set up a PC running Microsoft Windows to be an Ethereum development platform. Windows isn't the only operating system that supports Ethereum. You can just as easily set up a macOS or Linux computer to support Ethereum. If you're running macOS or Linux, each tool in this chapter will work on your computer, too, although the installation steps might be a little different. Each tool's website will provide detailed instructions for each operating system.

Installing the blockchain client

Start by installing an Ethereum client. I chose Go Ethereum (Geth) as the Ethereum client you'll use in this book. Geth is written in the Go language and allows you to run a full Ethereum node. Running a full Ethereum node means you'll have access to the complete Ethereum blockchain and also run a local EVM. Geth gives you the capability to mine ETH, create transactions and smart contracts, and examine any blocks that already exist on the blockchain. All remaining tools you'll install in this chapter will depend on Geth to provide the local EVM and allow access to the blocks on the blockchain.

TECHNICAL
STUFF

The Geth website provides prepackaged installers for Microsoft Windows, macOS, and Linux operating systems. You can also download the Geth source code and build it for your own custom environment. If you're interested in playing around with devices other than just computers, you can conduct an Internet search and easily find instructions on setting up Geth on smartphones or a Raspberry Pi. That's the beauty of using open-source tools.

Start by downloading and installing Geth, as follows:

1. **Launch your browser and navigate to** https://ethereum.github.io/go-ethereum, **and then click or tap the Downloads link at the top of the page.**

   Your web browser will look like Figure 5-1.

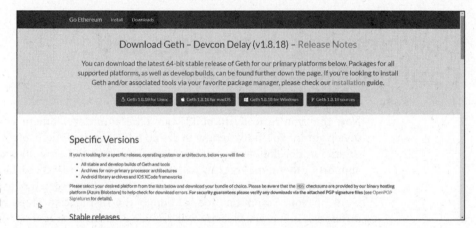

FIGURE 5-1:
The Go Ethereum
(Geth) Download
web page.

2. **Click or tap the Geth button for your operating system.**

   Because I'm setting up a Microsoft Windows computer in this tutorial, I selected Geth 1.8.18 for Windows. (When you set up your computer, a newer version of Geth might be available. You should download and install the latest version of each tool.)

3. **Launch the executable file you just downloaded.**

4. **Click or tap I Agree to the GNU General Public License.**

   Always read any license agreement before agreeing to its contents.

REMEMBER

5. **Select the Development Tools check box, and then click or tap the Next button.**

   Make sure that you choose to install the development tools in this window before continuing. Figure 5-2 shows what the Installation Options window will look like.

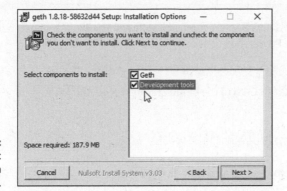

FIGURE 5-2:
Geth Setup:
Installation
Options window.

6. **If you want to install Geth to a different folder than the one that's displayed, change it to your desired destination folder.**

7. **Click or tap the Install button to start the installation process.**

8. **When the installation finishes, click or tap the Close button.**

After you've installed Geth, you can launch it to start the EVM and synchronize with the public Ethereum blockchain.

You learn about a few other Geth startup options in Chapter 7, but the only option you need for now is syncmode, which tells Geth how much of the blockchain to download. The syncmode option has the following three values. Note that you'll be using the light value for the syncmode option:

» **full:** Download and validate the entire blockchain. This option requires the most time and disk space but can provide the fastest response because a full node doesn't ever have to request missing blocks from other nodes.

» **fast:** Download and validate the block headers and data for the most recent 1000 transactions. This option is a good choice when you want to conserve some disk space but also want to store the most recent blocks locally.

» **light:** Download only the blockchain current state and request any missing blocks from other nodes as needed. This option allows you to operate Ethereum with minimal disk space requirements.

For the exercise in this book, you'll use the light syncmode option for Geth. To start Geth in light mode, follow these steps:

1. **Launch a command prompt or PowerShell prompt.**

To launch a command prompt, type **cmd** in the search bar at the lower-left corner of your desktop and then click or tap the Command Prompt option.

To launch a PowerShell prompt, type **PowerShell** in the search bar and click or tap the PowerShell option.

2. **Change the current working directory to the Geth install directory.**

   If you installed Geth to the default location, type the following and then press Enter:

   ```
   cd 'C:\Program Files\Geth\'
   ```

3. **Type the following, and then press Enter:**

   ```
   .\geth --syncmode "light"
   ```

   This command launches Geth in light mode. Make sure that you type two dashes before *syncmode*. Figure 5-3 shows the Geth command to start a light Ethereum node.

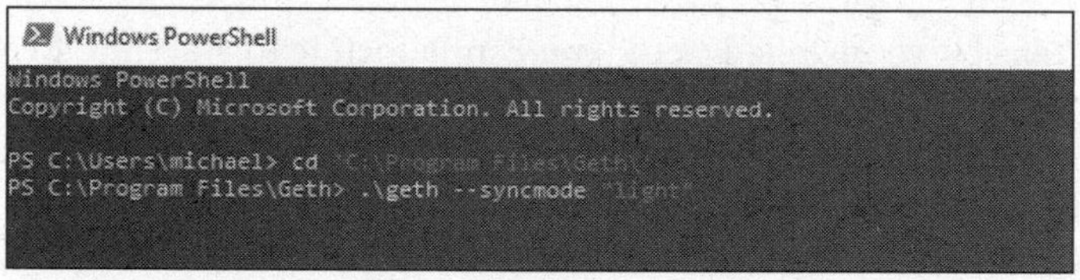

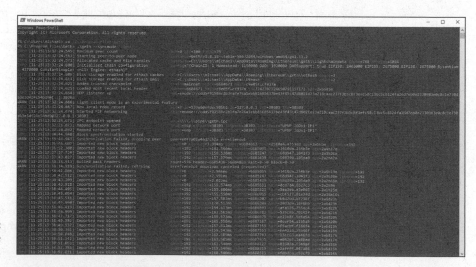

FIGURE 5-3: Geth light node startup command.

A Geth starts, it establishes a connection with the Ethereum network and begins synchronizing the current blockchain. Geth provides messages at each stage of its startup process to let you see what is happening. Figure 5-4 shows what the Geth messages looks like.

FIGURE 5-4: Geth runtime messages.

After Geth synchronizes the blockchain, you're ready to use the Geth blockchain client to develop and deploy your own dApps.

Installing the test blockchain

When you develop smart contracts and dApps, you don't want to deploy your code or data to the live blockchain until you're sure that everything works correctly. You have to test your code in some non-live environment. You'll need a blockchain to use during the development and testing process. Ethereum clients, Geth included, connect to the main public Ethereum blockchain by default, but you can connect to other blockchains as well. You can change the connection settings easily for development and testing.

Several tools make it easy to create and manage test blockchains. I chose Ganache for our test blockchain environment. According to the Ganache website (https://truffleframework.com/ganache), "Ganache is a personal blockchain for Ethereum development you can use to deploy contracts, develop your applications, and run tests."

TECHNICAL
STUFF

You aren't limited to the prebuilt Ganache images. Because Ganache is an open-source product, you can also download the Ganache source code and build it for your own custom environment.

To download and install Ganache, follow these steps:

1. **Launch your browser and navigate to** https://truffleframework.com/ganache.

   Your web browser will look like Figure 5-5. Click or tap the Download (Windows) button to download the Windows installer.

FIGURE 5-5:
The Ganache
Download
web page.

2. **Launch the executable file you just downloaded.**

   Click or tap the Install button to start the installation process. By default, Ganache launches when the installation finishes.

3. **Accept the default, as shown in Figure 5-6, or click or tap the Analytics Enabled toggle box to disable Analytics, and then click or tap the Continue button.**

   Because this is the first time you're launching Ganache, you are asked to allow Google Analytics tracking. You don't have to do this, but allowing analytics helps the Ganache development team learn how different people use Ganache.

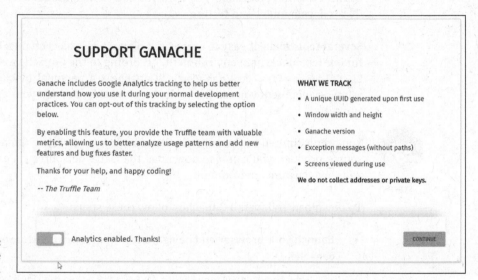

FIGURE 5-6:
Support Ganache
Analytics window.

When Ganache launches, you'll see the main window with basic server information and a list of accounts,. as shown in Figure 5-7. Because the reason to install Ganache is to create your own blockchain, you'll need at least one account to access the blockchain. Ganache creates 10 accounts for you, each with a balance of 100.0 ETH. You can create more accounts and give them all the ETH they need to test your smart contracts and dApps. Figure 5-7 shows the main Ganache Accounts window.

That's all it takes to create your own Ethereum blockchain in Ganache. Of course, this blockchain is local to your own computer and isn't distributed to any other nodes. Because there aren't any other nodes on this network, there aren't any miners. This blockchain is set to *automining*, which means that any new transactions are processed immediately. That setting makes it easy to test your smart contracts and dApps without having to pay miners to process your transactions.

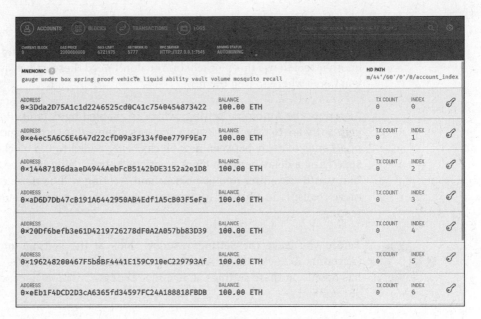

FIGURE 5-7:
Ganache
Accounts window.

When you're ready to start developing software for Ethereum, you'll need to tell your client and other tools which blockchain to use. Let's see where your new Ganache blockchain is located. In Ganache, click or tap the settings (gear) icon in the upper-right corner to launch the Ganache Settings window. Figure 5-8 displays the Server tab of the Ganache Settings window.

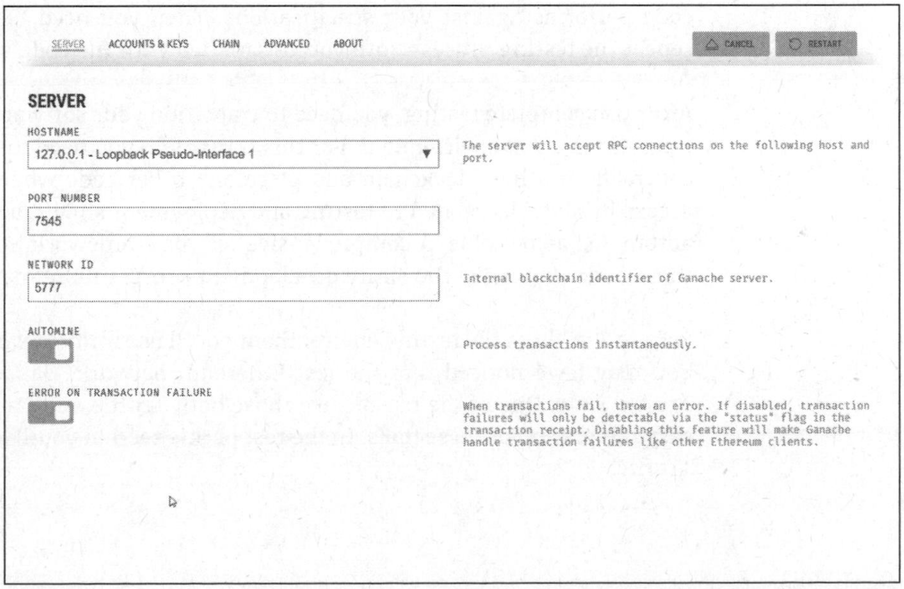

FIGURE 5-8:
Ganache Settings
window's
Server tab.

You can see where other tools can find your blockchain. The Hostname, Port Number, and Network ID values show you what you need any time you want another tool to use this blockchain. You don't need these values quite yet, but now you know where to find them.

Also note the Automine setting, which is enabled by default. Before you deploy your software to a live blockchain, you can disable this setting and enter a number of seconds to delay between new blocks being added to the blockchain. Manually specifying a delay between block creations helps to simulate the effect of miners that you'll encounter in a live blockchain. Testing will be more complex but also more realistic. In Chapter 10, you learn more about carrying out comprehensive testing.

TIP

Before you leave the Settings window, look at the settings on the other tabs (Accounts & Keys, Chain, Advanced, and About). The Ganache Quickstart guide has details on these settings at `https://truffleframework.com/docs/ganache/quickstart`.

Installing the testing environment

The software development process is made up of multiple steps. In Chapter 4, you learn about the four main phases of the Ethereum software development lifecycle. Although the lifecycle has only four phases, many different tasks need to be accomplished. In addition to just writing source code, you have to compile your code, deploy it to a test environment, test the code, and measure how well the code performs against your specifications. Then you need to fix any flaws and repeat the testing process until you're satisfied with the code's operation.

After you complete testing, you need to transition your software from a test environment to a live environment. For this transition, you need to submit your smart contracts to a live blockchain and place any other code where your clients can access it. All tasks related to testing and deployment should be repeatable and as automated as possible. A comprehensive testing framework helps to standardize these tasks and make the entire development process more manageable.

I chose Truffle as the testing environment you'll use for the examples in this book. You may have noticed that the test Ethereum network, Ganache, is part of the Truffle Suite. One of the reasons we chose both Truffle and Ganache is due to the easy integration of these tools. In the rest of this section you'll learn how to install Truffle.

Getting ready to install Truffle

Before you can install Truffle, you have to ensure that your computer meets the prerequisite. Open your browser and navigate to `https://truffleframework.com/docs/truffle/getting-started/installation` to see the Truffle installation requirements, which are shown in Figure 5-9.

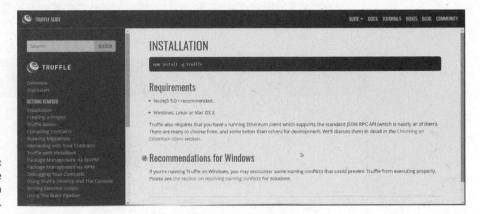

The main requirement for Truffle is to have NodeJS version 5.0 or higher installed. NodeJS is an open-source project that provides a runtime environment for code written in JavaScript. JavaScript was originally designed to run in web browsers, but NodeJS makes it easy to run JavaScript code outside a browser.

It's easy to find out whether NodeJS is installed. Open a command shell or PowerShell window, type the `node` command, and press Enter. You'll get a simple > prompt or an error message telling you that NodeJS is not installed. Figure 5-10 shows the error message you'll see in Windows PowerShell if you don't have NodeJS installed.

If you do have NodeJS installed, skip to the next section, "Downloading and installing Truffle." If you don't have NodeJS installed, follow these steps to download and install it:

1. **Launch your browser and navigate to** `https://nodejs.org/en/`.

Your web browser will look like Figure 5-11. The NodeJS website detects your operating system and suggests the versions for that operating system. Because I'm using Microsoft Windows, I saw download links for Windows.

FIGURE 5-11:
The NodeJS
Download
web page.

2. **Click or tap the button for the version you want to install to download the Windows installer.**

You can download the latest version or the latest stable (long term support, or LTS) version. I chose the LTS version for the examples in this book. (When you set up your computer, a newer version of NodeJS might be available. You should download and install the latest version of each available tool.)

REMEMBER

If you want to install NodeJS on a computer that isn't running Microsoft Windows or want to build your own version of NodeJS, click or tap the Other Downloads link. This link takes you to a page with options to download source code or installer packages for multiple operating systems.

3. **Launch the executable file you just downloaded.**

Click or tap the Next button to start the installation process.

4. **Read the End-User License Agreement, accept it, and then click or tap Next.**

5. **Select NodeJS installation options in the next three windows.**

   Enter the install destination (or accept the default), and then click or tap Next. In the Custom Setup window that appears, click or tap Next to accept the defaults. In the next window, click or tap the Automatically Install the Necessary Tools option and then click or tap Next.

6. **To install NodeJS, click or tap Install.**

7. **To complete the NodeJS part of the installation process, click or tap Finish.**

8. **Install the NodeJS tools.**

   Press any key in the next two windows to run the scripts to install the supplemental NodeJS tools.

You can verify that NodeJS is installed with a simple command. Open a command shell or PowerShell window, type the following command, and press Enter:

```
node --version
```

This time when you enter the node command, you should see a message showing you the installed NodeJS version. Figure 5-12 shows the version message in Windows PowerShell.

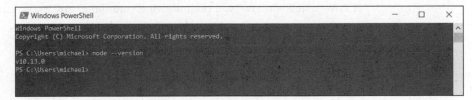

FIGURE 5-12: The NodeJS version message.

After you have NodeJS installed, you're ready to install Truffle.

Downloading and installing Truffle

The NodeJS environment makes it easy to find and download new packages, including Truffle. The Truffle installation process requires you to enter just a single command.

To install Truffle, open a command shell or PowerShell window, type the following command, and press Enter:

```
npm install -g truffle
```

Figure 5-13 shows what this command and the results. Truffle is installed and almost ready to be used.

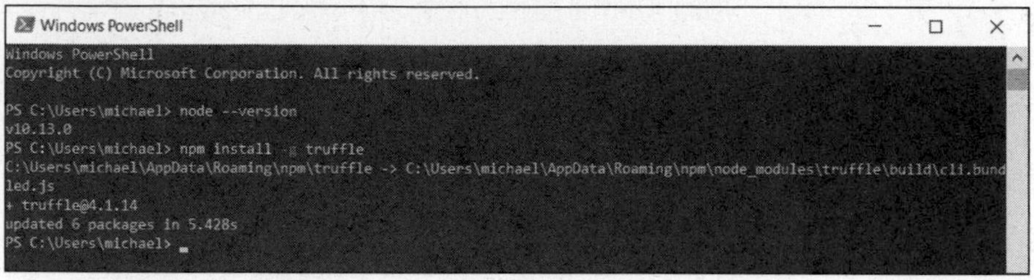

FIGURE 5-13:
Installing Truffle.

Truffle organizes development activities into projects. That way you can work on multiple projects with different configuration requirements. For example, you could set up a different testing blockchain for each of several projects. In Chapter 7, you learn more about configuring projects. Here, let's look at the basics of setting up a project in Truffle.

Each Truffle project needs its own folder. The first thing you need to do to set up a Truffle project is to create a project folder. If you'd rather download the project files instead of creating a new empty project, go to www.dummies.com/go/ ethereumfd and extract the project archive file to a directory of your choice. To create a new empty project named myProject, for example, open a command shell or PowerShell window type the following command, and press Enter:

```
mkdir myProject
```

Make the new project folder your current directory by typing the following command and pressing Enter:

```
cd myProject
```

Then, to initialize your new Truffle project, enter this command and then press Enter:

```
truffle init
```

Figure 5-14 shows these commands to initialize a new Truffle project.

That's it! You now have a new Truffle project named myProject. That's all you'll do at this point. You can use File Explorer or the dir command to look at the myProject folder to see the files and new folders that Truffle created. You learn more about how Truffle uses these to define projects when you start writing your own smart contracts. But for now, you're ready to install the last tool to complete your Ethereum development environment.

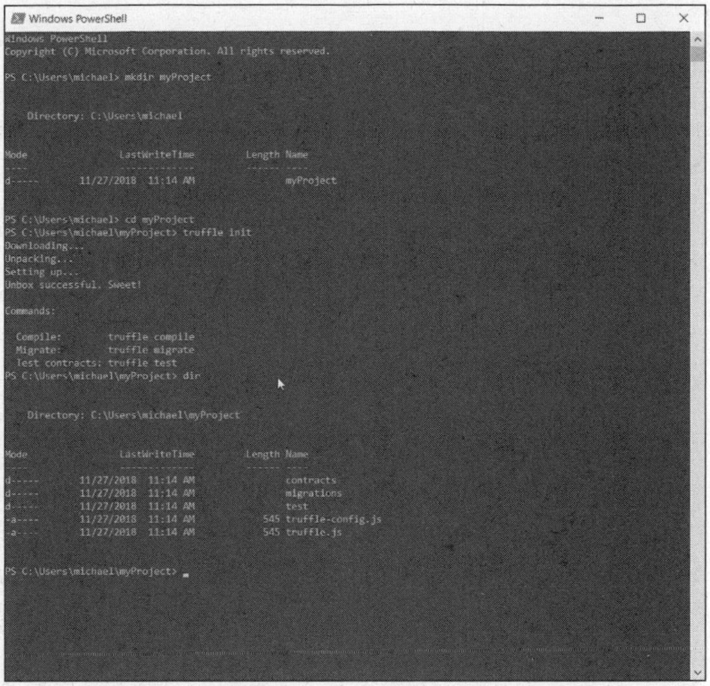

FIGURE 5-14:
Initializing a new
Truffle project.

Installing the IDE

Now that all foundational pieces are in place, you're just about ready to start writing code. The most visible part of software development is writing the source code. Many developers consider writing code to be the first "productive" step in the software development process, but that is far from the truth. Before you start writing any code, you should carefully and completely plan and design your application.

You'll save yourself far more time in the development process by taking the time up front to plan. Planning will reduce the number of times you'll have to rework your code when what you write the first time doesn't do everything that you need it to.

After you have a thorough plan and know what code you need to write to meet all your application's goals, you're ready to start writing the source code that will become your final application. Although you can use any text editor to write code in Solidity, many tools are available to make your development activities easier. An integrated development environment (IDE) is like a super editor. IDEs enable you to create and edit code as well as provide many supporting features, such as automatic code completion and syntax help, as you type. A good IDE can save you lots of time and help you write better code.

TIP

Use an editor or IDE that you find comfortable. Try out several options before you settle on the tool you'll use.

For the exercise in this book, you use Microsoft Visual Studio Code IDE to write source code. To download and install Visual Studio Code, follow these steps:

1. **Launch your browser and navigate to** `https://code.visualstudio.com/`.

Your web browser will look like Figure 5-15.

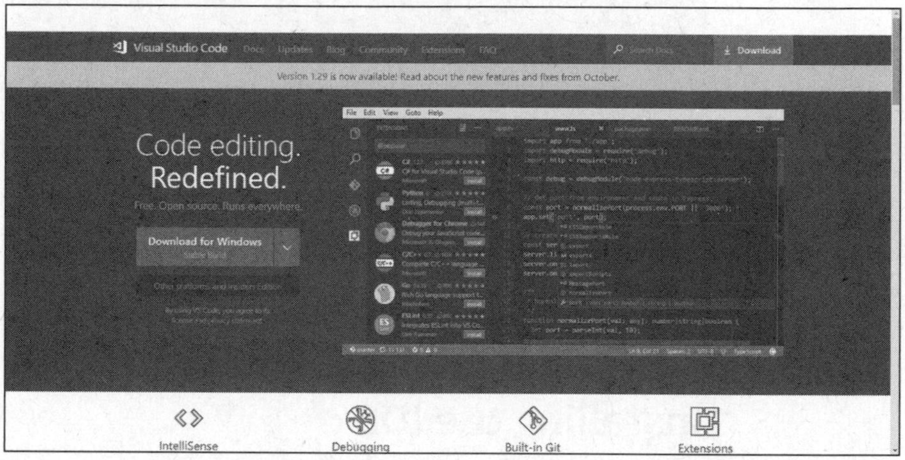

FIGURE 5-15:
Microsoft Visual
Studio Code
download
web page.

2. **Click or tap the Download for Windows button.**

If you want to install Visual Studio Code on a computer that isn't running Microsoft Windows, click or tap the down arrow next to the Download for Windows button. You'll see a list of links to download a Visual Studio Code installable file for macOS, Windows, or Linux.

3. **Launch the executable file you just downloaded by clicking the Next button on the Setup — Visual Studio Code window.**

4. **Read and accept the License Agreement, and then click or tap Next.**

5. **Select Visual Studio Code installation options in the next three windows.**

Enter the install destination (or accept the default), and then click or tap Next. In the Select Start Menu Folder window, click or tap Next to accept the defaults. In the next window, if you want to place a shortcut to Visual Studio Code on your desktop, click or tap the Create a Desktop Icon option. Then click or tap Next.

6. **To install Visual Studio code, review your install options (see Figure 5-16) and then click or tap Install.**

Your settings should look similar to the ones in Figure 5-16, with the exception of the destination location.

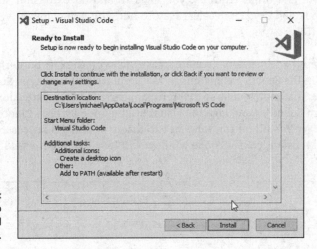

FIGURE 5-16:
Visual Studio
Code install
options window.

7. **When Visual Studio Code finishes installing, click or tap Finish to complete the installation process and launch the Visual Studio Code IDE.**

Visual Studio (VS) Code IDE is now installed. Figure 5-17 shows the default Visual Studio Code tabletop and Welcome window. The welcome window contains lots of helpful information for getting started using the VS Code IDE.

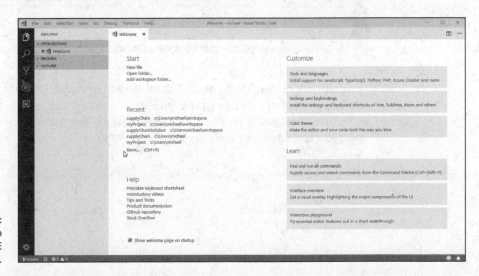

FIGURE 5-17:
Visual Studio
Code IDE
desktop.

TIP

If you close the Welcome window, you can always open it again from the Help menu. It's the top option in the Help menu.

You have one more step to complete the installation of your Ethereum development environment. To get the benefit of VS Code's syntax highlighting, code completion, and other features, you need to add an extension so that VS Code understands Solidity. The easiest way to add any extension to VS Code is right from the IDE.

Click or tap the Extensions (square image) icon on the left border of the VS Code tabletop. In the Search Extensions in Marketplace text box, type **Solidity**. A list of extensions that match your search term appears. Find the extension with the title "Ethereum Solidity Language for Visual Studio Code by Juan Blanco" and click or tap the green Install button for that extension. When you successfully install the Solidity extension, your VS Code window will look like Figure 5-18.

FIGURE 5-18: Visual Studio Code IDE with the Solidity extension.

Congratulations! You've successfully built an Ethereum Solidity application development environment. In Chapter 6, you learn how to set up and manage Ethereum accounts. Then you'll be ready to start learning how to write your own smart contracts and dApps for the Ethereum blockchain.

Chapter **6**

Establishing an Ethereum Wallet

When most people think of wallets, they think of folded leather cases for storing money, credit cards, identification, and even pictures. An *Ethereum wallet* is pretty much the same thing, except it stores the ways to access your valuable stuff on the Ethereum blockchain and can be either a physical or a virtual item.

In the blockchain world, you have to present private keys to access virtual currency and data. An Ethereum wallet holds the keys that allows you to access your content on the Ethereum blockchain. Simply put, an Ethereum wallet securely stores your private encryption keys.

Regardless what you're planning to do with Ethereum, you need a way to find and access data in blocks. That's where a wallet comes in. It stores your private keys, which allow you to buy and sell crypto-assets and to interact with smart contracts. Without a wallet, you wouldn't be able do anything other than just look at Ethereum blockchain blocks.

In this chapter, you discover the different types of Ethereum wallets and look at popular wallet options so you can select the best wallet for your needs.

Unlocking the Secrets of an Ethereum Wallet

Everything stored in an Ethereum block has an address so that the owner can find and access their data in blocks. Data stored in Ethereum blocks can be *crypto-assets,* such as ether or other tokens, smart contracts, or any other data. The address of the data identifies the owner of that data. And when it comes to crypto-assets, only the owner can access that data. Well, anyone could access encrypted data, but only the owner can decrypt the data and consume the asset. For more on crypto-assets, see Chapters 3 and 4.

The person who controls the private key used to encrypt data on the blockchain controls the data. The only way that you can claim any crypto-asset is to prove that you control the private key associated with a crypto-asset's address.

TECHNICAL
STUFF

You learn about hashes, keys, and Ethereum's Keccak-256 algorithm in Chapter 2. Addresses in Ethereum are the last (rightmost) 20 bytes of the hash of the owner's public key. To calculate an address, just calculate the Keccak-256 hash of a public key, and then copy the rightmost 20 bytes. The resulting value is the address for that account's public key. The code to calculate an address from a public key looks like this:

```
addr = right(keccak256(pubkey),20)
```

The only way to protect your crypto-assets is to protect your private keys. You need some mechanism to store your private key so that you can get to it, but no one else can. The primary function of a wallet is as a place to store one or more private keys used to access blockchain data.

The perfect wallet makes it really easy for you to get to your keys and impossible for anyone else to access your keys. All wallets balance these two goals and strike some compromise between utility (how easy it is to access your keys) and security (how safe your keys are from attack).

Examining the Types of Ethereum Wallets

Private keys can be stored in several ways, ranging from very secure to very easy to access. You should consider how important your private keys are and select a wallet type that works for you. The main categories of wallets follow:

>> **Software wallets** store private keys in data files, where users can easily access them.

>> **Hardware wallet** store private keys on a physical chip stored inside a device, such as a Ledger Nano S.

>> **Paper wallets** are pieces of paper with the keys printed on them.

Sorting out software wallets

Software wallets are programs that store private keys and make it easy for users to retrieve and use those keys. After setting up your wallet, you can access your keys by providing a user ID and password or an encrypted file that only you have. Software wallets can be further divided into two main categories: hot wallets and cold wallets.

Hot wallet

A *hot wallet* is one that stores your keys online. You can easily access your keys, and your Ethereum assets, from anywhere in the world. All you need is an Internet connection and access credentials. Although hot wallets are convenient, that convenience comes at a cost. If someone steals your access credentials, he or she can steal your Ethereum assets.

Also, you have to trust the wallet organization that stores your keys. If your wallet organization is hacked or goes out of business, you could lose everything. If that organization is a target of an investigation, your information could be divulged or your Ethereum assets could be frozen. You give up control to get convenience.

Cold wallet

A *cold wallet* is one in which you store your keys offline. You need to provide your keys only when you want to access your Ethereum assets. You can store keys offline in multiple ways, but this approach requires a few extra steps when you want to buy or sell crypto-assets or interact with smart contracts.

Although cold wallets are a little less convenient, they can be more secure. You have control over your keys with a cold wallet and can take whatever precautions you feel are necessary to protect your keys. Using a cold wallet gives you an alternative and mitigates the threat of an attacker hacking into your online wallet and harvesting lots of keys.

WARNING

With a cold wallet, you're responsible for protecting your keys. You have to make sure that every place you store your keys is as secure as possible. If you have a lot of value stored on the Ethereum blockchain, make sure that your key storage locations are as secure as possible and can't be accessed by anyone but you.

Choosing between hot and cold wallets

How do you decide whether to use a hot wallet or a cold wallet? If you want more convenience and trust the security of an online wallet vendor, a hot wallet might be the best choice. Also, if you don't plan to store anything of great value using a specific Ethereum account, a hot wallet is easiest and may make the most sense for that account.

On the other hand, if you distrust online vendors and are comfortable taking responsibility for securing your key storage, a cold wallet will give you more control. Or if you plan to store assets with substantial value, you should take responsibility for protecting your own stuff. You will have to sacrifice some convenience, but losing all your cryptocurrency is inconvenient itself.

Types of wallet client software

After you decide to store your keys in a hot or cold wallet, your next choice is the type(s) of wallet client software. If you choose an Ethereum software wallet to store your keys, you need to run that software somewhere. You have several choices:

>> **Web wallets:** Wallet software that you access by using a web browser.

>> **Desktop wallets:** Software that runs on a desktop or laptop computer. In most cases, desktop wallets run on computers running Microsoft Windows, macOS, or Linux.

>> **Mobile wallets:** Ethereum wallets for mobile devices. The most common wallet software runs on the iOS and Android operating systems for smartphones and tablets.

TIP

You don't have to choose just one type of Ethereum wallet. You can use multiple wallets, depending on your needs. Keys for high-value crypto-assets need to be protected more carefully, whereas keys for low-value crypto-assets could be stored online for easier access.

Handling hardware wallets

An Ethereum wallet option that is more secure than most software wallets is a hardware wallet. A *hardware wallet* stores private keys on a physical chip. You can connect the device housing the chip to many different types of computers and mobile devices, thus providing multiple ways to access the keys. Most hardware wallets also provide physical buttons to manage access to your keys.

The advantage of a physical wallet is the increased security. You connect your device to a computer only when you want to access your blockchain assets. When the device is not connected, your keys are safe inside the physical device. An attacker would have to physically steal your wallet device and know your access credentials to get to your keys.

The disadvantage of a physical wallet is the loss of convenience and redundancy. You must attach your physical wallet to a computer or device every time you want to access your blockchain assets. If you access assets frequently, this process could become annoying. Also, if you lose your physical device, you may not ever be able to recover access to your blockchain assets. For that reason, many physical wallet users make at least one backup copy of their keys and take extra care to store the copies in a secure location.

Perusing paper wallets

The last type of wallet can be the most secure. As the name implies, a *paper wallet* is literally just a piece of paper. After creating an Ethereum account and generating keys, one way of storing those keys is by simply printing them on paper. Most key generation options give you the choice of printing your keys. If you choose that option, you'll get a hard copy of the private and public keys, along with a QR code of each key. Figure 6-1 shows a paper wallet.

FIGURE 6-1: A paper Ethereum wallet.

Whenever you want to access your blockchain assets, such as to buy or sell Ether, you can either type in your private key or scan the QR code. Of course, the software that you're using to access Ethereum has to support QR scanning.

WARNING

Paper wallets are secure only if you keep your paper secret. Carefully guard that piece of paper. Anyone who can grab the paper, or even take a picture of it, can steal all of your Ethereum assets. And, just like with hardware wallets, it's a good idea to make a backup copy and keep it in a secure location.

Choosing an Ethereum Wallet

You have many choices for Ethereum wallets, and in this section, you learn about the most popular types. You can use this information to decide which wallet will best fit your needs.

If, after reading this section, you aren't sure which one is the best wallet, don't worry — choose the one that looks good and start using it. If you decide later to change to another wallet, the process is easy. And no rule dictates that you can't have multiple Ethereum wallets. (It's not like cramming multiple wallets into your back pocket!)

Software wallets

As mentioned, software wallets are simply programs that generate, store, and manage your keys Your options are web wallets, desktop wallets, and mobile wallets. The two primary differences among software wallet options are where they run and where they store your keys.

Web wallets

Web wallets are popular for casual Ethereum use. They are easy to use and make access to your keys convenient. To open your wallet, you need only an Internet connection, a web browser, and your login credentials. Table 6-1 lists popular web wallets.

TABLE 6-1

TABLE 6-1   ## Popular Web Wallets

Name	Description	Pros	Cons
MyEtherWallet, `www.myetherwallet.com`	Open-source, decentralized cold wallet. You locally control your keys.	Most popular Ethereum web wallet. Works well with hardware wallets.	Has been hacked and may be vulnerable to phishing attacks.
Coinbase, `www.coinbase.com`	Popular cryptocurrency exchange that provides a hot wallet as well.	Provides more than just wallet services. Long history handling cryptocurrency.	Limited tokens and coins supported. Keys stored online.
Guarda, `https://guarda.co`	Cold wallet that supports multiple cryptocurrencies and makes it easy to transfer funds between cryptocurrencies. Also offers a desktop wallet.	One of the first to support multiple types of coins and tokens. Doesn't store personal info.	User must manage local key storage.

Desktop wallets

Desktop wallets are software programs that run on a personal computer. Most desktop wallets store keys locally, so you need to have access to your computer to open your wallet. Table 6-2 lists popular desktop wallets.

TABLE 6-2   ## Popular Desktop Wallets

Name	Description	Pros	Cons
Exodus, `www.exodus.io`	First to offer multiple cryptocurrencies in a single wallet. Cold wallet with easy key backup and restore operations.	Visually appealing and informative, easy-to-use interface.	Source code is not open source.
Mist, `https://sourceforge.net/projects/ethereum-wallet.mirror`	Cold wallet and the official Ethereum wallet, developed by those who created Ethereum.	Created by the Ethereum Foundation, officially endorsed wallet.	Less user friendly than other wallets.
MetaMask, `https://metamask.io/`	Cold wallet running as a Firefox or Chrome extension. Supports easy switching between test and live Ethereum networks.	Partially funded by the Ethereum Foundation, easy to use in Chrome. Easy to switch between test and live networks.	Released only as a Chrome extension, making it possible for other websites to see that you have a wallet installed.

Mobile wallets

Mobile wallets are similar to desktop wallets, but the software runs on mobile devices. Your keys are commonly stored on the mobile device as well. A mobile wallet is a good option if you always want your keys with you. The drawback is that if you lose your mobile device, you could lose access to your Ethereum assets. (That's why backups are always good.) Table 6-3 lists popular mobile wallets.

TABLE 6-3 ### Popular Mobile Wallets

Name	Description	Pros	Cons
Jaxx, https://jaxx.io/	Cold wallet available on mobile devices and desktops (Windows, macOS, Linux).	Multi-platform support. Stores keys on specified device.	Code is not open source. Limited number of coins and tokens supported.
Coinomi, www.coinomi.com	Cold wallet for multiple cryptocurrencies currently available for only Android mobile devices.	Runs on Android, iOS, and desktops. Extensive list of supported coins and tokens. Focus on privacy.	Code is not open source.
Bread (BRD), https://brd.com/	Cold wallet for multiple cryptocurrencies that runs on iOS and Android mobile devices.	No central server. Easy to use and fast. Code is open source.	Limited number of supported coins and tokens. No two-factor authentication.

Hardware wallets

Hardware wallets provide an extra layer of security for your keys because they are stored on a physical chip inside the device. Most hardware wallets are USB devices. You access your keys by attaching the wallet device to a computer or a mobile device, and then running some software to access the keys. Depending on the device, the software could be web based or running locally on the computer or mobile device. Several software wallets provide the option to integrate with hardware wallets to make key storage even more secure.

Storing your keys on your own device means that you have to take measures to secure the device. Always be aware of the device's location and always have a backup in case the device goes missing. Table 6-4 lists popular hardware wallets.

TABLE 6-4   ## Popular Hardware Wallets

Name	Description	Pros	Cons
Ledger Nano S, www. ledger.com/products/ ledger-nano-s	Secure physical device that supports multiple cryptocurrencies and uses two-factor authentication.	Small. Most popular hardware wallet. Hardware designed for security. Supports over 700 types of coins and tokens.	Cost ($59). Requires client software to control crypto-assets.
Trezor, https:// trezor.io/	Secure physical device that supports multiple cryptocurrencies and uses two-factor authentication.	Established reputation. Physical buttons or touchscreen. Supports nearly 700 types of coins and tokens.	Cost ($49). Requires a web wallet to control some stored crypto-assets.
KeepKey, www. keepkey.com	Similar to the Ledger Nano S and Trezor features, but with a slightly larger screen.	Firmware is open source. Designed to meet current blockchain requirements.	Cost ($49). Relative newcomer. Limited number of supported coins and token types. Requires Chrome add-in.

Paper wallets

A *paper wallet* is the simplest type of wallet. After you create an account and generate your keys, you simply print the keys on a plain piece of paper. Your keys exist only on the paper you used to print them; you don't store them using software or on a hardware device.

The advantage to a paper wallet is that you have supreme control over your keys and no one else can touch them. That's the biggest drawback, too. You have to take extra precautions to securely store a backup copy in case something happens to your piece of paper. Table 6-5 lists popular paper wallets.

TABLE 6-5   ## Popular Hardware Wallets

Name	Description	Pros	Cons
ETHAddress, https:// github.com/ryepdx/ ethaddress.org	Open-source project with source code you can compile and run on your own computer to generate private and public keys.	Open-source code. Useful for creating multiple accounts and keys.	No easy to use interface. Must download and run code or use Chrome add-in.
MyEtherWallet, www. myetherwallet.com	Provides the option to print your keys instead of storing them. The easiest way to create your own paper wallet.	Easy-to-use web interface for creating accounts and keys.	You must protect generated keys.

Installing MetaMask, an Ethereum Wallet

The preceding section shows you lots of options for Ethereum wallets. In this section, I show you how to set up a MetaMask wallet. You could use any other option, but MetaMask is a popular wallet that provides some nice ease-of-use options for developing blockchain apps.

MetaMask is a desktop wallet that runs as an extension to the Chrome, Firefox, Opera, or Brave web browsers. For these installation steps, I use the Chrome browser.

To install MetaMask, follow these steps:

1. **Launch your browser and navigate to** https://metamask.io/.

   Your web browser will look like Figure 6-2.

FIGURE 6-2:
The MetaMask
website.

2. **On the MetaMask page, click or tap Get Chrome Extension.**

   If you're using another browser, select the link to get MetaMask for your browser.

3. **Click or tap the Add to Chrome button and confirm your choice.**

4. **After MetaMask installs, click or tap the MetaMask icon, and accept the license agreements.**

   The MetaMask icon is the fox in the upper-right corner of your web browser

5. **In the MetaMask Create Account window, shown in Figure 6-3, enter a secure password. Click or tap Create.**

   A screen appears where you can choose from several networks.

6. **From the network drop-down list, select Ropsten Test Network.**

   MetaMask makes it easy to interact with both test networks to develop and test your apps, and live networks when you're ready to deploy. Figure 6-4 show a list of the networks MetaMask supports.

You've installed the MetaMask Ethereum wallet. MetaMask automatically creates an account named Account 1. You can see the private key and QR code for your new account by clicking or tapping the menu icon and then the Show QR Code option.

You can't do very much with your wallet just yet, but in Chapter 7 you find out how to add ether to your account to fuel your blockchain activities.

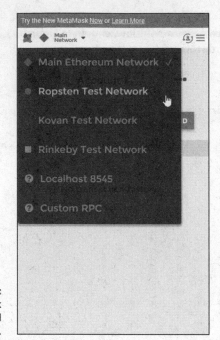

FIGURE 6-4:
The MetaMask
list of supported
networks.

3

Building Ethereum Distributed Blockchain Apps

Build a simple smart contract in Solidity.

Dig into the Solidity language.

Develop smart contracts that solve problems.

Chapter 7

Building Your First Ethereum Apps

The best way to learn how to write apps for the Ethereum blockchain is to start writing them. You can read about all the components and language syntax, but until you write some code, it won't sink in. You've already gone through the steps to set up your development environment, so why not start using it?

Don't worry about writing code before you know what you're doing — you start with small, simple Solidity apps. And you learn about syntax and process as you need it. The typos you enter and other issues you encounter will help you learn faster.

The code you'll write in this chapter is really simple. That's okay. You're going to learn how to write code in Solidity, and you're going to start from the very beginning. Whether you're new to programming or you already know several other programming languages, the exercises in this chapter will ensure that you have a working development environment and know how to write basic Solidity code.

Validating Your Ethereum Development Environment

When you installed the development environment components in Chapter 5, you installed each piece to operate separately. The Geth Ethereum client connects to the live Ethereum network by default. However, we don't want to use the live Ethereum network for app development and testing. For now, you won't need to launch Geth. You'll use Ganache to provide the blockchain for development and testing. You looked at the settings page when you installed Ganache to view your blockchain's host name, port number, and network ID. But you didn't do anything with that information — until now.

Truffle is the framework you'll use to develop and test your Solidity code. Before you can start writing code, you need to configure Truffle to use the Ganache blockchain. You do that by editing the Truffle configuration file.

Creating a Truffle project

Truffle organizes software activities into projects, and stores project files in directories. If you did not create a project in Chapter 5, follow the instructions in the section on installing and downloading Truffle. (If you'd rather download the project files, go to www.dummies.com/go/ethereumfd.) After initializing the new project, type **dir** to see a list of files and directories Truffle created. Figure 7-1 shows a newly initiated Truffle project.

Depending on the version of Truffle you're running, you may have two files in the project directory: truffle.js and truffle-config.js. If you open these two files, you'll see that their contents are the same. You should always use the configuration file named truffle-config.js. To keep things simple, if your version of Truffle created the file truffle.js, just delete it.

You'll be editing the file named truffle-config.js to configure Truffle to use the Ganache blockchain.

TECHNICAL STUFF

Because Truffle runs in Windows, macOS, and Linux, it has to handle subtle differences between the environments. The Windows operating system looks at a file with the js extension as an executable file. That means when you type the `truffle` command, Windows will find the local truffle.js file and try to execute it. That's why Truffle started including the truffle-config.js file as its default configuration file. Older versions of Truffle still use truffle.js as a default configuration filename, but I recommend that you not use it. Always use truffle-config.js or your own custom filename to avoid conflicts when you try to run Truffle in Windows.

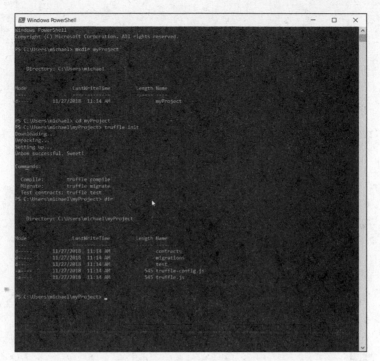

FIGURE 7-1:
Initiating a Truffle
project.

Editing the Truffle config file

You have to edit the Truffle config file to tell Truffle to use the Ganache block-chain. Follow these steps to hook up Truffle and Ganache:

1. **Get the blockchain address from the Ganache settings window.**

Launch Ganache, and then click or tap the Settings (gear) icon in the upper-right corner of the Ganache window. Note the hostname, port number, and network ID values. Figure 7-2 shows the Ganache settings window with default values. (You can get the host name and port number also from the main window.) The RPC SERVER value shows the host name and port number separated by a colon.

2. **Launch Visual Studio Code (VS Code) for your project.**

Open a Windows Command prompt or PowerShell (my favorite) and navigate to your project directory (myProject.) From here, type the following and then press Enter:

```
code .
```

The code command launches VS Code, and the period tells VS Code to use the current directory as the current project. Figure 7-3 shows what your VS Code window will look like when you launch it in your myProject directory.

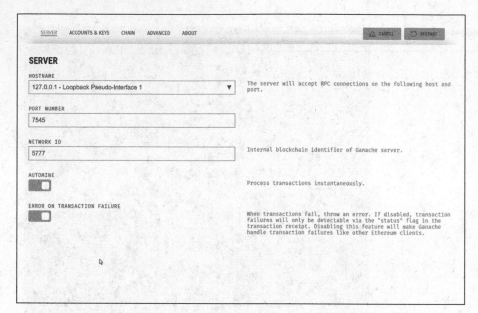

FIGURE 7-2:
Ganache Settings window.

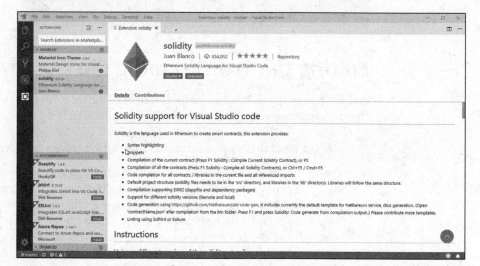

FIGURE 7-3:
Visual Studio Code in myProject.

3. **Modify your Truffle project configuration file to reference the Ganache blockchain.**

   Click or tap truffle-config.js on the left side of your VS Code window to open the file. Add the sections shown in Figure 7-4. Then save the file (choose File ⇨ Save or press Ctrl+S).

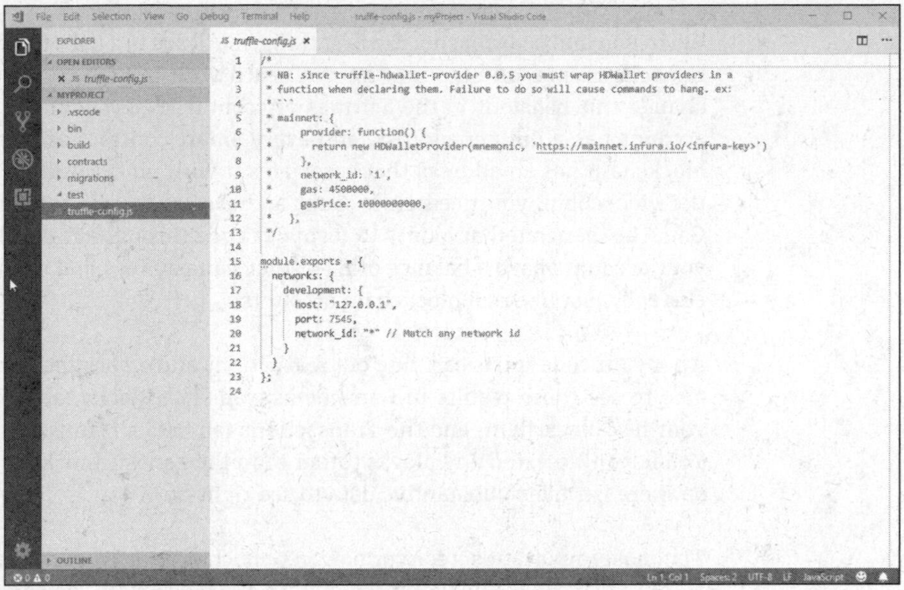

FIGURE 7-4:
Modified
Truffle project
configuration file.

When you finish editing the truffle.js file, the uncommented lines (lines that don't start with /*, *, or */) should look like this:

```
module.exports = {
  networks: {
    development: {
      host: "127.0.0.1",
      port: 7545,
      network_id: "*" // Match any network id
    }
  }
};
```

Exploring the Ganache Test Environment

Before you write any code in Solidity, you should take a look around Ganache. You'll be coming back to this component in your development environment from time to time, so it makes sense to take a few minutes to survey what Ganache offers. Remember that Ganache is your test blockchain. You'll need to simulate real blockchain interactions as you develop and test your code, and Ganache provides you with an environment that looks real.

When you launch Ganache, the first thing you'll see is a list of accounts. By default, Ganache creates 10 accounts for you, each with a balance of 100 ETH. You can change this behavior in the Settings⇨Accounts & Keys window. Every Ethereum account has a unique address, and every smart contract and transaction on the blockchain has an address that associates it with an account. So, to interact with the blockchain, you need an account address (or maybe several). You'll use the Ganache-generated accounts to test your code throughout development. Because your accounts have a balance of ETH, they can pay fees and even transfer cryptocurrency just like real blockchain accounts.

After your code starts carrying out real actions and creating transactions, you'll be able to see those results in Ganache as well. The Blocks tab shows all blocks on your test blockchain, and the Transactions tab lists all transactions in each block. You haven't created any blocks (other than the genesis block) or transactions yet, so there isn't any substantive data to see right now.

The most important screen for now in Ganache is the Accounts tab, which lists the accounts you'll use as you interact with the blockchain, as shown in Figure 7-5. You'll see these accounts again in this chapter.

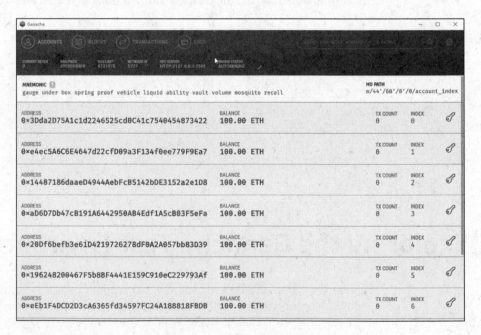

FIGURE 7-5:
Ganache accounts list.

Designing Simple Smart Contracts

Designing smart contracts is different than many other types of software development. You have to consider many blockchain nuances during all aspects of software design and development. For example, any time you access the blockchain or carry out operations, you have to pay a fee. You'll learn about paying for blockchain access later in this chapter, but for now just be aware that a cost is associated with storage and work, so storing too much data or doing too much work could cost a lot.

Another thing to consider is that after you deploy code to the blockchain, that code can't be changed. If you need to fix a bug or add functionality, you have to tell everyone to ignore the old code and use new code. (Well, you do if your new code works on old data. If not, you'll have to figure out how to bind code version to data version.) Plus, the entire process of getting your code from your editor out to the blockchain is a little different than in most development workflows.

Those are just some of the issues you'll need to keep in mind as you design and develop blockchain apps. For now, I keep things simple. The steps probably seem confusing if you're new to blockchain development, so I won't throw too much at you at once.

Your first smart contract is the familiar Hello World program. If you've ever written software in any language, chances are you wrote a simple program that displayed the message Hello World. The Hello World program is a tradition that has been around since the early days of computing. Writing this simple program will give you the concrete steps you have to follow for all your development activities.

You'll write a smart contract that displays the message *Hello World.* You might be surprised at the number of steps to display that simple message, but as your apps become more complex, you'll essentially follow the same process.

As you design your own smart contacts, consider what each one must do. Smart contracts are objects, so you can think about them as a combinations of data and functionality. Each smart contract can store some data and will always have actions it can perform. You can think of data as nouns and actions as verbs. Your HelloWorld smart contact has one data item, `helloMessage`, and can do one thing, `getHelloMessage()`. In Solidity, simple data items are variables and actions are functions.

That's all that your HelloWorld smart contract needs to do, so you're ready to start coding.

Coding Your First Smart Contract

Your HelloWorld smart contract has only five lines of code. To get started writing your first smart contract, right-click the Contracts folder in VS Code Explorer, and then click New File to create a new file in the Contracts folder.

Type **HelloWorld.sol** in the filename text box and press Enter. VS Code opens your new file in a new Editor tab. Type the following text in the VS Code editor:

```
pragma solidity ^0.4.24;

contract HelloWorld {
    string private helloMessage = "Hello world";

    function getHelloMessage() public view returns (string) {
        return helloMessage;
    }
}
```

The semicolons and curly braces may appear to be in random places, but they each have a purpose. Don't worry too much about punctuation right now. Just type the code as shown.

Let's look at each line of code. The first line is

```
pragma solidity ^0.4.24;
```

The first line of every smart contract is (or should be) the version pragma. It tells Solidity what version of the compiler is expected to be used to compile this smart contract. Solidity is still a new language, and it changes a little with each version. In fact, major version updates of the compiler often will not compile all Solidity written using earlier versions. The version pragma helps to avoid compilation failures just because you're using a newer Solidity compiler.

To use the version pragma, you provide the lowest version of the compiler that should compile this code. In the example, I provided the specific Solidity version, 0.4.24. I could have used 0.4.0, which means "the latest minor version within the 0.4 major version." Also note that I added the caret (^) to the beginning of the version. The caret tells Solidity to allow only minor versions of the compiler in the 0.4 major version range. In other words, don't use a 0.5.0 compiler.

TECHNICAL STUFF

If you want to see the version of the Solidity compiler that Truffle is using, open a terminal (in VS Code, click or tap Terminal ⇨ New Terminal from the top menu bar). Type the command `truffle version`. You'll see the Truffle and Solidity compiler versions.

The next line of code defines the smart contract:

```
contract HelloWorld {
```

At this point, all you need to provide is the keyword contract and the contract's name, HelloWorld.

After defining the smart contract and giving it a name, you define a data item:

```
string private helloMessage = "Hello world";
```

You want to store a string in memory, so you define a Solidity variable. You define the helloMessage variable as a string datatype. You'll learn about more datatypes in Chapter 8; for now, we'll use string. Before finishing this line of code, you store the value "Hello world" in the helloMessage variable. You need to use this variable only in the helloMessage function, so you tell Solidity that it is a private variable.

In the next line, you define the only action, or function, in your smart contract:

```
function getHelloMessage() public view returns (string) {
```

The function keyword tells Solidity that you're going to write some code that you'll execute by calling the function's name, getHelloMessage(). To declare a function, you provide the function keyword, the function name, who can see it and use it, the mutability modifier, and what type of data it returns to the caller. Your function is named getHelloMessage. You want anyone to be able to call it, so you tell Solidity that it is a public function. The view modifier tells Solidity that this function will be allowed to only read and return state variables. It cannot modify the blockchain. And finally, your function will return, or send back, a string to whatever calls it (returns).

The last line of code does all the real work:

```
return helloMessage;
```

This line of code tells the function to return control to the caller and pass the contents of the helloMessage variable back in the process. The two lines following the return statement are just closing curly braces to tell Solidity that the function and contract have ended. The closing braces are like closing parentheses when you write. They finish up whatever you're wrapping in curly braces.

You can save the file at any time by clicking or tapping File ⇨ Save on the top menu bar, or by pressing Ctrl+S. Go ahead and save your first smart contract.

Running Your First Smart Contract

The only thing left is to make your smart contract display *Hello World.* To do that, you have to run your smart contract. Here are the high-level steps for running code in the Ethereum environment:

1. **Write the smart contract source code.**

   Write the smart contract and any supporting code.

2. **Compile the smart contract.**

   This step creates the bytecode that the EVM executes.

3. **Deploy the compiled smart contract to the Ethereum blockchain.**

   This step writes your smart contract code to a block on the blockchain.

4. **Call (invoke) a function in the smart contract.**

   This step finds your smart contract code and carries out the actions you request.

Writing your code

You've already written the source code for your HelloWorld smart contract, but that isn't all you need to do. You also need a way get your code onto the blockchain. That process is called *deploying code* (as noted in Step 3 in the preceding steps). The deploy step runs *deployment,* or *migration, code.*

You should go ahead and write it now while you're still in code editing mode:

1. **In VS Code, right-click the Migrations folder in Explorer, and then click New File to create a new file in the Migrations folder.**

2. **Type** 2_contracts_migration.js **in the filename text box and press Enter.**

   VS Code opens your new file in a new Editor tab.

3. **Type the following text in the VS Code editor:**

   ```
   var HelloWorld = artifacts.require("HelloWorld");
   module.exports = function(deployer) {
       deployer.deploy(HelloWorld);
   };
   ```

We won't go into many details of this JavaScript code. This file finds the Hello-World compiled bytecode and calls a deploy function to place the code in a block on the blockchain. You learn more about deploying smart contracts when you write more complex smart contracts. For now, just enter the preceding code to set up your project to deploy your new smart contract.

Compiling your code

You can compile your smart contract code at any time in VS Code by pressing the F5 key. When the compile starts, VS Code opens a new view at the bottom of your window with four tabs: Problems, Output, Debug Console, and Terminal. I hope the compile completes without errors. If you do see errors, go back and make sure that your code looks exactly like the example HelloWorld smart contract in the preceding section.

Sometimes you'll get errors because of a mismatch between compiler versions. The safest option when learning Solidity is to ensure that your VS Code extension and Truffle use the same Solidity compiler version. You already know how to find the Truffle compiler version (type **truffle version** at a PowerShell prompt). Click or tap the Output tab in the new view that opened when you started the compile. It should display the compiler version it uses for compiling code in VS Code. If the version doesn't match your Truffle Solidity version, you should change it in VS Code to match the Solidity version that Truffle uses.

If you need to change the Solidity compiler version that VS Code uses, you can do that from within VS Code:

1. **Find the version of the compiler you need by launching your browser and navigate to** https://github.com/ethereum/solc-bin/tree/gh-pages/bin.

   This page lists all Solidity releases.

2. **Scroll down until you find a file named soljson-v followed by the version of the compiler that you want.**

   In the case of HelloWorld, the version is 0.4.24. You'll see a list of files for each version.

3. **Find the file that has +commit after the version. Click or tap the description next to the filename.**

4. **In the next window, copy the complete compiler version.**

   The version will start with *v0*. For the HelloWorld smart contract, the version is v0.4.24+commit.e67f0147.

5. **Back in VS Code, click or tap the .vscode folder in Explorer view, and then click or tap settings.json to open the file in the VS Code editor.**

6. **Click or tap User Settings in the upper-right window, and scroll down in the middle window until you see Solidity Configuration.**

7. **Click or tap Solidity Configuration and then click or tap solidity. compileUsingRemoteVersion.**

8. **Type the following three lines in the upper right window (right under the *Place your settings here to overwrite the Default Settings* message):**

```
{
    "solidity.compileUsingRemoteVersion": "v0.4.24+commit.e67f0147"
}
```

Replace v0.4.24+commit.e67f0147 with the compiler version that you copied in Step 4 above.

9. **Save the file and close it (by clicking or tapping the X on the tab for this file).**

Now your VS Code compiler should match the version Truffle uses.

After your smart contract compiles in VS Code, you can proceed to the next step.

Deploying your code

After you have finished writing your smart contract code, it's time to test it and eventually place it into production. As mentioned, the process of copying smart contracts to the blockchain is called *deployment.* When you deploy smart contracts, you copy the code into a new block. The new smart contract gets an address and can be run on the EVM.

Because you're using the Truffle framework, the process to deploy your smart contracts is simple. Open the Terminal window (click or tap Terminal in the menu bar), and type the following:

```
truffle deploy --reset
```

WARNING

Make sure that Ganache is running before you type the deploy command. If you use Microsoft Windows and Ganache isn't running, click or tap the Windows button and then type **Ganache**. The Windows Search function should find Ganache and highlight its shortcut. Click or tap the Ganache shortcut to launch the Ganache program. Because the purpose of building dApps is to send smart contracts to the blockchain, a blockchain has to be available.

Truffle compiles your smart contracts and then uses the JavaScript files in the Migrations folder of your project to migrate, or deploy, your smart contracts to the blockchain. Figure 7-6 shows the output of the `deploy` command. Note that Truffle places each smart contract into a block and returns the address of the smart contract. You'll use this address to find the smart contract again and invoke its functions.

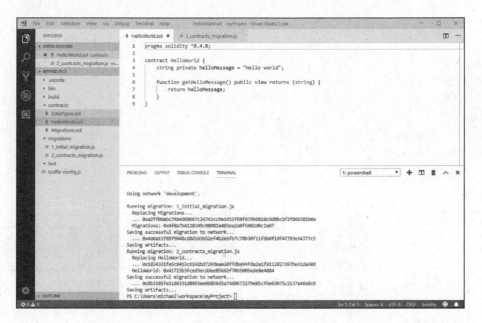

FIGURE 7-6:
Truffle
deployment
results.

This is the first time you've interacted with the blockchain. The deployment process created a new block and placed your smart contract code into it. To see this activity, click or tap the Blocks tab in Ganache to see the blocks on your blockchain.

Each action in the deployment process created a new block with a single transaction. At least four blocks should be on the blockchain now. Figure 7-7 shows the blocks view in Ganache.

You can see the bytecode for smart contracts, too. Click or tap the Transactions tab to list the transactions in your blockchain. Click or tap a Contract Creation button to view the contents of a smart contract. Figure 7-8 shows the contents of a smart contract in the Ethereum blockchain. TX Data contains the bytecode for the smart contract.

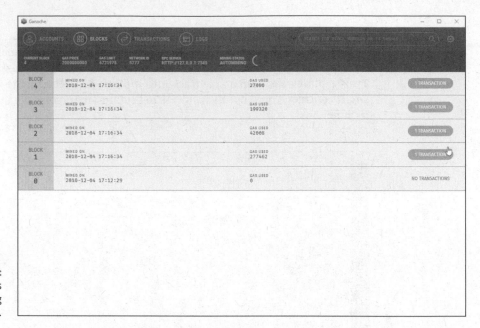

FIGURE 7-7:
Ganache blocks
after deploying
smart contracts.

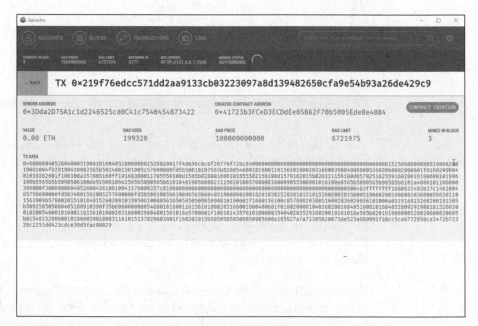

FIGURE 7-8:
Contents
of a smart
contract block.

Invoking your code's functions

The final step in running smart contract code is to invoke one or more functions in your smart contract. You have only one function, `getHelloMessage()`, in your smart contract, so that's the one you'll invoke.

Before you can invoke code in a smart contract, you have to know where it resides on the blockchain. First, let's get some information about the smart contract, including its address from the blockchain. In your Terminal window, launch the Truffle console. Type the following command and then press Enter:

```
truffle console
```

The Truffle console allows you to interact directly with the blockchain. Type the following command at the Truffle console prompt and then press Enter:

```
HelloWorld.deployed().then(function(instance) {return instance });
```

This command goes to the blockchain and reads an instance of the HelloWorld deployed smart contract. It creates a lot of output, including the bytecode and the original source code of your smart contract.

Figure 7-9 shows the Terminal window with the results of the preceding command. Note the deployedBytecode and source values.

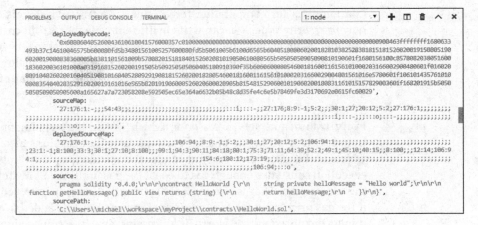

FIGURE 7-9:
Smart contract instance information.

Now that you have an instance of your smart contract (that is, a pointer to where your smart contract is running in memory), you can use it to invoke any of its functions. Type the following command at the Truffle console prompt, and then press Enter:

```
HelloWorld.deployed().then(function(instance) {return instance.
    getHelloWorld() });
```

This command invokes the getHelloMessage() function in the HelloWorld smart contract and displays the results. You should see the *"Hello world"* message in the

CHAPTER 7 **Building Your First Ethereum Apps** 123

Terminal window. That may seem like a lot of work just to display a message, and it is. But the process you just learned is one that you'll use over and over to develop, test, and deploy smart contracts, regardless of how complex they may be.

Paying as You Go

You may have noticed in Ganache that blocks and transactions each have a Gas Used value. The Ganache main window also shows the Gas Price and Gas Limit for the blockchain. You learn a lot more about gas in Chapter 8, but you need to know a little about transaction costs now, before you start writing bigger and more functional smart contracts.

Gas is a unit of value in Ethereum. Every operation that a smart contract carries out costs some number of gas units. For example, you have to pay 30 gas to calculate a Keccak256 hash, plus another 6 gas for every 256 bits (not bytes) of data you want to hash. The amount you pay for operations is called the *gas cost*.

Charging gas for computation forces smart contract developers to think about how they write code. You can write inefficient code, but it will cost you. Also, gas provides a great way to keep malicious code from taking over EVMs. Every transaction has a gas limit, and when the EVM reaches that limit, it stops the contract. Gas limits protect EVMs from many types of denial of service (DoS) attacks.

Every transaction sets a *gas price*, which is the highest amount of ETH that transaction is willing to pay for each gas unit. Transactions also set a *gas limit*, which is the maximum amount of gas the transaction is willing to pay. If the execution consumes enough gas to equal the gas limit, the EVM stops execution of the transaction. That is one reason a transaction may not succeed. Alternatively, if the gas price is set too low, a transaction may never be added to a block because miners did not want to waste their processing time on a transaction with too small of a reward. Miners generally try to mine blocks with transactions that have a high enough gas price to make the mining process profitable.

The takeaway is that creating transactions in the Ethereum blockchain requires a fee. That fee is charged in gas units and can be limited to a range with which you are comfortable. Paying more gas often means getting your transaction processed quicker, but paying too much wastes money. As you write smart contract code, pay attention to the operations that incur gas cost. As you learn more about Solidity in Chapter 8, you'll learn ways to write code that conserves operations that require gas.

IN THIS CHAPTER

» Describing Supply Chain and its challenges

» Exploring a blockchain solution to supply chain

» Handling data and computation in Solidity

» Coding to limit gas cost

» Controlling execution flow and responding to errors

Chapter **8**

Learning about Smart Contracts

Smart contracts are the functional part of any blockchain solution. Just like the objects you learn about in Chapter 7, a blockchain solution is a combination of data and actions on that data. The data is the content of the blocks on the blockchain. You already know that after data is added, it stays there forever. (Although you could technically change blockchain data, doing so without any other node detecting your change is next to impossible.) Because blockchain data is immutable, it is important to carefully control how that data is added.

The actions that operate on the blockchain data are the smart contracts. You already know that smart contracts, like the data, are stored in blocks on the blockchain. But smart contracts execute on all EVMs and have to work the same way and produce the same results on all EVMs. Smart contracts govern the way that data is added to the blockchain and how that data can be used.

In Chapter 7, you wrote a simple smart contract, but it didn't do anything useful. The only way to create a smart contract to do anything useful is to identify a real-world problem and then create a blockchain solution that solves the problem. One use case that is a good fit for a blockchain solution is supply chain management.

In this chapter, you learn about some supply chain challenges and how blockchain can address some of them. You also learn more about Solidity smart contracts by developing a solution to a current supply chain problem.

Introducing Supply Chain and Common Challenges

In today's economy, nearly every product you use or service you consume comes from some other source. Although you might grow your own vegetables and herbs, you likely don't raise livestock as a meat source as well. Everything that you buy comes from an original producer. In the case of food products, the original producer could be a grower, a rancher, a fisherman, or a producer of any other type of food.

As society has moved from being self-sufficient to relying on others to supply products services, consumers have become detached from producers. Geographic distances, regulations, and the suppliers' desires for greater reach and higher profits have given rise to aggregators and middlemen to handle goods. These middlemen provide benefits to producers and consumers but also require fees for their services. These fees increase the consumer price, and the processing may slow down the time it takes for goods to arrive to the market or consumer.

Describing supply chain

Consider what happens when you buy fish. If you live near the coast, you might go to the docks and purchase fish directly from the fishing boat. However, it is more likely that you bought the last fish you ate from a market or a restaurant. That means one or more parties were between the fishermen (the producer) and you (the consumer). The framework that connects consumers to producers, along with the system that manages it, is called a *supply chain*. A supply chain might have only a single participant between the producer and consumer, or it might contain many participants along the way. A supply chain manages all assets, along with handling the payments tendered in exchange for the products or services.

In a simple supply chain, fishermen may sell their fish directly to markets near the docks where their ships bring a fresh catch each day. Consumers shop at the markets and purchase fish from a single middleman. If you don't live near a market like that, the fish may go to a processor, then to a shipper, then on to a warehouse, and finally to a retail store, where the consumer purchases the fish. That is an example of a common supply chain. As consumers demand more options, supply chains exist to help producers provide the products and services that consumers demand.

Supply chain participants provide value to small and large producers. For the small producers, an aggregator can collect product from multiple producers and provide larger shipments to processors or warehouses. Large producers benefit from having local points of entry into the supply chain, without having to handle point-to-point shipments to all outlets for their products.

Consumers benefit as well because the supply chain makes available a wide variety of products from many producers.

Explaining difficulties when implementing a supply chain

So far, a supply chain sounds like a great way to get products and services to a wide variety of consumers. And it does do all that. But the current supply chain approach has obstacles, or limitations. In general, five types of obstacles are encountered in today's supply chain implementations, as listed in Table 8-1.

TABLE 8-1   **Supply Chain Obstacles**

Obstacle	Description
Lack of transparency	Today's supply chain participants often manage their own data systems and don't publish their internal data. Separately managed data systems makes it difficult to see how items are processed at each step in the chain.
Lack of traceability	With limited transparency at each step, the data required for tracing products to their origin is often not available, making authenticity claims and recall notices for points of origin difficult or impossible.
Transfer time lags	Transferring products from one participant to another requires synchronization between organizations and might not occur in real time. Many transfers occur in batches based on scheduled operations. This can cause delays at every stage, resulting in cumulative delays throughout the chain.
Translation data loss	Each participant receives, manages, and passes along its own core set of data. Even with decades-old standards, such as Electronic Data Interchange (EDI), some data items might not be passed along from one participant to another, resulting in granular data loss along the supply chain. Also, any data that must be re-keyed because it isn't passed along is subject to human error.
Nonstandard/ unavailable status tracking	Because each participant generally manages its own data, status updates might not be available at each stage. Some participants might either decline to provide status updates or provide them in a manner that is incompatible with status updates from other participants. In the latter case, the status update requestor is required to assimilate status updates in various formats and harmonize them into meaningful output.

The items in Table 8-1 represent just some of the obstacles in supply chain implementations in production today. These problems tend to be more pronounced as the complexity of a supply chain increases. But as many markets mature and become more global, supply chains nearly always become more diverse and complex. Pursuing solutions to these obstacles is important to global commerce.

Examining How Blockchain Can Help Resolve Supply Chain Problems

Blockchain technology can help address many of the supply chain obstacles. While no single solution is a perfect fit for any situation, blockchain, and Ethereum is particular, can help resolve the majority of the shortcomings of today's supply chain implementations. Table 8-2 lists the obstacles from the previous section, and how Ethereum can help resolve each one.

TABLE 8-2   Ethereum Solutions to Supply Chain Obstacles

Obstacle	Description
Lack of transparency	Blockchain technology does not have a central authority. All transactions are published to the shared blockchain. Any participating node can view transactions and verify their authenticity.
Lack of traceability	Because all nodes have access to all transactions on the blockchain, linking transactions is almost trivial. Any node can easily construct a complete chain of transactions between the original producer and the final consumer.
Transfer time lags	Smart contracts provide the capability to assess the current blockchain state and make decisions on demand. Legacy solutions often require human interaction, which depends on set working hours. Blockchain introduces the opportunity for smart contracts, not humans, to make certain decisions immediately. This benefit can remove the need for human intervention in some types of decisions.
Translation data loss	Ethereum smart contracts define data needed for each transaction and ensure that all participants provide the same input. In short, every node uses the same rules — the rules don't change from participant to participant as you move along the supply chain.
Non-standard/ unavailable status tracking	Instead of each participant responding individually to status update requests, all necessary information is in blocks on the blockchain. Anyone who can access the blockchain can determine the current status of any digital asset.

Ethereum provides a level playing field for many uses, including supply chains. In an environment that includes participants who do not fully trust one another, or are even competitors, Ethereum makes it possible to conduct business in a fair manner. Supply chain implementations can be far more comprehensive than just tracking how products move to the consumer. Participants along the supply chain can also add their own value.

For example, an elaborate supply chain can operate like a distributed manufacturing or assembly line. High-end corporate aircraft often undergo customizations after the aircraft leaves the manufacturer but before delivery to the customer. For example, the aircraft might go to several other companies for interior fitting, painting, and even aftermarket performance upgrades. Each step likely includes additional services and products that add to the original aircraft — for a fee.

Ethereum makes it possible to track and control products through multiple steps, and provides a secure way to provide transparency and traceability for all products to all parties.

Describing a Blockchain Supply Chain Solution

You've learned about what an Ethereum supply chain solution can do, but you still need to see how it will operate before you start writing code. For the rest of this book, you'll implement a simple supply chain solution in Solidity. This solution will provide the absolute basic actions you'll need to track and manage products and payments from initial production to the final consumer.

Your supply chain solution will consist of two smart contracts. One smart contract will handle payments and the other will handle the asset tracking and management. Because you'll be focusing on learning about smart contracts, your solution won't implement every imaginable supply chain function. But when you're done, you'll appreciate how powerful Ethereum is and, I hope, be motivated to write your own smart contracts to solve your own problems.

Paying for supply chain services

Each link in a supply chain provides a service. A supply chain participant might ship goods from one place to another, store goods in a warehouse, add value to products, or even place goods on shelves at retail locations. Unless your organization is a non-profit, the main goal for participating in supply chain is to make money. That means you'll have to pay every time a product moves from one participant to another.

Although you could use traditional payment processing, you're going to learn how to do it using Ethereum! The easiest way to send and receive funds in Ethereum is by using a token. An *Ethereum token* is a type of cryptocurrency for a particular dApp. You'll be creating a supply chain token based on the popular ERC-20 Ethereum token standard.

TECHNICAL STUFF

Although several Ethereum token standards are available, ERC-20 is by far the most popular. You can see how many tokens exist by navigating to `https://etherscan.io` and click or tapping Tokens — ERC-20 Top Tokens. At the time of this writing, there were more than 155,000 different ERC-20 tokens.

You can think of a token as a college student ID with money in a special account. To avoid carrying around cash or multiple cards, many college students pay for things on campus using their IDs. The "college cash" attached to their ID is good only on campus, but it's convenient and makes it easy for on-campus vendors to identify students and offer special pricing.

Your token smart contract will contain all the rules to manage your balance of cryptocurrency. You'll write the code to check your balance, transfer funds to another Ethereum address, and receive funds from another Ethereum address.

Managing assets on the supply chain

The main smart contract for your supply chain will contain the core functions to manage assets. From a technical sense, Ethereum can't manage physical assets. It can manage only digital assets. Think about tracking your bags when you fly on a commercial airline. Many airlines provide status updates via a mobile app. They tell you when your bag gets loaded on the airplane and where to pick it up when you arrive at your destination. However, the airline isn't tracking your bag — they're tracking the tag on your bag. The tag is a generated version of a digital asset that the airline tracks.

The difference between a physical asset and a digital asset is obvious on one hand but subtle on the other hand. Continuing the airline luggage example, problems can occur at the cyber-physical barrier. If the human or device that attaches the tag to the bag doesn't get it right, nothing works from there on. When I recently flew from San Antonio, Texas to Atlanta, Georgie, I arrived but my bag did not. When the airline baggage representative investigated, we found that my baggage tag was attached to another traveler's bag. Because the airline tracks and manages their tags, they sent the wrong bag (with the right tag) to Atlanta. Unfortunately, my bag (with the other traveler's tag attached to it) went to Mexico City. It took me almost a week to get my bag back.

That story should help point out how important it is to maintain the cyber-physical relationship. Physical goods have to be associated with a digital asset to be managed in any computing environment. In many cases, that means the entry point of the supply chain creates a tag or other method of positively identifying the physical asset. Regardless of the identification option you choose, you'll need a number or an identifier that corresponds to a single physical asset. Table 8-3 lists a few options for associating physical assets with their digital mirror assets.

TABLE 8-3   **Connecting Physical Assets to Digital Assets**

ID Method	Pros	Cons
Engraving an identifier on each product	Unique to each item and difficult to alter	Expensive and slow
Attaching a printed label to each product	Unique to each item and useful for a wide variety of products	Labels can be damaged or lost
Attaching a printed label to a box of products	Fast for products managed in batches	Difficulty handling opened boxes with missing product
Using a manufacturer-generated identifier	Integrates with manufacturer's data, and fast if identifier can be scanned	Potentially different formats or locations for different manufacturers, and depends on external data provider
Attaching an RFID tag	Fast and easy to scan	More expensive than printed labels, and tags can detach

Your supply chain smart contract assumes that some external device or other entity creates a trusted digital string or number that uniquely identifies a physical asset. After you have a digital asset ID, your smart contract will define functions that will carry out these actions:

>> **Creating a new supply chain participant:** Validates a new participant and authorizes the participant to become part of the supply chain process.

>> **Adding a new product to the supply chain:** Puts a product into the supply chain process.

>> **Transferring ownership of a product to another participant:** Carries out the main action of transferring a product from one supply chain participant to another.

>> **Tracking a product:** Provides status updates of a product and its history on the supply chain.

Your two smart contracts will work together every time a product transfers from one participant to another. At the moment a product's owner changes, the participants making the transfer will use the ERC-20 token to exchange funds to pay for the asset. Figure 8-1 show how your supply chain process will work.

Digging into Solidity

Solidity is the language you'll use to write smart contracts in the examples in this book. Solidity was proposed by Gavin Wood in August 2014. Although it isn't the only language you can use to write smart contracts, it is the most popular language for writing smart contracts that run in the Ethereum. It enjoys solid support from the Ethereum community and was developed by the Ethereum project's Solidity team.

Solidity was designed to be similar to JavaScript and was influenced by a few other popular programming languages as well, including C++ and Python. The goal of Solidity is to provide a language that is familiar to web application developers but targeted at smart contract development. Solidity isn't intended not as a general-purpose language but to support blockchain specific operations with code that runs in the EVM.

Before your code can run in the EVM, you have to compile it. That's why one of the components you installed when building your development environment was a Solidity compiler. You first write your Solidity source code in an editor. Then you compile it into bytecode, which are the instructions that run in the EVM. After you deploy your smart contract bytecode, it runs on all Ethereum nodes.

Because smart contracts run on all nodes, Solidity must enforce *determinism*, that is, the results must be the same for all nodes running your smart contract code with the same input. If you look at the Solidity documentation, you won't find a `random()` function. That omission is specifically to support Solidity's determinism. Your code gets run first by the node that mines a new block, but then all nodes verify the block and run the code to ensure that they don't get a different result.

In many ways, Solidity is similar to other programming languages. The biggest differences are in how the programs are run and how Solidity deals with data. You'll learn more about Solidity data handling later in this chapter. But for now, note that Solidity deals with data only in the EVM or the blockchain.

Solidity doesn't interact with the outside world much, but it is possible. Solidity supports the concept of an *oracle*, which is a trusted source of information from the outside world. Calling an oracle is easy. One problem is being able to trust the oracle. Another problem is dealing with oracle data that may return different data each time it's called. Before using any oracles, you must ensure that the data source is trustworthy and consistent. It is common for oracles to return data and some proof of authenticity.

 The concept of trust with respect to oracles is just an extension of blockchain trust. Remember that blockchain technology provides a trusted ledger of data in an environment of trustless network nodes. Because trust is such a foundational property of blockchain, it isn't surprising that trusting an oracle is an important concern.

TIP

Describing Basic Smart Contract Syntax

You've already seen a little Solidity syntax. Now it's time to learn some more. When you write Solidity source code, you save that code in a file with the extension .sol. You may recall from Chapter 7 that you stored your Hello World smart contract in the file HelloWorld.sol.

A Solidity program has several main sections, as follows:

>> **Pragma:** This tells Solidity what versions of the compiler are valid to compile this file.

>> **Comments:** Developers should use comments for documenting code.

>> **Import:** An import defines an external file that contains code that your smart contract needs.

>> **Contract(s):** This section is where the body of your smart contract code resides.

Declaring valid compiler version

The `pragma` directive should be the first line of code in a Solidity file. Because the Solidity language is still maturing, it is common for new compiler versions to include changes that would fail to compile older programs. The `pragma` directive helps avoid compiler failures due to using a newer compiler.

Here is the syntax for the `pragma` directive:

```
pragma Solidity <<version number>>;
```

Here is a sample `pragma` directive:

```
pragma Solidity ^0.4.24;
```

REMEMBER

All statements in Solidity end with a semicolon.

The version number starts with a 0, followed by a major build number and a minor build number. For example, the version number 0.4.24 refers to major build 4 and minor build 24. The caret symbol (^) before the version number tells Solidity that it can use the latest build in a major version range. In the preceding example, Solidity can use a compiler from any build in the version 4 build range. This is a way to tell readers that your program was written for 0.4.24 but will still compile for subsequent version 4 builds.

TIP

Although using the caret in the `pragma` directive provides flexibility, it is a better practice to drop the caret and tell Solidity exactly what compiler version you expect.

Commenting your code

Adding comments to your code is an extra step that adds a professional look and feel to your code. A well-commented source code file is easier to read and understand and helps other developers quickly understand what your code is supposed to do. Even simple comments can cut down on the time required to fix bugs or add new functionality. Comments can also provide input for utilities to generate documentation for your smart contracts.

You can use single-line or multiline regular comments. Single-line comments start with two forward slashes. Multiline comments start with the /* characters and end with the */ characters. Here is an example of Solidity comments:

```
// Here is a single line Solidity comment

/* I have a lot more to say with this comment, so I'll
```

```
use a multiline comment. The compiler will ignore
everything after the opening comment characters, until
it sees the closing comment characters. */
```

A third type of Solidity comment is called the *Ethereum Natural Specification* (*NatSpec*) directive. You can use NatSpec to provide information about your code for documentation generators to use to create formatted documentation the describes your smart contracts. NatSpec directives start with three forward slashes and include special tags with data for the documentation. Here is an example of using NatSpec directives:

```
/// @title Greeter smart contract
/// @author Joe Programmer
/// @notice This code takes a person's name and says hello
/// @param name The name of the caller
/// @return greeting The greeting with the caller's name
```

You can find NatSpec documentation and additional information at https://github.com/ethereum/wiki/wiki/Ethereum-Natural-Specification-Format.

Importing external code

The import section is optional but can be powerful. If your smart contract needs to refer to code in other files, you'll have to import those other files first. Importing files makes it as though you copied the other code into the current file. Using imports helps you avoid actually copying code from one place to another. If you need to access code, just import the Solidity file that contains it.

The syntax for importing other files is simple. You use the import keyword and then provide the filename for the file you want to import. For example, to import the file myToken.sol, use this syntax:

```
Import 'myToken.sol';
```

Defining your smart contracts

In the last main section of Solidity, you define the contents of your smart contract. It starts with the keyword contract and contains all of the functional code in your smart contract. You can have multiple contract sections in Solidity. That means a single .sol file can define multiple contracts. Here is an example contract section (you might recognize this code from Chapter 7):

```
contract HelloWorld {
    string private helloMessage = "Hello world";
```

```
function getHelloMessage() public view returns (string) {
    return helloMessage;
  }
}
```

Inside the contract section is where you define all of your variables, structures, events, and functions. There's a lot more to the contract section of your code, but for now, you know how to set up a Solidity smart contract. In the next section you learn more about what goes into the contract section.

Handling Data in Solidity

Solidity is particular about where you can store data. You generally define two types of variables in Solidity: state variables and local variables. You define state variables in the contract section, and those variables are available anywhere in the smart contract. These variables store the state of your smart contract by saving the values in a block on the blockchain. You define local variables inside functions. Local variables don't save their values between function calls. Those values aren't stored on the blockchain and go away when the function ends.

Solidity defines three places for storing data:

>> **Stack:** Where Solidity stores local simple variable values defined in functions.

>> **Memory:** An area of memory on each EVM that Solidity uses to store temporary values. Values stored here are erased between function calls.

>> **Storage:** Where state variables defined in a smart contract reside. These state variables reside in the smart contract data section on the blockchain.

Variable storage location is one of the more confusing aspects of Solidity. I cover the basics now, and come back to some finer points in Chapter 9. The Solidity language doesn't have a stack keyword but does have memory and storage keywords. Solidity uses its own defaults, depending on where you define variables and how you use them, but you can override some of these defaults and also use the keywords to modify how Solidity treats variables.

Here are a few rules that help keep things straight when learning about storing data in Solidity:

>> State variables are storage by default (values are stored in the blockchain).

>> Local variables in functions are memory by default (values are stored temporarily in memory).

>> Structs are storage by default (values are stored in the blockchain).

Solidity can handle different types of data and provides different types of variables to handle each type. When you define variables, you have to specify the datatype of the variable. The datatype tells Solidity how much space to allocate for the value you will store in the variable and how to treat the data. Table 8-4 lists the data types that Solidity supports.

As your smart contracts become more complex, you'll probably need to represent more complex types of data. For example, you might want to define a physical address type that contains several pieces of information, including street address, city, state, and postal code.

You also might need to store tables or lists of data. Solidity allows you to create your own data structures with the `struct` complex data type. You can also define arrays that store groups of similar data items. Solidity arrays can be groups of simple data types or groups of structs. You use `structs` and arrays in the smart contracts you write in Chapter 9.

Here is a smart contract that demonstrates some of Solidity's simple data types. In this example, you're using only state variables, which means you're writing to the blockchain. Defining all of your variable as state variables is not a good idea unless you want to store data forever. Data stored to the blockchain requires expensive operations and shouldn't be used unless you need to store your data persistently. For now, you'll use state variables, but in Chapter 9 you learn how to define local variables as well.

Open VS Code for the myProject project:

REMEMBER

To open VS Code in the myProject project, open a Windows Command prompt or PowerShell (my favorite) and use the `cd` command to navigate to your project directory (myProject.) From here, just enter the following command and press Enter:

```
code .
```

TABLE 8-4   **Solidity Data Types**

Data type	Comments	Example	When to use

uint	32-byte (256 bit) unsigned integer. You can also define smaller uints as uint8, unit16, ... up to uint256 (which is the same as uint).	uint x = 10;
		
		uint16 x = 44;
			To store positive integers. Using smaller uints (such as uint8) saves storage space and processing cost.

int	32-byte (256 bit) signed integer. You can also define smaller ints as int8, int16, ... up to int256 (which is the same as int).	int x = −10; int32 x = 45;	To store integers with negative and positive values. Using smaller ints (such as int8) saves storage space and processing cost.
byte	A single byte. You can also define arrays of 1–32 bytes using the type bytes2, byte3, ... up to bytes32.	byte singleChar = 't'; bytes16 msgHello = 'Hello, world!';	To store any number (up to 32) bytes. The bytes datatype makes it easy to access and manipulate array contents.
string	32-byte array of characters. This datatype is most often used to store strings of UTF-8 characters.	string myString = "Hello, world!";	To store character strings. Solidity strings are difficult to manipulate directly. In most cases, using bytes is more convenient.
bool	Boolean, or logical, values (yes/no or true/false).	bool isOK = true;	To store yes/no, true/false values.
address	20 byte Ethereum address.	address myAddress;	To store an Ethereum address.
mapping	A dictionary that relates key to a value. Mappings provide an easy method to lookup a value that corresponds to a key.	mapping (address => uint) balances;	To lookup data for a specific key, such as finding the balance of an account.
enum	Enumerated list of options.	enum surveyResult { StronglyDis-agree, Disagree, Neutral, Agree, StronglyAgree };	To store meaningful values from a limited set of choices.

Then type the following code. (If you'd rather download the project files, go to www.dummies.com/go/ethereumfd.)

```
pragma solidity 0.4.24;

/*
 * @title Solidity data types
 * @author Michael Solomon
```

```
 * @notice A simply smart contract to demonstrate simple data types available in
   Solidity
 *
 */

contract DataTypes {
    uint x = 9;
    int i = -68;
    uint8 j = 17;
    bool isEthereumCool = true;
    address owner = msg.sender;   //Ethereum address of the message sender
    bytes32 bMsg = "hello";
    string sMsg = "hello";

    function getStateVariables() public view returns (uint, int, uint8, bool,
    address, bytes32, string) {
        return (x, i, j, isEthereumCool, owner, bMsg, sMsg);
    }
}
```

REMEMBER

The steps to deploy and test your smart contract are the same as the steps you learned in Chapter 7. Go to that chapter for details.

Before you can deploy and test your new smart contract, you need to add it to the migration JavaScript script. In VS Code, open the 2_contracts_migrations.js file in the Migrations directory. Then add the two lines with comments so your file looks this:

```
var HelloWorld = artifacts.require("HelloWorld");
var DataTypes = artifacts.require("DataTypes");                    // Add this line

module.exports = function(deployer) {
    deployer.deploy(HelloWorld);
    deployer.deploy(DataTypes);// Add this line
};
```

Don't forget to save your file after adding the new text!

Here are the steps you can use to deploy and test your new smart contract:

1. **Make sure you have Ganache running.**

2. **In VS Code, click or tap the Terminal tab, type the following, and then press Enter:**

```
truffle deploy --reset
```

3. **Type** truffle console **and press Enter.**

4. **At the Truffle console prompt, type the following and press Enter:**

```
DataTypes.deployed().then(function(instance) {return
    instance.getStateVariables() });
```

Figure 8-2 shows the values that your new smart contract returns. Truffle displays the return values in an interesting way. Numbers are returned as `BigNumber` objects. You can call functions in a `BigNumber` library to convert them, but for now just read the values directly. For the numeric returned values, the first value, `s:` is the sign of the number, and the third value, `c:` is the unsigned value the function returned. Also note that the address and bytes32 values are in hexadecimal format.

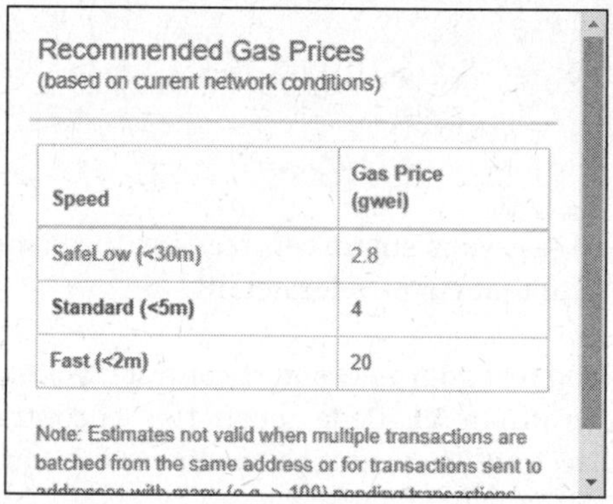

Recommended Gas Prices
(based on current network conditions)

Speed	Gas Price (gwei)
SafeLow (<30m)	2.8
Standard (<5m)	4
Fast (<2m)	20

Note: Estimates not valid when multiple transactions are batched from the same address or for transactions sent to addresses with many (e.g. > 100) pending transactions

FIGURE 8-2:
Smart contract
return values.

Learning about Computation and Gas

One of the difficulties encountered when writing distributed applications is balancing the workload among participating nodes. The way blockchain technology is designed, all nodes do the same amount of work. In fact, all nodes duplicate the same work. This redundancy is necessary to ensure consensus among the nodes.

Workload balance isn't a problem, but node overload is a big problem. Consider what would happen if a malicious user submitted a smart contract that consumed so much computing power that the node running the code couldn't do anything else. That would be a denial of service (DoS) attack. And what's worse, every node would be required to do the same amount of work. If malicious smart contracts were allowed to run, they could render the entire blockchain network unusable.

To avoid DoS attacks and to reduce the overall work network nodes have to carry out, Ethereum introduced the concept of paying for the work required to carry out a transaction. Ethereum also includes a charge for storing data on the blockchain. These requirements encourage smart contract developers to use the blockchain only when necessary, thereby keeping the blockchain from growing unrestrained. Requiring transaction creators to pay for usage is a way of promoting conservative use of shared resources.

As you learned earlier, Ethereum measures the work required for operations by using *gas.* The amount of work required for each operation is used to calculate the fee to carry out the operations that make up a transaction. According to the Ethereum Yellow Paper (the formal Ethereum definition), every transaction requires a minimum of 21,000 gas units to complete.

TECHNICAL
STUFF

The Ethereum Yellow Paper contains the formal definition of Ethereum. You can find the Yellow Paper by opening your browser and navigating to this address: `https://github.com/ethereum/yellowpaper` .

Miners are nodes on an Ethereum network that carry out the intensive mathematical calculations to find a nonce value that satisfies the hash requirements for the block. You learn about mining, hashes, and nonce values in Chapter 2. Paying gas provides an incentive to miners to commit their computing power (and electricity) to the blockchain. Every user that submits a transaction pays a fee in gas, and miners in turn select transactions they think will be profitable and build new blocks with those transactions. The miner that is successful in solving the mathematical puzzle gets the gas fees for the transactions in that block.

So, who pays all these fees to miners? Well, we all do! Every Ethereum transaction requires a small processing fee. Although this might sound like the middlemen that blockchain is supposed to replace, Ethereum fees are tiny compared to existing systems in use today. However, even a relatively tiny Ethereum gas process can grow to be not so tiny during times of heavy network congestion.

Calculating gas fees requires several inputs, including gas price, gas limit, and gas (computation) cost. The user who submits a transaction (that is, initiates some action that invokes a smart contract) sets the highest acceptable gas price and the total limit of gas he or she will agree to pay. The total fee is the amount of gas used in the transaction multiplied by the gas price the miner charges. All of these values can change from transaction to transaction. Table 8-5 lists the main components of gas charges and how they contribute to transaction fees.

If you want to know how much gas will cost, open your browser and navigate to `https://ethgasstation.info`. This web page shows gas statistics for recent Ethereum transactions. Figure 8-2 shows the recommended gas prices at the time of this writing. Note that a safe low gas price is 2.8 Gwei, the standard gas price is 4 Gwei, and if you want your transaction picked up quickly, you should set your gas price to 20 Gwei. 1 ETH is worth 1 billion (1,000,000,000) Gwei, so 4 Gwei is worth 0.000000004 ETH. At the time of this writing, 1 ETH is worth $89.40 USD, so the standard gas price of 4 Gwei (a standard gas price) is worth $ 0.0000003576. If a transaction requires a minimum of 21,000 Gwei, a transaction costs at least 0.0000003576 * 21,000 = $0.0075096. That's less than a penny.

TABLE 8-5   **Ethereum Gas Charges**

Component	Comments
Gas price	The highest price per gas unit a transaction originator is willing to pay. Miners use this limit to determine if the transaction is worth including in a block. If the value is too low, the transaction might not be profitable. If too many transactions are selected with very high gas prices, it might take too long to mine the block and the miner might lose to another node.
Gas limit	The total number of gas units the transaction originator is willing to pay. It must be high enough to allow all operations to complete. If this value is too low, the EVM will terminate the transaction and undo all of its operations. Also, each block has a gas limit, so miners can't just choose the transactions with very high gas limits — they have to choose transactions with gas limits that are cumulatively lower than the block gas limit.
Gas cost	The cost of a single operation. For example, the ADD operation costs 3 gas and the MUL operation costs 5 gas.
Transaction fee	The total fee for computations in a transaction. The formula is: transaction fee = total gas cost * gas price.
Unused gas	The amount of unused gas returned to the transaction originator if the gas limit for the transaction is greater than the actual gas cost.

TECHNICAL STUFF

You can find the gas cost for operations in Ethereum in a spreadsheet located at: `https://docs.google.com/spreadsheets/d/1m89CVujrQe5LAFJ8-YAUCc NK950dUzMQPMJBxRtGCqs/edit#gid=0` .

Although the minimum transaction fee doesn't look like it is very expensive, the fees do add up if you waste computation. From a strict cost per computation, it isn't hard to pay for your own node to carry out calculations. But what you're paying for is transparency and validity among a large number of untrusted participants.

Exploring Access Modes and Visibility of Smart Contract Functions and Data

You can restrict who can invoke Solidity functions and who can access variable values. These access keywords are called *visibility modifiers*. You can use four visibility modifiers when you define functions and variables, as shown in Table 8-6.

TABLE 8-6   **Solidity Visibility Modifiers**

Visibility	What It Means for Functions	What It Means for Variables
`public`	Anyone can call this function.	Anyone can access this variable's value.
`external`	Only external functions can call this function.	This doesn't apply to state variables, and only external functions can access this local variable's value.
`internal`	Only functions in this contract and any contract deriving from it can call this function.	Only functions in this contract and any contract deriving from it can access this variable's value.
`private`	Only functions in this contract can call this function.	Only functions in this contract can access this variable's value.

TECHNICAL STUFF

The Solidity compiler automatically creates a `getter` function for each `public` state variable, which provides an easy way to fetch the value of any variable. The name of the function is the same as the name of the variable. When the `getter` function is called, it returns the value stored in the `state` variable. So if you define a public `state` variable of type `uint` named `myVar`, the function `myVar()` will return a `uint` that is the current value of `myVal`.

Solidity visibility modifiers make it possible to write functions and define variables that are available only to a specific subset of users. You might want some functions and variable to be available only to other functions in the same contract, say, for internal maintenance. In other cases, you might want other functions or variables to be available to anyone. A `getter` function (function that gets the value of some data item and returns it) is often a `public` function. That makes it available to anyone, while an `internal` function that manages a contract's date may be a `private` or `internal` function.

In addition to providing visibility modifiers, you can specify function access modifiers. *Access modifiers* restrict how functions are allowed to access `state` variables. Older versions of Solidity used a single access modifier, `constant`, to indicate that a function did not modify any `state` variable. Starting with Solidity 0.4.17, two new access modifiers replace the `constant` modifier: `view` and `pure`. A function that exceeds its access modifier will result in a compiler error.

Here are the meanings of each access modifier:

» **constant:** This access modifier, which was deprecated in Solidity 0.4.17, was used to inform the compiler that the function would not modify any `state` variables.

» **view:** This access modifier, introduced in Solidity 0.4.17, is a replacement for `constant` and informs the compiler that the function will not modify any `state` variables.

>> **pure:** This access modifier, introduced in Solidity 0.4.17, is more restrictive than `view` and informs the compiler that the function will not even read any state variables.

Controlling Execution Flow

The simple smart contract code that you've seen so far doesn't do much. It just executes from the top of the code to the bottom. Programs that do something useful have statements in them that alter the flow of execution based on input and calculations. Some statements, called *conditional statements*, enforce conditional expressions and execute only under certain circumstances. Other statements, called *iteration statements* or *loops*, repeat sections of code a certain number of times.

These types of statement are called *flow of execution statements.* Solidity implements many of the flow of executions statements you'll find in JavaScript. Table 8-7 lists the conditional and iteration statements in Solidity.

TABLE 8-7 **Solidity Conditional and Iteration Statements**

Statement	What it does	Example

if–else	Executes a group of statements if a condition is true, and optionally executes another set of statements if the condition is false (else).	`numDonuts = purchasedQty;`
		
		`if (numDonuts >= 12)`
		
		`    giveDozenPrice = true;`
		
		`else`
		
		`    giveDozenPrice = false;`

While	Executes a group of statements zero or more times until some condition is true (pre-test repetition structure.)	`numDonuts = 1;`
		
		`giveDozenPrice = false;`
		
		`While (numDonuts < purchasedQty)`
		`{`
		
		`    numDonuts++;`
		
		`    if (numDonuts >= 12)`
		
		`        giveDozenPrice = true;`
		
		`        break;`
		
		`}`

Statement	What it does	Example

do–while	Executes a group of statements one or more times until some condition is true (post-test repetition structure.) Note that a do–while loop always executes at least once.	`numDonuts = 1;`
		
		`giveDozenPrice = false;`
		
		`do {`
		    `numDonuts++;`
		    `if (numDonuts >= 12)`
		        `giveDozenPrice = true;`
		        `break;`
		`} (while numDonuts < purchasedQty);`

for	Executes a group of statements zero or more times until some condition is true (pre-test repetition structure.) This differs from a while loop in that the test condition is defined in the statement.	`giveDozenPrice = false;`
		
		`for (numDonuts=1;`
		`numDonuts<=purchasedDonuts;`
		`numDonuts++) {`
		    `if (numDonuts >= 12)`
		        `giveDozenPrice = true;`
		        `break;`
		`}`

Handling Errors and Exceptions

The last topic in your introduction to Solidity smart contract development is knowing how to handle errors and exceptions. By far the best way to handle errors is to avoid them in the first place. A naïve and unproductive way to handle errors is to leave it completely up to the user interface. A much better design practice is to anticipate as many errors and exceptions as possible and design your code to handle them. If you can envision an error during the design phase, you can develop code to handle it and even develop a test to ensure that your code handles it properly.

In versions of Solidity before 0.4.10, the only way to handle an error was to throw an exception when something bad happened. For example, pre 0.4.10 code to ensure that a code segment would run only if initiated by the code's owner might look like this:

```
if (msg.sender != owner( { throw(); }))
```

If a smart contract ever encountered a throw() function, all changes to state variables would be undone, the contract would return to the caller passing back an invalid opcode error, and all remaining gas would be used up. In other words, if your code encountered a throw() function, you would never get any gas back. And to make matters worse, you didn't get anything done for that gas.

Starting with Solidity version 0.4.10, you have more options for handling error conditions. Current smart contracts can use the revert(), assert(), and require() functions to proactively handle errors. Table 8-8 lists each of the new guard functions and what each one does.

TABLE 8-8   ## Error-handling Guard Functions

Function	What It Does	Example
revert()	Undoes all state changes, allows a return value, and refunds remaining gas to the caller. You should use this function to catch expected conditions that indicate that a transaction should be terminated.	`if (msg.sender != owner( { revert(); }))`
assert()	Undoes all state changes and uses up all remaining gas — that is, like the legacy throw() function, does not return unused gas. You should never encounter this function in properly functioning code.	`assert(msg.sender == owner);`
require()	Undoes all state changes, allows a return value, and refunds remaining gas to the caller. You should use this function to proactively execute code when prerequisite conditions have not been met.	`require(msg.sender == owner);`

Although there is far more to Solidity than what you've seen here, you've learned enough to get started writing your own code. Before you know it, you'll be ready to create your own Ethereum dApps.

Chapter **9**

Writing Your Own Smart Contracts with Solidity

You learn about the basics of developing Solidity smart contracts for Ethereum in Chapter 8. You also learn about difficulties encountered with traditional supply chain applications and how Ethereum can help address some of those problems. Developing distributed applications, or dApps, for the Ethereum blockchain may look similar to writing code in other languages, but it does have specific advantages over non-blockchain environments. However, you have to approach the software development process a little differently when working with blockchain.

Before starting to write a dApp for the Ethereum blockchain, make sure that you understand what your dApp should do and why a blockchain environment is a good fit. Getting these points cleared up in the beginning can help you avoid mistakes that waste time and money. Knowing the tips and tricks of blockchain development before you start writing your own dApps will help you develop better software than just learning as you go.

Ethereum dApps focus on providing some functionality that interacts with data stored in the blockchain environment. Due to the design of blockchain technology, each interaction with the blockchain has an associated cost. Understanding how your dApp will have to pay for blockchain access is critical to getting it right the first time. In this chapter, you learn how to use Solidity to write effective smart contracts for the Ethereum blockchain environment.

Reviewing Supply Chain Design Specification

As you discover in Chapter 8, a *supply chain* is a framework that connects producers to consumers and manages how products and services make their way toward the consumers. In simple cases such as a farmer's market, consumers buy their produce directly from the growers. But in most other cases, at least one intermediary helps get products from producers to consumers. Intermediaries can provide transportation, warehousing, retailing, and other value-added services.

Implementing a supply chain solution in a blockchain environment can reduce the overall cost of providing products and services to consumers and make the entire process more transparent. If you store every step of a product's journey on the blockchain, anyone can track the product along its way.

The first step in developing a supply chain dApp is to look at the data and actions the dApp will need to provide the required functionality. For your supply chain dApp to do its job, you need at least four types of data. Here is a list of the types of data you'll need:

>> **Products:** This data uniquely identifies a specific product that is eventually bought by a consumer.

>> **Participants:** This type of data is a description of all supply chain participants, including manufacturers, suppliers, shippers, and consumers.

>> **Registrations:** This type of data is a snapshot of which participant owns a product at a specific point in time. Registrations track products along the supply chain.

>> **Payment token:** Participants use payment tokens to pay one another for ownership changes of products. For example, a supplier can purchase a product from a manufacturer and use a payment token to pay the manufacturer.

To provide minimal functionality, your supply chain dApp needs to include the following capabilities:

>> **Initialize tokens:** Establish an initial pool of payment tokens.

>> **Transfer tokens:** Move tokens between accounts (that is, pay for products with tokens).

>> **Authorize token payments:** Allow an account to transfer tokens on behalf of another account.

>> **Create products:** Create products and show product details.

>> **Create participants:** Create participants and show participant details.

>> **Move products along the supply chain:** Transfer product ownership to another participant.

>> **Track a product:** Show a product's supply chain history.

The data and functionality your supply chain dApp will support fits nicely into two groups: payment tokens and supply chain. Some of the data and functionality applies to the supply chain, and other data and functionality applies to paying for supply chain activity. You'll separate your data and functionality into two smart contracts.

Payment token smart contract

The *payment token smart contract* handles anything related to payments. Your supply chain participants will buy and sell products by using tokens instead of traditional currency. Although Ethereum includes its own currency, Ether, you will implement your own token for supply chain participants to use. Although you could just have participants pay each other by using Ether, a custom token helps you to manage the entire process.

Defining your own token helps ensure that you limit supply chain participation to only valid supply chain participants and can make transfers simpler. Instead of allowing any Ethereum account to interact with your supply chain, only accounts that own your tokens can pay for products. Therefore, the only way a participant can enter the supply chain is to gain the trust of another participant. You have to either sell your products to an existing participant or exchange some other currency for your tokens.

TIP

Many businesses use the token concept. Arcades often set up their games to use physical tokens instead of real coins or paper money. You buy tokens using real currency and then use the tokens to play each game. This approach makes breaking into game consoles less attractive because the games contain only tokens — not real money. The tokens have value only inside the arcade. (Also, any lost or misplaced tokens mean a profit for the house; a nice benefit if you're issuing the tokens.)

Multiple proposed standards for Ethereum tokens in the form of *Ethereum Request for Comments (ERC)* documents exist. Ten of these proposals have been accepted to become *Ethereum Improvement Proposals (EIP)*. ERC-20 (now EIP-20) defines one of the early standards for defining tokens for Ethereum. You'll use the ERC/EIP-20 standard for your tokens.

TECHNICAL STUFF

ERC and EIP are used interchangeably. Technically, *EIP* refers to finalized ERC documents. However, even though a proposal is finalized, such as EIP-20, you still will see it referred to as ERC-20.

Your token smart contract will allow participants to acquire tokens and then transfer them to other participants in exchange for moving products along the supply chain. To complete this process, you need several data items and functions. The data items you'll define follow:

>> `totalSupply:` The total number of tokens in circulation

>> `name:` A descriptive name for your token

>> `decimals:` The number of decimals to use when displaying token amounts

>> `symbol:` A short identifier for your token

>> `balances:` The current balance of each participating account, mapped to the account's address

>> `allowed:` A list of number of tokens authorized for transfer between accounts, mapped to the sender's address

Your token smart contract will define six functions that allow users to manage token transfers. The functions you'll define are as follows:

>> `totalSupply():` Returns the current total number of tokens

>> `balanceOf():` Returns the current balance, in tokens, of a specific account

>> `allowance():` Returns the remaining number of tokens that are allowed to be transferred from a specific source account to a specific target account

>> `transfer():` Transfers tokens from the caller to a specified target account

>> `approve():` Sets a number of tokens that are allowed to be transferred from a specific source account to a specific target account

>> `transferFrom():` Transfers tokens from a specified source account to a specified target account

Supply chain smart contract

Your second smart contract will contain the data and functionality to manage the product, participant, and product transfer data. In other words, it will handle all supply chain activity that isn't related to payment. As you learn how to implement supply chain functionality, you'll probably think of more things that you'd like your dApp to handle. That's okay. The smart contracts you'll develop in this book are just a starting point. You can extend them to handle many more use cases.

To store the supply chain data necessary for managing product migration toward consumers, you'll define the following data items:

>> **product structure:** This data item stores data that defines a unique product (model number, part number, serial number, product owner, cost, manufactured time).

>> **participant structure:** The participant structure stores data that defines a unique participant (user name, password, participant type, Ethereum address).

>> **registration structure:** The registration structure stores data that records a transfer of a product from one owner to another as the product moves toward the consumer (product ID, owner ID, transaction time, product owner Ethereum address).

>> **p_id:** The product ID uniquely identifies a product and is mapped to a product structure.

>> **u_id:** The participant ID uniquely identifies a participant and is mapped to a participant structure.

>> **r_id:** The registration ID uniquely identifies a registration and is mapped to a registration structure.

Now that you know the data and functions you'll need in your smart contracts, the next step is to start writing code in Solidity.

Creating New Smart Contracts

In this section you create the files you need to implement the token and supply chain smart contracts. To get started, follow these steps to create a new project named SupplyChain, initialize it in Truffle, and launch VS Code for your new project:

REMEMBER

You learn how to create projects, initialize them in Truffle, and use VS Code to edit files and code for projects in Chapters 5 and 7. Review those chapters if you need details for each step. (If you'd rather download the project files instead of creating a new empty project, go to www.dummies.com/go/ethereumfd and extract the project archive file to a directory of your choice.)

1. **Open a command shell or PowerShell window.**

2. **Type the following to create a new project folder:**

```
mkdir SupplyChain
```

3. Change the current folder to the new project folder:

```
cd SupplyChain
```

4. Initialize the new project in Truffle:

```
truffle init
```

5. Launch VS Code for the new SupplyChain project:

```
code .
```

In VS Code, create three new smart contracts as follows. Click or tap SUPPLYCHAIN, then Contracts, and then the New File button next to SUPPLYCHAIN. Type the following filenames to create each new file (make sure your filenames appear under Contracts and look exactly like these). (If you download the project files, you don't have to do this.)

» erc20Interface.sol

» erc20Token.sol

» SupplyChain.sol

Now click or tap SUPPLYCHAIN and then Contracts to display your contracts. Your VS Code Explorer view should look like Figure 9-1.

FIGURE 9-1:
Supply chain starting smart contracts in VS Code.

TIP

Don't worry if you mistype a filename. Changing filenames in VS Code is easy. Just click or tap the filename in VS Code Explorer, and press F2. Now you can type the new filename. If you created your files in the wrong folder, you can fix that in VS Code as well. Just drag them to the right place (under Contracts).

ERC-20 token interface

The first file you'll edit is the interface for the ERC-20 token. An *interface* looks just like a smart contract but doesn't contain any executable code. Developers use interfaces to define minimum functionality for groups of programs. When you define an interface, you define the minimum data items and functions that you want to be common among smart contracts that implement the interface.

TECHNICAL
STUFF

ERC-20 tokens aren't the only type of tokens in Ethereum. Another token standard that looks like it may challenge ERC-20's popularity is ERC-223. You can find out more about the ERC-223 token standard at https://medium.com/kinblog/the-new-erc223-token-standard-8dddbf1a5909.

In our case, we're going to use the standard ERC-20 (or EIP-20) token interface. Every ERC-20 token that uses this interface is guaranteed to have the same minimum data and functions. That's the purpose of an interface. Your implementation may have more data and functions, but you can count on the fact that it has at least everything defined in the interface. In fact, if you use an interface and forget to define a data item or function, the compiler generates an error and refuses to compile the program.

To make sure that your token complies with the ERC-20 token standard, you use the ERC-20 token interface. Click or tap the erc20Interface.sol tab in VS Code and enter the following code:

```
// -----------------------------------------------------------
// ERC Token Standard #20 Interface
// https://github.com/ethereum/EIPs/blob/master/EIPS/eip-20.md
// -----------------------------------------------------------
pragma solidity ^0.4.24;

contract ERC20Interface {
    uint256 public totalSupply;

    function totalSupply() public view returns (uint);
    function balanceOf(address tokenOwner) public view returns (uint balance);
    function allowance(address tokenOwner, address spender) public view returns
    (uint remaining);
```

```
    function transfer(address to, uint tokens) public returns (bool success);
    function approve(address spender, uint tokens) public returns (bool
    success);
    function transferFrom(address from, address to, uint tokens) public returns
    (bool success);

    event Transfer(address indexed from, address indexed to, uint tokens);
    event Approval(address indexed tokenOwner, address indexed spender, uint
    tokens);
}
```

This interface defines the single variable, six functions, and two events that every token contract must implement to support the ERC-20 token standard. You'll learn what each line of code does in the next section, where you implement the interface. At this point, just note that each line of code defines a variable, a function, or an event. There is no code that actually does anything.

ERC-20 token smart contract

After you define the interface, you can implement the code to make your token smart contract work. Click or tap the erc20Token.sol tab in VS Code and enter the following code:

```
// ------------------------------------------------------------------------
///Implements EIP20 token standard: https://github.com/ethereum/EIPs/blob/
    master/EIPS/eip-20.md
// ------------------------------------------------------------------------

pragma solidity ^0.4.24;

import "./erc20Interface.sol";

contract ERC20Token is ERC20Interface {
}
```

You learned about the `pragma` statement in Chapter 7. The `import` statement tells Solidity to open an external file and read it into this file to compile it, just as if you had copied the contents of erc20Interface.sol into this file. You can use the `import` statement as your projects grow to help you keep any single source code file from growing too large to manage easily. If any source code file starts to get too big, you can spilt it into multiple smaller files and import the pieces in the main file.

The last line in the code segment defines the smart contract. You use the `contract` statement to define a smart contract named `ERC20Token`. When you define the contract as `ERC20token is ERC20Interface`, you are telling Solidity that you intend to implement ERC20Interface in this file. Therefore, the compiler will check to make sure that every item defined in the interface is implemented in this file.

The first step to make your token work is to add the data items you'll need. Add the following code between the two curly braces (after the contract statement):

```
uint256 constant private MAX_UINT256 = 2**256 - 1;
mapping (address => uint256) public balances;
mapping (address => mapping (address => uint256)) public allowed;

uint256 public totalSupply; // Total number of tokens
string public name;         // Descriptive name (i.e. For Dummies Token)
uint8 public decimals;      // How many decimals to use to display amounts
string public symbol;       // Short identifier for token (i.e. FDT)
```

These lines of source code define the data you'll store on the blockchain for your token. The first data item, MAX_UINT256, is defined as a constant, which means that the value you assign to it can't be changed at runtime. Solidity uses the ** symbol to denote exponentiation, so 3 squared is 3**2 in Solidity. The value of 2 raised to the 256 power minus 1 is stored in the MAX_UINT256 constant. Defining MAX_UINT256 is a convenient way to store the largest possible value in a uint256 variable.

The balances and allowed data items are mappings. They exist to make it easy to look up a balance or a list of token transfer allowances for an Ethereum account address. The remaining data items are state variables that describe attributes of your token.

TECHNICAL
STUFF

State variables are stored in the blockchain, and storing data in the blockchain costs gas. So you can conserve gas by minimizing how much and how often you store blockchain data. Don't define more state variables than you need. It is good practice to declare the smallest uint size for the data you'll store, which is why the decimal variable is defined as uint8. When you define more complex data using structs, size matters even more.

Supply chain smart contract

The next step in writing developing your supply chain dApp is to begin the definition of the supply chain smart contract. Click or tap the SupplyChain.sol tab in VS Code and enter the following code:

```
pragma solidity ^0.4.24;

contract supplyChain {
```

```
    uint32 public p_id = 0;     // Product ID
    uint32 public u_id = 0;     // Participant ID
    uint32 public r_id = 0;     // Registration ID
}
```

This smart contract starts like the other smart contracts you've seen so far. Inside the contract body, you define three state variables to store the highest ID for products, participants, and registrations. The next sections define the details of each type of supply chain data.

Product structure

The product structure defines the details for each unique product. Type the following code after the state variable definitions in the preceding section:

```
struct product {
    string modelNumber;
    string partNumber;
    string serialNumber;
    address productOwner;
    uint32 cost;
    uint32 mfgTimeStamp;
}

mapping(uint32 => product) public products;
```

In addition to the product structure, the products mapping allows users to look up a product from its product ID (p_id).

Participant structure

The participant structure defines the details for each unique participant. Type the following code after the products mapping in the preceding section:

```
struct participant {
    string userName;
    string password;
    string participantType;
    address participantAddress;
}
mapping(uint32 => participant) public participants;
```

In addition to the participant structure, the participants mapping allows users to lookup a participant from its participant ID (u_id).

Registration structure

The registration structure defines the details for each unique registration. A *registration* is defined as the point in time when a product's owner changes from one participant to another. Each registration represents a product moving along the supply chain.

Type the following code after the `participants` mapping in the preceding section:

```
struct registration {
    uint32 productId;
    uint32 ownerId;
    uint32 trxTimeStamp;
    address productOwner;
}
mapping(uint32 => registration) public registrations; // Registrations by
Registration ID (r_id)
mapping(uint32 => uint32[]) public productTrack;  // Registrations by
Product ID (p_id) / Movement track for a product
```

In addition to the product structure, the `registrations` mapping allows users to look up a registration from its registration ID (r_id). The `productTrack` mapping returns the supply chain movement history for a specified product (p_id).

Coding Primary Functions

After defining the basic contract structure and data items, the next step in developing your smart contracts is to write the code for each smart contract function. *Functions* provide the actions of your smart contracts and define what your smart contracts can do.

ERC-20 token functions

To define the actions your ERC-20 token smart contract should carry out, you need to define its functions and provide the code for the body of each function. Remember that your ERC-20 token smart contract implements an interface, so you have to at least define the functions required in the interface. Note that you can define more functions than those in the interface.

Click or tap the erc20Token.sol tab in VS Code and enter the code for each of the following functions. (Start entering function source code after the symbol state variable definition.)

ERC-20 token constructor

A *constructor* is a special type of function that runs when the smart contract is deployed to the blockchain. In the constructor, you place initialization steps that are executed only when the contract is first stored in the blockchain. In the case of the ERC-20 token, the constructor initializes the token's attributes and allocates the supply of tokens to the Ethereum address that deploys the smart contract.

Enter the following code to define the smart contract's constructor:

```
constructor(uint256 _initialAmount, string _tokenName,
    uint8 _decimalUnits, string _tokenSymbol) public {
    balances[msg.sender] = _initialAmount; // The creator owns all tokens
    totalSupply = _initialAmount;          // Update total token supply
    name = _tokenName;                     // Token name
    decimals = _decimalUnits;              // Number of decimals
    symbol = _tokenSymbol;                 // Token symbol
}
```

TIP

You can use any naming convention for function parameters and variables. Many Solidity developers use the underscore character as the first character for function parameter names. That convention makes it easy to tell whether a data item is a variable or a parameter passed into a function. In this book, parameter names start with the underscore character.

The constructor code for the ERC-20 token is simple. When you deploy the smart contract code to the blockchain, the smart contract assigns the token data items to the provided parameters and assigns all initial tokens to the Ethereum account address that deployed the smart contract.

Defining the `transfer()` function

The `transfer()` function transfers tokens from the calling address to a specified address. Enter the following code after the constructor:

```
function transfer(address _to, uint256 _value) public returns (bool
success) {
    require(_value >= 0,"Cannot transfer negative amount.");
    require(balances[msg.sender] >= _value,"Insufficient funds.");
    balances[msg.sender] -= _value;
    balances[_to] += _value;
    return true;
}
```

The `transfer()` function introduces the Solidity `require()` function, which prevents functions from continuing unless a specific condition is met. If the `require()`

condition is not satisfied, it returns a message to the caller and refunds any unused gas. It provides a polite way to stop smart contract execution. In the case of the transfer() function, you can transfer tokens only if the sender has a sufficient balance to transfer. The require() condition validates that the sender has at least as many tokens as the transfer requires; otherwise, it returns the "Insufficient funds." string.

If the sender does have the required funds, you decrease the balance of the sender and increase the balance of the receiver by the amount to transfer, and then return a true value that tells the caller that the transfer was completed successfully.

Defining the transferFrom() function

The transferFrom() function transfers tokens from one specified address to another specified address. Enter the following code after the transfer() function:

```
function transferFrom(address _from, address _to, uint256 _value) public
returns (bool success) {
    uint256 allowance = allowed[_from][msg.sender];
    require(balances[_from] >= _value && allowance >= _value,"Insufficient
funds.");
    balances[_from] -= _value;
    balances[_to] += _value;
    if (allowance < MAX_UINT256) {
        allowed[_from][msg.sender] -= _value;
    }
    return true;
}
```

The transferFrom() function transfers up to a pre-approved amount from one address to another. The function looks up the pre-approved amount from the allowed mapping and stores that value in the allowance variable. The function calls the require() function to verify that the sender has a sufficient token balance to transfer, and then adjusts the balances of the sender and receiver. The last step is to query the allowance variable and, if it is set, subtract the amount transferred from the remaining allowance.

Defining the balanceOf() function

The balanceOf() function returns the number of tokens owned by a specified address. Enter the following code after the transferFrom() function:

```
function balanceOf(address _owner) public view returns (uint256 balance) {
    return balances[_owner];
}
```

Defining the `approve()` function

The `approve()` function grants permission to transfer a specified number of tokens from one address to another specified address. Enter the following code after the `balanceOf()` function:

```
function approve(address _spender, uint256 _value) public returns (bool success) {
    allowed[msg.sender][_spender] = _value;
    return true;
}
```

Defining the `allowance()` function

Th `allowance()` function returns the remaining number of approved tokens that can be transferred from one address to another specified address. Enter the following code after the `approve()` function:

```
function allowance(address _owner, address _spender) public view returns (uint256 remaining) {
    return allowed[_owner][_spender];
}
```

Defining the `totalsupply()` function

The `totalSupply()` function returns the total number of tokens in circulation. Enter the following code after the `allowance()` function:

```
function totalSupply() public view returns (uint256 totSupp) {
    return totalSupply;
}
```

Supply chain functions

To define the functionality of your supply chain smart contract, you need to define its functions and provide the code for the body of each function.

Click or tap the SupplyChain.sol tab in VS Code and enter the code for each of the following functions. (Start entering function source code after the `productTrack` mapping definition.)

Defining the participant functions

The `createParticipant()` function increments the participant ID (`u_id`), creates a new participant, and sets its attributes to the passed-in parameters. Enter the following code after the `productTrack` mapping:

```solidity
function createParticipant(string _name, string _pass, address _pAdd,
            string _pType) public returns (uint32){
    uint32 userId = u_id++;
    participants[userId].userName = _name ;
    participants[userId].password = _pass;
    participants[userId].participantAddress = _pAdd;
    participants[userId].participantType = _pType;


    return userId;
}
```

The `getParticipantDetails()` function returns the attributes of the specified participant (`p_id`). Enter the following code after the `createParticipant()` function:

```solidity
function getParticipantDetails(uint32 _p_id) public view returns
            (string,address,string) {
    return (participants[_p_id].userName,participants[_p_id].participantAddr
ess,participants[_p_id].participantType);
}
```

Defining the product functions

The `createProduct()` function increments the product ID (`p_id`), creates a new product, and sets its attributes to the passed-in values. Enter the following code after the `getParticipantDetails()` function:

```solidity
function createProduct(uint32 _ownerId, string _modelNumber, string _
partNumber, string _serialNumber, uint32 _productCost) public returns
(uint32) {
    if(keccak256(abi.encodePacked(participants[_ownerId].participantType))
== keccak256("Manufacturer")) {
        uint32 productId = p_id++;

        products[productId].modelNumber = _modelNumber;
        products[productId].partNumber = _partNumber;
        products[productId].serialNumber = _serialNumber;
        products[productId].cost = _productCost;
        products[productId].productOwner = participants[_ownerId].
participantAddress;
```

```
        products[productId].mfgTimeStamp = uint32(now);

        return productId;
    }

    return 0;
}
```

TIP

Unlike many other languages, you can't directly compare strings in Solidity. You have to first calculate a hash value of the string and then compare that number to the hash value of another string. If the two hash values are equal, the strings are equal. Solidity includes the keccak256() function to calculate hashes. To calculate a hash value that you can use in a comparison, you have to call the convert to string function by using the api.encodePacked() function, and then call the keccak256() function on the encoded string.

The getProductDetails() function returns the attributes of the specified product (p_id). Enter the following code after the createProduct() function:

```
function getProductDetails(uint32 _productId) public view returns
        (string,string,string,uint32,address,uint32){
    return (products[_productId].modelNumber,products[_productId].partNumber,
            products[_productId].serialNumber,products[_productId].cost,
            products[_productId].productOwner,products[_productId].
mfgTimeStamp);
    }
```

Defining the supply chain movement functions

The transferToOwner() function records movement along the supply chain. This function transfers the ownership of a specified product from one supply chain participant to another. It creates a new registrations struct, based on r_id, assigns its data items from the passed-in parameters, and pushes the new struct onto the productTrack list. Enter the following code after the getProductDetails() function:

```
function transferToOwner(uint32 _user1Id ,uint32 _user2Id, uint32 _prodId)
        public returns(bool) {
    participant memory p1 = participants[_user1Id];
    participant memory p2 = participants[_user2Id];
    uint32 registration_id = r_id++;

    registrations[registration_id].productId = _prodId;
    registrations[registration_id].productOwner = p2.participantAddress;
    registrations[registration_id].ownerId = _user2Id;
```

```
            registrations[registration_id].trxTimeStamp = uint32(now);
            products[_prodId].productOwner = p2.participantAddress;
            productTrack[_prodId].push(registration_id);

            return (true);
    }
```

TIP

You define two local variables, p1 and p2, to temporarily hold the source and target participant data. However, Solidity would create these by default as storage variables because they directly reference storage structs. You have to tell Solidity to make these variable local by using the memory modifier. That reduces the gas cost of your smart contract.

The getProductTrack() function returns the registration history for a specified product. This function shows the path a product has taken along the supply chain from its original producer. This function provides the current status of any product in the supply chain. Enter the following code after the transferToOwner() function:

```
function getProductTrack(uint32 _prodId) external view returns (uint32[]) {

    return productTrack[_prodId];
}
```

The getRegistrationDetails() function returns the attributes of the specified registration (r_id). Enter the following code after the getProductTrack() function:

```
function getRegistrationDetails(uint32 _regId)  public view returns
        (uint32,uint32,address,uint32) {

    registration memory r = registrations[_regId];

    return (r.productId,r.ownerId,r.productOwner,r.trxTimeStamp);
}
```

Using Events

Smart contract code runs on each EVM across the Ethereum network. It is essentially server-side code. One of the difficulties you encounter when running server-side code is communicating with the client. Smart contracts don't just run arbitrarily — they have to be called by a client or another smart contract.

Communication is pretty easy when a client or smart contract calls another smart contract function. The caller sends input parameters and waits to receive any return values.

TECHNICAL STUFF

One of the more interesting features of Solidity is that its functions can return multiple values. Many languages allow functions to return only a single value, so developers have to figure out ways to pack multiple data items into return strings and unpack them on the client side. Take a look at your `getProductDetails()` and `getParticipantDetails()` functions in the SupplyChain.sol file to see how Solidity passes back multiple return values.

Sometimes the caller doesn't want to wait around for a function to finish. Many programs operate under a different flow control model. In an *event-driven* model, one program waits for something to happen and then responds. VS Code operates in an event-driven model. Figure 9-2 shows VS Code as you edit the SupplyChain.sol smart contract.

FIGURE 9-2: Editing SupplyChain.sol in VS Code.

Your VS Code window should look like the one in the figure. The program is running, but it isn't doing much right now. In fact, VS Code is waiting on you to do something. After you launch VS Code and open SupplyChain.sol, VS Code just waits for you to tell it what to do. You can type text into the editor, click or tap menu items or buttons, or press function keys of control key combinations.

You can code event-driven programs in Solidity, too. Solidity allows you to define *events* in your smart contracts and then *trigger* those events whenever you want to. If your calling program is waiting, or listening, for these events, it can respond to the events and carry out some of its own functions. In the case of VS Code, it is listening for many events, including the Ctrl+S keystroke event. When VS Code sees that the Ctrl-S event has occurred, it runs its Save File function. You can code your smart contracts the same way.

TECHNICAL STUFF

Event-driven programming is often described as a *publish-subscribe* approach to program flow. The called programs generate, or publish, events when interesting things happen. The called program doesn't care what programs are listening for the events, if any. Publishing events allows the called programs to communicate *asynchronously* with any listening programs. Programs that want to listen for, and respond to, events must subscribe to those events. It works just like subscribing to a local newspaper. The newspaper publishes a paper every day, but only its subscribers receive the paper.

There are three steps to implanting events in Solidity:

1. **Define the event.**

   Use the Solidity event statement to define the event, give it a name, and define the data it passes when it triggers.

2. **Trigger the event.**

   Use the Solidity `emit` statement to trigger a previously defined event and pass data to it.

3. **Receive and respond to the event.**

   You learn how to receive and respond to events in Chapter 10.

Defining events

Your supply chain smart contracts will use three events. The ERC-20 token interface requires that you implement two of the events, and you'll define the other one in the main supply chain smart contract.

Click or tap the erc20Interface.sol tab in VS Code to switch to the ERC-20 interface code. Look at the last two lines of code:

```
event Transfer(address indexed from, address indexed to, uint tokens);
event Approval(address indexed tokenOwner, address indexed spender,
          uint tokens);
```

These lines define the `Transfer` and `Approval` events. When the `Transfer` event triggers, it tells any program that is listening for this event that a transfer has just occurred, and that the transfer consisted of send tokens from one address to another. When the `Approval` event triggers, it tells any program that is listening for this event that a new approval was just authorized for a token owner to transfer up to some number of tokens to a specific sender. It is up to the listening programs to do something with these events. Your smart contracts need to only define and trigger the events.

Click or tap the SupplyChain.sol tab in VS Code to switch to the supply chain smart contract code. Scroll down to the definitions for the two mappings after the `registrations` struct. This should be around line 35. Type the following text on a new line:

```
event Transfer(uint32 productId);
```

After you enter this new code, the last few lines of your SupplyChain.sol code should look like Figure 9-3.

```
27    struct registration {
28        uint32 productId;
29        uint32 ownerId;
30        uint32 trxTimeStamp;
31        address productOwner;
32    }
33    mapping(uint32 => registration) public registrations;  // Registrations by Registration ID (r_id)
34    mapping(uint32 => uint32[]) public productTrack;   // Registrations by Product ID (p_id) / Movement track for a product
35
36    event Transfer(uint32 productId);
37
```

FIGURE 9-3:
Defining an event in VS Code.

You will use your new `Transfer` event every time you create a new registration. That means you'll use the event to let any listening program know that a product has just been transferred from one supply chain participant to another. The `Transfer` event sends the transferred product ID to the listening program to tell it what product just moved. The event mechanism makes it easy for external programs to monitor changes that your smart contracts carry out.

Triggering events

After you define the events you'll need in your smart contracts, the next step is to trigger each event at the right time. All you really have to do here is trigger the event in your code when you carry out the action you want to communicate. In other words, you should trigger the `Transfer` event at the point where your code carries out the transfer action.

In Solidity, you use the `emit` statement to trigger an event. When you use the `emit` statement, it is like calling a function. You tell Solidity what event to trigger, and then you provide parameter values, as you do with a function.

Click or tap the erc20Interface.sol tab in VS Code to switch to the ERC-20 smart contract code. Update your `transfer()`, `transferFrom()`, and `approve()` functions to include the `emit` statements shown here (new code is in bold):

```
function transfer(address _to, uint256 _value) public returns
        (bool success) {
    require(balances[msg.sender] >= _value,"Insufficient funds for transfer
            source.");
    balances[msg.sender] -= _value;
    balances[_to] += _value;
    emit Transfer(msg.sender, _to, _value);
    return true;
}


function transferFrom(address _from, address _to, uint256 _value) public
        returns (bool success) {
    uint256 allowance = allowed[_from][msg.sender];
    require(balances[_from] >= _value && allowance >= _value,"Insufficient
            allowed funds for transfer source.");
    balances[_to] += _value;
    balances[_from] -= _value;
    if (allowance < MAX_UINT256) {
        allowed[_from][msg.sender] -= _value;
    }
    emit Transfer(_from, _to, _value);
    return true;
}
function approve(address _spender, uint256 _value) public returns
        (bool success) {
    allowed[msg.sender][_spender] = _value;
    emit Approval(msg.sender, _spender, _value);
    return true;
}
```

You can call the emit statement anywhere in your smart contract code. In your
ERC-20 token smart contract, you have added the emit statement in three places
to signal that some notable action has just occurred.

Click or tap the SupplyChain.sol tab in VS Code to switch to the supply chain smart
contract code. Update your transferToOwner() function to include the emit
statement shown here (new code is in bold):

```
function transferToOwner(uint32 _user1Id ,uint32 _user2Id, uint32 _prodId)
        onlyOwner(_prodId) public returns(bool) {
    participant memory p1 = participants[_user1Id];
    participant memory p2 = participants[_user2Id];
    uint32 registration_id = r_id++;

    registrations[registration_id].productId = _prodId;
```

```
        registrations[registration_id].productOwner = p2.participantAddress;
        registrations[registration_id].ownerId = _user2Id;
        registrations[registration_id].trxTimeStamp = uint32(now);
        products[_prodId].productOwner = p2.participantAddress;
        productTrack[_prodId].push(registration_id);
        emit Transfer(_prodId);

        return (true);
    }
```

Introducing Ownership

One of the difficulties you'll encounter when developing blockchain applications is restricting the execution of sensitive functions. Remember that your smart contract code runs on all EVMs. All EVMs have the complete code for your smart contracts, so limiting execution requires careful planning.

Modifiers can make data items and functions unavailable for external entities to access or run. Don't make the mistake of thinking modifiers make smart contracts secure. They can help reduce the availability to external programs, but they don't provide complete security. Remember that data on a public blockchain is there for anyone to see.

Every smart contract invocation has a caller address. Each EVM knows which account carries out each action. In Solidity, you can access the calling account by referencing msg.sender. Open the erc20Token.sol smart contract and look at the first line of the constructor body:

```
    constructor(uint256 _initialAmount, string _tokenName,
    uint8 _decimalUnits, string _tokenSymbol) public {
        balances[msg.sender] = _initialAmount;  // The creator owns all tokens
        totalSupply = _initialAmount;           // Update total token supply
        name = _tokenName;                      // Token name
        decimals = _decimalUnits;               // Number of decimals
        symbol = _tokenSymbol;                  // Token symbol
    }
```

The first thing you do when the constructor executes (that is, when you deploy this smart contract), is to assign the total initial number of tokens to the calling address's balance value. Solidity stores the value of the caller's address in the msg.sender value, so you can use that to refer to the sender in your code.

You can use the `msg.sender` value also to define ownership and enforce access restrictions in your smart contract code. In your supply chain smart contract, you don't want anyone to be able to transfer a product to another participant. Doing so would allow one participant to steal products from others. The transfer process in your supply chain smart contract transfers the ownership of a product as the product moves along the supply chain. It makes sense that only the current owner should be allowed to transfer a product to another owner.

TIP

Ownership is a common concern when buying and selling products. If you sell a car, you have to sign the title over to the new owner. Possession of the car's title proves ownership. As the car's current owner, you must ensure that no one else can transfer the title of your car to another owner.

Solidity provides modifiers to help make the task of enforcing ownership easier. A modifier is like a lightweight function. It has a name, input parameters, and a body, but it doesn't support return values.

Open the SupplyChain.sol smart contract in VS Code and add the following code after the `createProduct()` function:

```
modifier onlyOwner(uint32 _productId) {
    require(msg.sender == products[_productId].productOwner );
    _;

}
```

This code defines the `onlyOwner` modifier. You can use this modifier on any function to allow only a product's current owner to execute that function. The modifier takes a product ID as an input parameter and checks to see if the `msg.sender` is the same address as the product's current owner address. If the two values match, the modifier is satisfied and the function proceeds. If the two address values do not match, `msg.sender` is not allowed to run the function and control returns to the caller.

TIP

When you write modifiers, don't forget to add the `_;` line as the last line in the modifier body. This tells Solidity to proceed to the function that you have modified. You'll only get to that line if the modifier body is satisfied (that is, the condition in the body is `true`.)

You invoke modifiers by adding them to existing functions. Scroll to the trans-
ferToOwner() function in the supply chain smart contract code and add the
onlyOwner(_prodId) modifier to the function header. Your modified function
header should look like this:

```
function transferToOwner(uint32 _user1Id ,uint32 _user2Id, uint32 _prodId)
                  onlyOwner(_prodId) public returns(bool) {
```

This modifier tells Solidity that before you execute the transferToOwner() function, execute the onlyOwner() modifier. The modifier determines whether the
function caller (msg.sender) is the owner of product prodId. If msg.sender is the
product owner, the transferToOwner() function proceeds. If not, it just returns
without transferring the product.

You can use modifiers to carry out any validation steps that should occur before
you run code in a function. Validating ownership is one of the more common uses
of modifiers.

Designing for Security

Solidity smart contract code can be as insecure as any other software. Just because
your code runs in a blockchain environment doesn't mean that it's secure. You
have to keep security in mind throughout the entire software development process. Although you need to consider many things when developing secure software in any environment, developing blockchain dApps requires that you pay
special attention to the distributed nature of the blockchain.

TIP

For a great online resource for Ethereum Smart Contract Security Best Practices,
go to https://consensys.github.io/smart-contract-best-practices. Read
through the explanations and recommendations in this resource for a more complete understanding of security issues in Ethereum application development.

When you're developing Ethereum dApps, you'll have to avoid many security
weaknesses. Table 9-1 lists a few of the most common security mistakes new
Ethereum developers tend to overlook.

TABLE 9-1 ## Common Ethereum Security Mistakes

Security Mistake	Description	How to Avoid
Lack of randomness	Because smart contract code runs on every EVM, generating random numbers can cause code to run differently on different EVMs.	Use only random numbers that do not affect stored data or smart contract execution flow.
Allowing re-entrancy	The `call` function forwards all the received gas to the called function. If your code allows a function to run multiple times before changing state data, that code could allow multiple changes, such as multiple withdrawals.	Always update state data before transferring control to another function.
Not checking for over-flow and underflow	Incrementing an integer larger than its maximum value or decrementing an integer smaller than the minimum value causes an error that reverts a smart contract.	Always check to make sure that increment and decrement operations do not overflow or underflow.
Permitting `delegate-call` with visible functions	`Delegatecall` allows a smart contract to execute a function from another contract, running it using the calling contract's address. Public or external functions that modify state may be able to do so without being detected.	Limit the use of public and external functions that modify state data.

Implementing Minimal Functionality

If you've followed the discussion throughout this chapter, your ERC-20 and supply chain smart contracts should be complete and clean. That is, they should compile with no errors. In VS Code, press the F5 key to start the Solidity compiler. Figure 9-4 shows the results of the Solidity compiler.

Note that the Output tab shows a warning. In the SupplyChain.sol smart contract's `transferToOwner()` function, you defined the p1 variable but never used it in the function.

REMEMBER

The compiler warns you that you left an unused variable in your code. Although this is a harmless warning, don't make a habit of ignoring compiler warnings. They exist for good reasons, and you should fix each one.

Click or tap the Problems tab to see a list of all problems the compile encountered, as shown in Figure 9-5. Click or tap any problem. VS Code highlights the problem and highlights the line in your source code that corresponds to the problem. If you hover your cursor over the problem or the line of code, more help appears in a pop-up. VS Code provides multiple ways to help you identify and fix problems with your code.

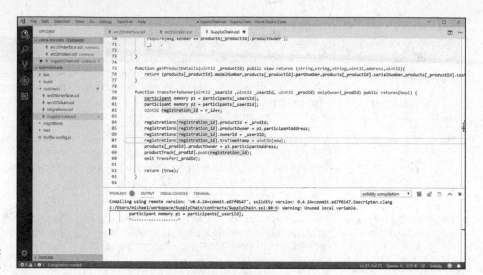

FIGURE 9-4:
Compiler output.

FIGURE 9-5:
Compiler problems.

If your smart contracts don't compile cleanly, review the code to make sure that what you entered is exactly what you see in the book. Pay attention to capitalization — it matters. Another common problem is copying code and pasting it into an editor. Make sure that you copied just what you expected, and look closely at copied quotes. In many cases, copied and pasted quotes result in a quote that won't compile. If you suspect that problem, just backspace over any pasted quotes and type them directly.

Because it is so easy to introduce minor errors that can stop code from compiling, keep your code as simple as possible As you develop your own smart contracts, implement only the minimal functionality first. You can always add more features after you get the simple code working.

4

Testing and Deploying Ethereum Apps

Test Ethereum apps.

Debug and maintain your Ethereum apps.

Integrate legacy applications with Ethereum apps.

Chapter **10**

Testing Ethereum Apps

In Chapter 9, you learn about writing smart contract software in Solidity. Although writing source code is the most visible phase in the software development lifecycle, it is only one part of the complete process. Of course, before you write any code, you should spend time planning and designing your application. Those phases should leave you with a clear specification document that contains the requirements your software must satisfy. After you have an application that compiles, you're ready to test it to see whether it does what it's supposed to do.

Testing software is more than just seeing whether it runs without obvious errors. Testing software ensures that it does what it is supposed to do, doesn't do what it isn't supposed to do, and fulfills the requirements set for the software in the first place.

All too often, a customer agrees to pay for software that does tasks A, B, and C, but ends up getting a different program that carries out tasks C, D, and E. It may be somewhat similar to what was intended, but software developers have a tendency to augment customer requests or at least interpret the needs differently. Software testing doesn't alter or control the scope of a software project, but it does help validate that the software meets its design goals. Meeting design goals ensures that all stakeholders in the software development process are satisfied with the result of the development process. Testing is the only way to see if your software really does what it's supposed to do. In this chapter you learn how to test your smart contracts in a blockchain environment.

Understanding Ethereum dApp Testing

Testing software that runs in a blockchain environment is a little different from testing traditional software applications. Because smart contract code runs in the EVM, you must have an EVM running first. Then you compile your smart contracts and deploy them to your blockchain. After that, you create transactions that call your smart contracts and cause them to carry out tasks. With careful planning, your tests should be able to simulate how your smart contracts will operate in a production environment.

Writing tests from the beginning

The smart contract testing process must start even before you write any software. Waiting to develop tests until after you write the code will take longer and leave more potential gaps in your test coverage. The best time to design tests for your software is when you define the requirements for your software because it makes you think through the code execution and boundaries, which results in better code design. For example If you know you'll be testing to see if you can overflow a variable, you'll likely be more apt to write the code up front that doesn't overflow.

Choosing the right test blockchain

You have several blockchain options for testing your smart contracts, and each one has advantages and disadvantages. Table 10-1 lists the smart contract test blockchain options and the pros and cons of each one.

TABLE 10-1 Smart contract test blockchain options

Type of blockchain	Pros	Cons
Live, public	The environment is live — no simulations	Slow transactions; costly
Test, public (for example, Ropsten)	Similar to a live environment, but far less costly	Somewhat slow transactions; little or no mining activity
Local, private (for example, Ganache)	Fast, free transactions; easy to reset to a new blockchain	No mining activity; difficult to simulate the effect of many network nodes

Most smart contract developers test their software first using a local private network and then using a public test network. Then they finally deploy to the live blockchain. Using this graduated approach makes it possible to find and fix many of the bugs found in smart contracts before deploying the code to networks, where many users can see it and you have to pay for transactions.

Learning the steps in the testing lifecycle

The process of testing smart contracts is the same, regardless of the type of network you choose. You'll follow these steps over and over again to test your smart contracts running on the Ethereum blockchain:

1. Write smart contract code and test cases.
2. Compile code.
3. Deploy code to a blockchain.
4. Run test cases.
5. Identify failure causes and propose changes to address failures.
6. Go to Step 1.

Although most software developers think that the code they write the first time is correct, testing often finds bugs. These bugs can be the result of sloppy programming, a lack of understanding of what was requested, or simply oversights. Regardless of the cause, bugs allow software to operate in ways that do not meet its design goals.

Testing should be thorough enough to execute software in a manner that validates how it operates in a variety of situations. These situations should simulate the activities of both benevolent and malicious users. For every bug encountered, you must try to determine the cause of the flaw, and then return as much information as possible to developers so that they can change the application to remove all flaws found in testing. This process often iterates multiple times, until all tests complete successfully, at which point your software is ready for production.

Testing for software quality

Test cases can be simple commands to check how well functions work or elaborate sets of programs and scripts that run automatically to exercise your smart contract functions. Either way, the point is to run your software in a way that lets you validate that it works as intended and helps you identify any gaps in functionality.

Don't skimp on testing your smart contract code. Any code that you deploy to the live blockchain is immutable — and so are any bugs. The only way to mitigate bugs in smart contract code is to just stop using that code.

If you do deploy smart contracts with bugs, you'll have to tell your clients to stop using the bad code and use the new, fixed code that you deployed to a new address. You'll need to do this in a way that ensures that all old data written to the blockchain (before you fixed your bug) is still valid and accessible, and that the old buggy smart contract code is never used again. In short, it is much easier to find all bugs in testing before you deploy to a live blockchain.

Deploying a dApp to a Test Ethereum Blockchain

Before you can test your smart contracts, you must deploy them to the blockchain. In the last section, you learned that you can use multiple blockchains to test your smart contracts. In Chapter 5, you downloaded and installed the Ganache personal blockchain. You'll use that blockchain for your initial smart contract tests. Ganache makes it easy to set up and launch your own personal blockchain, which works well as a live blockchain simulator.

Telling Truffle to use the Ganache blockchain

The first step in setting up tests on a private local blockchain is to let Truffle know how to connect to the blockchain network. In Chapter 7, you set up a new project and modified the truffle-config.js file to tell Truffle to use the Ganache blockchain. You'll need to edit the truffle-config.js file for each project you use to write smart contract code, including the supplyChain project you used in Chapter 9 and will continue to use in this chapter.

Follow these steps to hook up Truffle and Ganache:

1. **Get the blockchain address from the Ganache settings window.**

    Launch Ganache, and then click or tap the gear (Settings) icon, in the upper-right corner of the Ganache window. Note the hostname, port number, and network ID values. Figure 10-1 is the Ganache settings window with default values. You can also get the host name and port number from the main window. The RPC SERVER value displays the host name and port number separated by a colon.

2. **Launch Visual Studio Code (VS Code) for your project (SupplyChain).**

    Open a Windows Command prompt or PowerShell (my favorite) and navigate to your project directory (SupplyChain.) From here, just enter the following command:

    ```
    code .
    ```

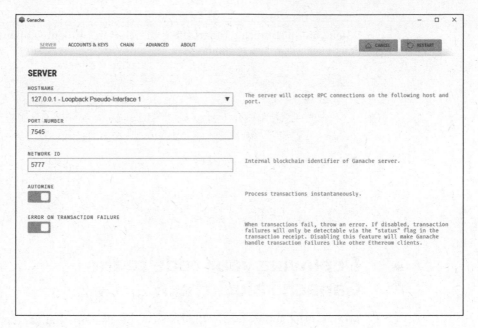

FIGURE 10-1:
Ganache settings
window.

The code command launches VS Code, and the period tells VS Code to use the current directory as the current project.

3. **Modify your Truffle project configuration file to reference the Ganache blockchain.**

Click or tap truffle-config.js on the left side of your VS Code window to open the file. Add the sections shown in Figure 10-2. Then save the file (choose File ⇨ Save or press Ctrl+S).

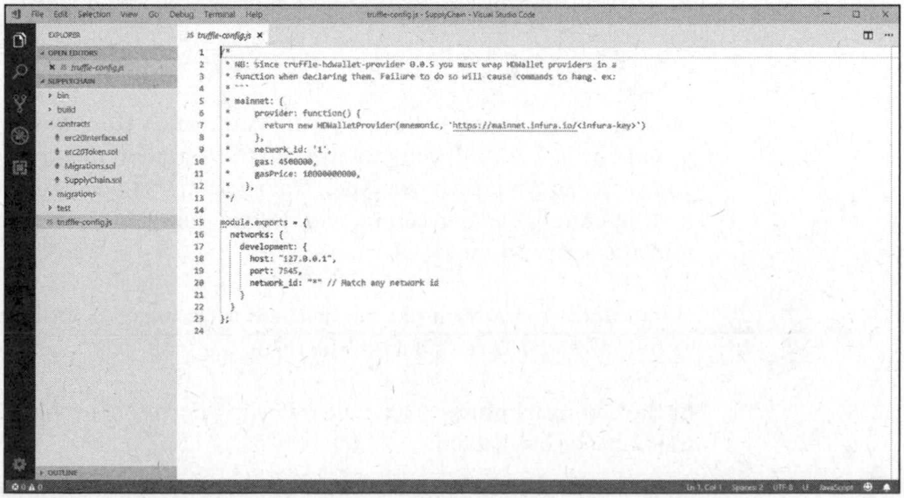

FIGURE 10-2:
Modified Truffle
project
configuration file.

When you finish editing the truffle.js file, the uncommented lines (lines that don't start with /*, *, or */) should look like this:

```
module.exports = {
  networks: {
    development: {
      host: "127.0.0.1",
      port: 7545,
      network_id: "*" // Match any network id
    }
  }
};
```

Deploying your code to the Ganache blockchain

After Truffle knows to use the Ganache blockchain, you can deploy your smart contract code to the Ganache test blockchain. Truffle will deploy your smart contracts based on JavaScript instruction files you place in the migrations folder.

Make sure that you have a file in your migrations folder named 2_contracts_migrations.js with the following contents:

```
var erc20Token = artifacts.require("./erc20Token.sol");
var SupplyChain = artifacts.require("./SupplyChain.sol");

module.exports = function(deployer) {
    deployer.deploy(erc20Token, 10000, "MGS Token", 18, "MGS");
    deployer.deploy(SupplyChain);
};
```

Although you can enter the following commands from any Windows command prompt or PowerShell, you can also use the Terminal tab in VS Code (which gives you access to Windows PowerShell from within VS Code.) All three options let you type operating system commands. (Make sure that your SupplyChain project folder is your current folder.)

TIP

If you don't see a terminal tab at the bottom of your VS Code window, choose Terminal ⇨ New Terminal from the menu bar.

At the command prompt, type the following to compile your code and deploy it to the Ganache blockchain:

```
truffle deploy --reset
```

This command returns the addresses of each newly deployed smart contract. The --reset option tells Truffle to replace your smart contracts if they have already been deployed. After you deploy each of your smart contracts, you're ready to start testing them.

Writing Tests for Ethereum dApps

You have three common options for writing tests for Solidity smart contracts:

>> Command line interaction

>> Solidity smart contracts

>> JavaScript

To define tests, command line interaction and Solidity smart contracts use the Solidity language, and the third option uses the JavaScript language. In this section, you learn how to write tests using Solidity at the command line and JavaScript. The main advantage of using Solidity is that you'll be using the same language for testing that you used to develop your code.

The third option, JavaScript, is also a popular option for writing tests. The Java Script approach provides many more options for writing complex test cases.

Testing using the command line

If you need to carry out a simple test of a smart contract, command line testing may be sufficient. It's quick and flexible but not easily repeatable. You should be writing formal test cases for each smart contract as you develop the smart contract. You'll learn about how to do that in the next section. However, you will commonly need to create a quick test to see if some aspect of your smart contract is doing what it should be doing. Command line testing may be the easiest way to create a simple, one-time test.

The first step in creating a command line test is to get the smart contract's address. You need that address to access any of the smart contract's public data or functions. Take a look at the output you saw when you deployed your smart contracts. Figure 10-3 shows the output of deploying the SupplyChain contracts.

Note the two *Saving artifacts. . .* messages. Those messages tell you that Truffle saved the addresses and other descriptive information related to each deployed smart contract. If you want to find the address of any deployed contract, you only have to ask Truffle for it.

FIGURE 10-3:
Deployment
output.

You can interact with your smart contracts from the Truffle console. From your operating system command prompt, type the following command to start the Truffle console:

```
truffle console
```

From here, you'll enter your commands to test smart contracts.

REMEMBER

Remember that you can enter commands at the Windows command prompt, at the Windows PowerShell, or by using the Terminal tab in VS Code. As long as your current folder is your project folder, you can enter commands in any of these three shells.

At a truffle console prompt, enter the following command:

```
supplyChain.deployed().then(function(instance) {return instance })
```

This command tells Truffle to search the artifacts for deployed smart contracts and return the address of the smart contract named supplyChain in the variable named instance. After you know the address of your smart contract, you can access its data and functions.

The next step is to access your smart contract's data and functions to see if your code is operating properly. In general, you want to write tests that ensure that your code is doing what it should be doing and doesn't do anything it shouldn't do. The second goal is much harder to accomplish. You need to think of all the things users could try that could cause your code to do things it shouldn't do.

Here is a brief list of things you should test for with each smart contract:

» **Overflows and underflows:** Make sure that your code doesn't allow numbers to become larger than the largest valid value or smaller than the smallest valid value. Either situation will cause an error.

» **Valid return values:** Ensure that each function returns values that are valid for the caller. In some cases the return value is calculated. Your tests should ensure that any calculated return values are always valid.

>> **Boundary conditions:** Always test that your code handles data that meets or exceeds expected limits.

>> **Iteration limits:** Test each looping structure to ensure that it doesn't iterate more times than you intend and burn up all your gas.

>> **Input and output data formats:** Test your code to make sure that it handles data provided or returned in unexpected formats.

>> **Input and output data validation:** Ensure that your code either sanitizes or rejects invalid characters or sequences of characters.

After you know the objectives for testing your code, you can invoke your smart contract's functions and examine the return values. If you need to provide different Ethereum account addresses, remember that Ganache provides you with ten addresses by default. Figure 10-4 shows the main Ganache window with the first seven accounts listed.

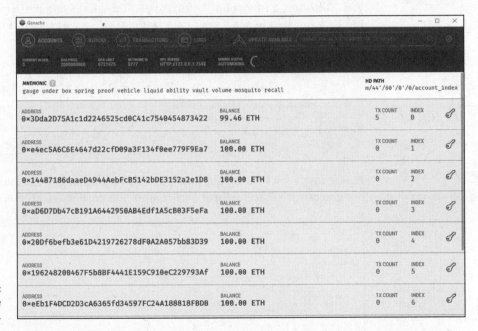

TECHNICAL STUFF

Note in the figure that the balance of the first account is lower than the rest. You used the first account by default to deploy your smart contracts. The cost of deploying those smart contracts was deducted from that account's ETH balance.

You'll use the account addresses from Ganache to define supplyChain participants. Enter the following three commands at the Truffle console prompt to create three supplyChain participants:

```
supplyChain.deployed().then(function(instance) {return instance.createParticipan
            t("A","passA","0x436f6e677261747320796f7520666f756e642045",
            "Manufacturer") });
supplyChain.deployed().then(function(instance) {return instance.createParticipan
            t("B","passB","0x6173746572722065576772120452d6d61696c20676d",
            "Supplier") });
supplyChain.deployed().then(function(instance) {return instance.createParticipan
            t("C","passC","0x61726b40676d61726b2e636f6d20746f2077696e",
            "Consumer") });
```

You can look at the details returned from each of these commands to see what happened, but you don't need to read through everything at this point. The easiest way to see if your functions worked as planned is to ask your smart contract to tell you. You wrote a function to return to you the details of a participant, so you can use that function to see if your data was stored. Type these commands to get the participant details for the three participants you just created:

```
supplyChain.deployed().then(function(instance) {return instance.
            getParticipantDetails(0)});
supplyChain.deployed().then(function(instance) {return instance.
            getParticipantDetails(1)});
supplyChain.deployed().then(function(instance) {return instance.
            getParticipantDetails(2)});
```

Figure 10-5 shows the output from these three commands. The output isn't pretty, but you can see that the three participants you created are all there.

FIGURE 10-5:
Results of
getParticipant
Details().

You can use the syntax of these commands to write your own simple tests to see how your smart contracts function. Before you learn about more complex tests, you'll need to know one important feature of command line testing. Enter these commands to add a product, and then transfer that product to participant B (the supplier):

```
supplyChain.deployed().then(function(instance) {return instance.createProduct(0,
            "prodABC", "100", "123", 11) });
supplyChain.deployed().then(function(instance) {return instance.transferToOwner
            (0, 1, 0) });
```

Now you want to transfer product 0 from the supplier (participant 1) to the consumer (participant 2). But the transferToOwner() function allows only the product's owner to transfer ownership to another owner. By default, all commands you enter at the Truffle console run as the first Ganache account. If you want to run a test command as another account (and you do), you have to tell Truffle. Enter the following command to transfer product 0 from the supplier (participant 1) to the consumer (participant 2):

```
supplyChain.deployed().then(function(instance) {return instance.transferToOwner
            (1, 2, 0, {from: "0x61737465722065567672120452d6d61696c20676d"
            }) });
```

Adding the from: clause allows you to use a different address as the transaction's sender.

Writing test cases in JavaScript

You can test your smart contracts from the command line, but your options are limited. Every time you test your code, you have to either type each command or copy it from a saved file. A much better way to test code is to write test cases for each contract as you write the contract. If you do this, Truffle will help you organize your test cases and run them at the same time. That way, you can run comprehensive tests any time you make changes to your smart contracts.

Note that your project folder includes a subfolder named test, which is where you'll put your test code. But you don't have to create any script files to test your code on your own. Truffle will help you get started. Enter the following commands at the operating system command prompt (with your project folder as the current folder) to create initial test files for the ERC-20 token and supplyChain smart contracts:

```
truffle create test erc20token
truffle create test supplyChain
```

Click or tap the test folder in VS Code Explorer. You should see two new files, erc-20token.js and supply_chain.js. These two new files are the starting JavaScript test cases that Truffle created for you. You enter your test case statements into each of these files to test your smart contracts. Open each of these JavaScript files in VS Code. The default files don't do much. They just fetch the deployed address of the smart contract and then return. You can add code in these files to run functions, access blockchain data, and run your smart contracts through their paces.

The first step in making these test cases functional is to import the smart contract you're testing. Open the supply_chain.js file and add the following line of code to the top:

```
var SupplyChain = artifacts.require('./SupplyChain.sol');
```

This line of code fetches the address of the deployed smart contract and stores it in the SupplyChain variable. After the test case has the smart contract address, you can automate many of the tests you ran at the command line. Replace the remaining lines in the supply_chain.js file with the following lines of code to carry out the same tests from the previous section:

```
contract('SupplyChain', async accounts => {
  it("should create a Participant", async () => {
    let instance = await SupplyChain.deployed();
    let participantId = await
             instance.createParticipant("A","passA","0x436f6e677261747320796f
             7520666f756e642045","Manufacturer");
    let participant = await instance.participants(0);
    assert.equal(participant[0], "A");
    assert.equal(participant[2], "Manufacturer");

    participantId = await
             instance.createParticipant("B","passB","0x6173746465722206567672120
             452d6d61696c696c620676d","Supplier");
    participant = await instance.participants(1);
    assert.equal(participant[0], "B");
    assert.equal(participant[2], "Supplier");

    participantId = await
             instance.createParticipant("C","passC","0x61726b40676d61726b2e63
             6f6d20746f2077696e6e","Consumer");
    participant = await instance.participants(2);
    assert.equal(participant[0], "C");
    assert.equal(participant[2], "Consumer");
  });

  it("should return Participant details", async () => {
    let instance = await SupplyChain.deployed();
    let participantDetails = await instance.getParticipantDetails(0);
    assert.equal(participantDetails[0], "A");

    instance = await SupplyChain.deployed();
    participantDetails = await instance.getParticipantDetails(1);
    assert.equal(participantDetails[0], "B");
```

```
    instance = await SupplyChain.deployed();
    participantDetails = await instance.getParticipantDetails(2);
    assert.equal(participantDetails[0], "C");
  })
});
```

One of the advantages of using JavaScript over command line tests is that you can not only run functions and access blockchain data, but also test data to see if it matches expected values. That's what the `assert()` function does. You can see that both the `participant` mapping and the `getParticipantDetails()` function returns structures of data. JavaScript can access individual data items as if they were in an array. That's why `participant[2]` refers to the *participantType* from the participant data structure.

You can carry out many more complex types of tests using JavaScript. This brief introduction just scratches the surface.

After you have you test cases written using JavaScript, Truffle will run them all with one command. Enter the `truffle test` command at the operating system command prompt to run all your test cases. Figure 10-6 shows the output of a successful run of the tests just listed.

FIGURE 10-6:
Truffle test
results.

Each time you change a smart contract, you can run your test cases to ensure that your application meets its design goals and runs without errors. If your tests do encounter errors, you'll see which test failed, along with information that helps you determine why it failed and what you need to do to fix the problem.

Logging and Handling Errors

Unlike many other languages, Solidity doesn't provide a direct way to output messages to a log file that you can use to test your code and follow along with its execution. Most languages let you at least output messages to a console or local file, but not in an Ethereum environment.

If Solidity allowed you to write to a local file, you could write to the filesystems of every EVM — outside the blockchain. Writing to every EVM's local filesystem would increase the workload and decrease the security of participating nodes and make running a blockchain node less desirable. Because you can't just write messages to local files, you have to carefully design your smart contracts to report errors and status to clients in other ways.

Handling errors in Solidity

Client software can determine if any return data was sent back from the EVM, and what the return code was. If a smart contract returns as a result of a revert() or a failed require(), the EVM can send a string, but your smart contract code has to send something that makes sense and the client UI has to use it to determine what happened. Following is an example of a simple smart contract and test code that uses a try/catch block to handle errors:

Here is the code for the basicMath smart contract, which is stored in the contracts/BasicMath.sol file:

```
pragma solidity ^0.4.24;

contract basicMath {
    uint256 constant private MAX_UINT256 = 2**256 - 1;

    function add(uint256 _numberA, uint256 _numberB) public pure returns(uint256) {
        return _numberA + _numberB;
    }
}
```

Here is the code for the JavaScript test case code to test the basicMath smart contract, which is stored in the test/basic_math.sol file:

```
contract('BasicMath', function(accounts) {
  it('the sum should not overflow', async () => {
    try {
      // Try to add 2^256 and 5 (should overflow and throw an exception)
      const addResult = contractInstance.add((2**256 - 1), 5)
      assert.ok(false, 'Threw an exception instead of overflowing.')
    } catch(error) {
      assert.ok(true, 'Caught the exception.')
    }
  })
});
```

In the preceding example, the `try/catch` structure can catch errors from the EVM and determine what to do with them. It is important that client software handle errors, but it is even more important that your smart contracts handle as much as possible without resorting to generic error conditions. As much as possible, your code should use the `revert()` and `require()` functions, which means your code is anticipating problems and handling them in a way that you have thought through and included in your application design. That's why writing test cases while you write smart contracts makes sense. The more you plan for errors, the better your smart contracts will be in handling those errors.

Logging activity in smart contracts

Although Ethereum does not have a traditional logging facility, the event feature comes pretty close. In fact, some careful planning can give you good execution information without having to pay full price for storage access. Every time you emit an event, that event and its parameters are stored in a blockchain block. You can query the blockchain for events, and even get a list of all events in an address range. You can use that information as a lightweight application logging feature.

In Chapters 11 and 12, you learn about integrating your smart contracts with other software. You'll always need some external software, generally some type of client software, to invoke smart contract functionality. One of the things client software can do is wait for events to occur.

Recall that you created a single event for your `supplyChain` smart contract. That event triggers every time your transfer a product from one participant in the blockchain to another. You could write the following JavaScript code to do that:

```
var transferEvent = SupplyChain.Transfer({_prodId});

transferEvent.watch(function(err, result) {
  if (err) {
    console.log(err)
    return;
  }
  // return result.args to UI
})
```

This code responds only to transfers that occur after the code runs. But if you want to see any prior transfers for a product, you can use the event indexing feature of Ethereum. You first have to change your event definition. In the SupplyChain.sol file, change the `Transfer` event definition to this:

```
event Transfer(uint32 indexed productId);
```

Adding the indexed keywork tells Ethereum that this event should be stored in a way that is easy to find. You can index up to three arguments for each event. Your JavaScript code can use the indexed arguments to fetch ranges of event data. Just change the first line of your event watcher code to the following to fetch all prior `Transfer` events:

```
var depositEvent = cryptoExContract.Deposit({_prodId,
    {fromBlock: 0, toBlock: 'latest'});});
```

Adding the `fromBlock` and `toBlock` modifiers tells the EVM to search multiple blocks for `Transfer` events and returns the details of each event. Using events this way can provide valuable runtime logging. And, as an added feature, event data is far less costly than storage.

Fixing Bugs in a dApp

You test your code so you can identify flaws in it. Software flaws, or bugs, are any bits of code that do not function the way they are supposed to. Bugs that cause errors are generally easy to spot, but silent bugs — those that do not cause compiler or runtime errors — can be much harder to find.

The first step in removing bugs from your smart contracts is getting all of your smart contracts to compile. That step should fix *syntax errors,* which are errors in the way you write statements in the language itself that the compiler can find and report. A syntax error could be a mistyped line of code or a missing parenthesis. The Solidity compiler will find obvious errors as well as code that might cause a future error. For example, if you define a variable but never use it, the compiler will generate a warning. You could ignore the warning, but it is poor practice or a mistake to define a variable that is not used. The best approach is to modify your code to remove all compiler warnings.

The other type of bug is a *semantics error*, in which a line of code is syntactically correct and does not generate compiler warnings, but the code doesn't generate the result you expect. Many times, this type of error shows up only under certain conditions. Successfully finding semantic errors is the main reason testing is crucial to the development process. You don't want bad code to make it to production, especially in a blockchain environment. Testing should be as extensive as possible to find as many of the bugs in your code as possible before you deploy that code to a live blockchain. The quality of your smart contracts is directly related to the quality of your testing.

Chapter **11**

Deploying and Maintaining Ethereum Apps

In Chapter 10 you find out how to test your dApp. You learn how to deploy your smart contracts to a test blockchain and then interact with them. You see how smart contracts respond to different types of data and how to call smart contract functions. Your tests are an important part of the software development lifecycle. You should test your smart contracts thoroughly before you allow them to be deployed to a production environment.

After you complete thorough testing, you're ready to make the transition to production. It's time to deploy your code to a live blockchain, called *mainnet.* Your live environment may be the main live Ethereum blockchain, another public Ethereum blockchain, or perhaps your own organization's private blockchain. Each blockchain has its own characteristics and provides a different operating ecosystem. You must understand the target environment for your dApp when you design its functionality.

Deploying a dApp isn't the last step. As with all software, tasks are required to maintain the dApp's ongoing operation. It's important to validate your smart contracts and ensure that they're working properly in the live environment. You'll also likely need to update features or perhaps fix newly discovered bugs in your code. When this happens, you need a plan to address the process of updating your code, testing the new functionality, and then deploying the new code to replace the old code. You learn about all these tasks in this chapter.

Test Blockchain Options versus Live Blockchains

In Chapter 10 you test your smart contracts by using the Ganache test blockchain. This blockchain is a common choice for the initial testing of Ethereum blockchain code because you can control the testing environment and can easily clean up to start testing again without having leftover data from previous tests. Although one of the basic features of blockchain technology is that blocks are immutable, sometimes it's necessary in testing to just remove everything you've done and start over. Although a clean redo isn't possible on a live blockchain, you can do it pretty easily if you're using a local blockchain that you control, such as Ganache.

TECHNICAL STUFF

You may have noticed that every time you quit Ganache, you lose all blocks on your test blockchain. By default, Ganache starts with a new blockchain every time it starts. Although this behavior makes it easy to start over for testing, sometime you want to save your blockchain between Ganache sessions. To do so, use `ganache-cli --db /path/to/db` to specify a location for Ganache to save the blockchain state. When you start Ganache again, it will initialize its new blockchain from the previously saved state, instead of creating a new blockchain.

Testing with the Ganache blockchain

Ganache does a great job of simulating how your smart contract code will execute. In fact, it provides the local blockchain and the EVM that executes the code. Although the pieces are good at simulating a live blockchain, it can't realistically simulate the effect of other nodes on the blockchain network. Real blockchain networks have miners and other nodes that communicate and share information around the network. Transactions almost always take longer to complete on a live network than on a test network because a live network has more participants and more work to do.

When you start Ganache, you automatically get the same 10 accounts by default, and each account starts with a balance of 100 ETH. Ganache sets up these defaults to make it fast and easy to start testing your code. You can easily change these defaults in the Ganache settings page if you need more or different accounts, or if your accounts need more ETH.

Ganache also defaults to automining mode, which means that the Ganache EVM processes each transaction as soon as it is received. Although testing your smart contracts without having to wait for each test is helpful, it isn't realistic. When running on a live blockchain, transactions aren't processed until a miner adds them to a new block and then satisfies the consensus requirement. Remember that Ethereum uses the Proof of Work (PoW) consensus protocol, so miners compete to find a nonce value that, when hashed with the previous block's header, results in a hash value that satisfies the current complexity requirements.

Ethereum adjusts the difficulty of the hashing process with each block to ensure that new blocks are added to the Ethereum blockchain every 10 to 19 seconds. If blocks get added faster than every 10 seconds, the difficulty is increased, and if blocks take 20 seconds or longer, the difficulty is reduced. As miners join or drop off the network, the relative available mining computing power changes and can affect how fast miners can mine new blocks. Advances in hardware and software techniques can also affect mining capabilities. Regardless of the available computing power, the Ethereum blockchain automatically reacts to keep the mining rate within 10 to 19 seconds per block.

Your Ganache test blockchain can either automine or provide a simulated delay. If you turn off Ganache's Automine option in the settings window, you can enter the number of seconds for Ganache to wait between mining new blocks. This wait time helps to simulate the delay your code will encounter on a live blockchain. Figure 11-1 shows the Ganache settings window with Automine turned off and a delay of 14 seconds between block creations.

Deploying your code to other test blockchains

Although Ganache can help simulate block mining delays, the artificial delays are constant and don't reflect what you'll encounter in a live blockchain environment. Also, it's difficult to share your code with other developers or testers when you use only a local test blockchain. Therefore, the next step in testing your smart contracts for a live environment is to use one of the several public test blockchains. Most blockchain software developers choose a public test blockchain after testing code locally using Ganache or some other blockchain simulator. A public test blockchain allows more people to get involved in the development and testing process.

Public test blockchains are closer to a true live blockchain but still don't give you the exact experience. Public test blockchains do consist of multiple nodes, as you'll find on the live blockchain, but the mining process is simulated. Additionally, different test blockchains use different consensus protocols. The most popular public test blockchains you'll encounter follow:

- » **Ropsten:** A test blockchain similar to the live Ethereum blockchain
- » **Rinkeby:** An alternative test blockchain that uses a different consensus algorithm and steady block generation time
- » **Kovan:** A test blockchain similar to Rinkeby but with a faster block generation time

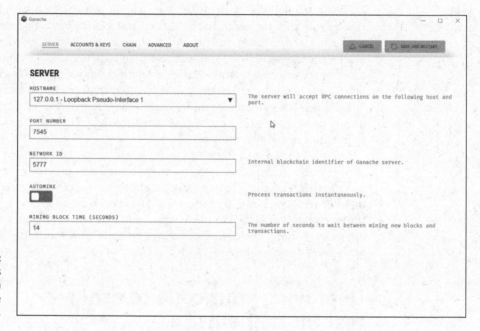

FIGURE 11-1:
Ganache settings window with Automine disabled.

Test blockchains give you the ability to deploy and run your code in environments that are close to live environments. You can pay for your code to execute with cheap or free money. The ability to generate ether or request as much of it as you want for free makes it possible to run as many tests as you need but can also lull you into a false sense of wellness. It's easy to ignore the effect of gas cost when you don't have to pay for it. Test networks are great at evaluating code functionality but don't require the same gas conservation skills that live networks do.

Ropsten

The *Ropsten test blockchain* is one of the most popular test blockchains. It uses a PoW consensus algorithm similar to the one that the public live Ethereum blockchain uses. Miners can earn a small amount of ETH for mining new blocks, and new blocks are added to the Ropsten blockchain approximately every 30 seconds. Geth and Parity Ethereum blockchain clients support Ropsten, and it is a good choice if you want to observe the effect of mining on your smart contracts.

Rinkeby

The *Rinkeby test blockchain* uses a different consensus algorithm than the live public Ethereum and Ropsten blockchains. Rinkeby uses a Proof of Authority (PoA) consensus algorithm and adds new blocks to its blockchain every 15 seconds. Before you can get ether, PoA requires that you prove your existence. All ether is pre-mined and you simply withdraw the amount you need from a faucet after proving your existence, generally by posting to a social media outlet and providing the evidence of the post. (A *faucet* is simply a mechanism that dispenses free ether.) Geth supports Rinkeby but not Parity.

Kovan

If you've decided to use the Parity client, you can choose the *Kovan test blockchain.* Kovan supports Parity but not Geth. It uses the same PoA algorithm as Rinkeby, but adds new blocks at a faster rate of every 4 seconds.

Anticipating Differences in Live Environments

Regardless which test blockchain you choose, it will only be a simulation of a live blockchain. In a live blockchain environment, miners compete for the reward paid to add new blocks. You will likely encounter many more miners and more node diversity in a live blockchain environment. This diversity can lead to unexpected delays and even an unexpected transaction order. A transaction that pays a higher reward because it uses more gas could be selected by miners before an earlier transaction that doesn't pay as well.

These considerations are just some of the ones to take into account when transitioning from a test environment to a live environment. Thorough testing will identify most of your software's flaws, but there will always be a leftover that you won't find until you deploy to a production blockchain. That's why maintaining your software after you deploy it is still important.

The biggest difference between test networks and mainnet, the live network, is that mainnet uses real money. All of the ether you use for testing on test networks is essentially worthless. You can get more by changing your configuration for local blockchain, or by requesting it from a test network faucet. Before you deploy anything to mainnet, however, the account you use must own real ether. You can purchase that through any exchange, such as coinbase.com, but it has to be in your account before you try to deploy your dApp.

The other primary difference with mainnet (or public test networks) is that all changes you make to the blockchain are immutable and persist forever. If you deploy a smart contract with a bug, you'll never be able to change it. The best you can do is to deploy a new version of your smart contract with the bug removed, and then ensure that no one uses the smart contract at the old address. And in the case of mainnet, you'll have to pay real money to deploy a new version of your code, which is another good reason to invest in thorough testing before you deploy your code.

Preparing Your Configuration for Deploying to Different Networks

You already know how to set up Truffle to deploy to the Ganache blockchain. Before you can deploy to a public test network or mainnet, you have to extend the Truffle configuration to support more networks. To make most of the changes, you edit the contents of your `truffle-config.js` file. You need to tell Truffle how to connect to each of the networks you'll use to deploy your code.

One of the pieces of information that Truffle needs is the account to use when accessing the network. You've already seen how to use Ethereum addresses to determine ownership. When you use Ganache, Truffle records the Ganache accounts in an array named `eth.accounts[]`. If you don't provide an account, Truffle assumes that you're using the first account from Ganache, which is stored in `eth.accounts[0]`. This approach keeps you from having to manage accounts during development and initial testing.

REMEMBER

When you want to use a public test network or mainnet, you have to use a valid address on each network. The good news is that Ethereum addresses are generic and valid on any network. However, remember that any crypto-assets you own are network-specific. If you 100 ETH on Ropsten, that doesn't mean you own 100 ETH on mainnet. You can use the same account for multiple networks, but crypto-assets owned by that account are not shared across networks.

One easy way to manage access to multiple networks without having to set up full nodes for each one yourself is to sign up for an Infura account. Infura maintains their own infrastructure that provides easy access to multiple blockchain networks. Infura accounts allow you to deploy code and interact with mainnet, Ropsten, RinkeBy, and Kovan networks. Your Infura account provides you with unique project keys (API keys) for multiple projects that you create. You use each project key to manage a unique dApp. Navigate to https://infura.io to explore Infura's offerings and set up your own account.

Launch VS Code for your SupplyChain project and click or tap the New File button next to SupplyChain in Explorer, then type **secrets.js** and press Enter. A new file is created in the project root directory named secrets.js. You'll use this new file to store sensitive account information.

WARNING

Make sure that you protect this file and don't share it with anyone. If you publish your code to any other location, make sure that you exclude the secrets.js file from any publish operations.

Type the following text in the editor for the secrets.js file:

```
var infuraProjectID = "Project ID from Infura";
var accountPK = "Your Ethereum account private key";
var mainnetPK = accountPK;
var ropstenPK = accountPK;
module.exports = {infuraProjectID: infuraProjectID, mainnetPK:
        mainnetPK, ropstenPK: ropstenPK};
```

Replace "Project ID from Infura" with the project ID that you got for the project you created on the Infura website. Also replace "Your Ethereum account private key" with the private key for the Ethereum account you want to use. In this case, use the same account for the Ropsten and mainnet networks.

The secrets.js file stores the private key (or keys) for blockchain network access, but you need another component to securely use your private key to access crypto-assets. To accomplish that task, you need a wallet provider that Truffle can call. Open a Windows command prompt or a Windows PowerShell window, and type the following command to install the Truffle wallet provider:

```
npm install truffle-hdwallet-provider
```

Next, click or tap truffle-config.js in Explorer to open the truffle-config.js file in the VS Code editor. Replace the contents of the truffle-config.js file with the following text:

```
let secrets = require('./secrets');

const WalletProvider = require("truffle-hdwallet-provider");
```

```
const Wallet = require('ethereumjs-wallet');

let mainNetPrivateKey = new Buffer(secrets.mainnetPK, "hex");
let mainNetWallet = Wallet.fromPrivateKey(mainNetPrivateKey);
let mainNetProvider = new WalletProvider(mainNetWallet,
    "https://mainnet.infura.io/");
let ropstenPrivateKey = new Buffer(secrets.ropstenPK, "hex");
let ropstenWallet = Wallet.fromPrivateKey(ropstenPrivateKey);
let ropstenProvider = new WalletProvider(ropstenWallet,
    "https://ropsten.infura.io/");

module.exports = {
  networks: {
    development: { host: "localhost", port: 7545,
                   network_id: "*", gas: 4465030 },
    ropsten: { provider: ropstenProvider,
                   network_id: "3", gas: 4465030 },
    live: { provider: mainNetProvider,
                   network_id: "1", gas: 7500000 }
  }
};
```

Previously, you defined only a network named development. The development network connects to your locally running Ganache blockchain. The new networks definition you just added now supports Ganache, Ropsten, and mainnet. The code before the networks section uses the Truffle wallet provider to instantiate objects that provide access to the Ropsten and mainnet blockchain networks. After you set up your Truffle configuration file, Truffle handles the rest.

TECHNICAL
STUFF

For more information on configuring Truffle for other networks, navigate to https://truffleframework.com/tutorials/using-infura-custom-provider.

Deploying a dApp

After you decide on a test network or are ready to deploy to mainnet, you need to complete just three steps to get your code deployed to the blockchain:

1. **Get some ether.**

   You must have enough ether to at least pay for the transaction to save your smart contracts to the blockchain.

2. **Compile your code.**

   Ensure that all your code cleanly compiles into bytecode.

3. **Deploy your code.**

Submit your smart contract code to your chosen blockchain.

Getting enough ether

You get ether in your account to pay for deployments and any other blockchain use in two ways. Just ask for ether or buy it. If you're deploying to mainnet, you'll have to buy ether. You can buy ether from any exchange that supports Ethereum (such as Coinbase, Gemini, or CEX-IO), and then you can use your wallet to manage access to your ether. (See Chapter 5 for more on wallets and exchanges.)

TIP

If you're not sure where to buy ether, check out the Coin Central resource on buying ether and how to select an exchange. Navigate to https://coincentral.com/how-to-buy-ethereum-and-best-exchange-ratings to find this resource.

If you're deploying to a test network, you can just ask that network for some free ether. Because there isn't any value associated with ether on a test network, getting what you need for free is easy. The common technique for getting ether for a test network is to request it from that network's faucet. Each test network has its own method getting ether from its faucet.

Getting ether for the Ropsten network

The Ropsten network ether faucet is the most straightforward. You simply navigate to https://faucet.ropsten.be, enter your account address, and click or tap Send Me Test Ether. In a matter of minutes your account balance shows that you now own Ropsten ether. Figure 11-2 shows the Ropsten Ethereum faucet.

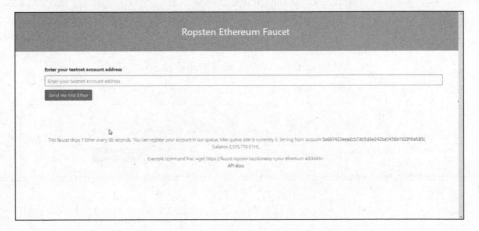

FIGURE 11-2:
Ropsten network
Ethereum faucet.

Getting ether for the Rinkeby network

Getting ether for the Rinkeby network from its faucet requires a few more steps. You can't simply enter your address. Rinkeby attempts to discourage malicious users by requiring simple authentication for ether requests. To satisfy the authentication requirements, you initiate ether requests from a social media account by sending a tweet or publishing a public post on Google+ or Facebook that includes your account. Navigate to `https://www.rinkeby.io/#faucet` to read the full Rinkeby faucet instructions or to provide a social media URL with your Ethereum address. Figure 11-3 shows the Rinkeby Ethereum faucet.

FIGURE 11-3:
Rinkeby network Ethereum faucet.

Getting ether for the Kovan network

The Kovan network requires that you have a valid GitHub account before you can request ether for their network. Navigate to `https://faucet.kovan.network` and log in with your GitHub credentials. Then enter your Ethereum account address to initiate the ether request. To remind you that Kovan is a test network, they call their ether *Kovan Ethere*, or *KETH*. Figure 11-4 shows the Kovan Ethereum faucet (after you log in with your GitHub credentials).

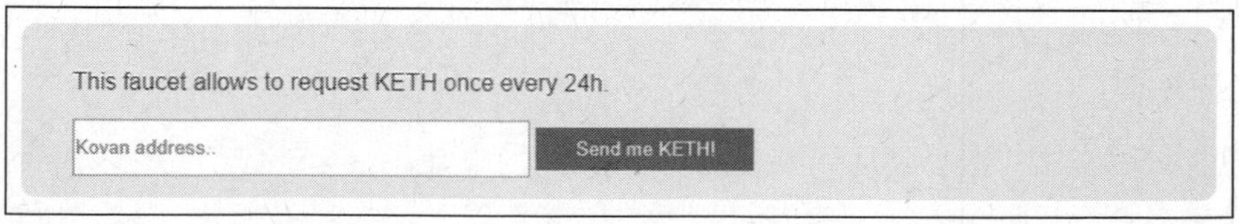

FIGURE 11-4:
Kovan network Ethereum faucet.

Verifying your ether

In Chapter 6, you installed the MetaMask Ethereum wallet. MetaMask makes it easy to manage accounts and crypto-assets from any of the networks you learned about in this chapter. You can change from one network to another by simply selecting a different network from the network drop-down list.

Launch MetaMask in Google Chrome and click or tap the network list in the upper-left corner of the MetaMask window. Figure 11-5 shows the networks you can choose in MetaMask.

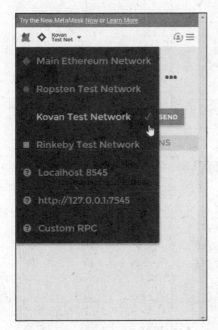

FIGURE 11-5:
MetaMask
Ethereum
network choices.

If you have a GitHub account, you can log in to the Kovan faucet and request ether. If you don't know your account address, MetaMask will copy it to your clipboard for you. From the network drop-down list, select Kovan Test Network. You should see your current account balance. Click or tap the menu icon (three dots on the right side of the window) and then click or tap Copy Address to Clipboard (see Figure 11-6). You can then paste your address into the appropriate input field in the Kovan faucet web page.

After a few minutes, 1.000 ETH will appear in your Kovan Test Net account in MetaMask. From the network drop-down list, select Kovan Test Network to see your updated account balance, as shown in Figure 11-7.

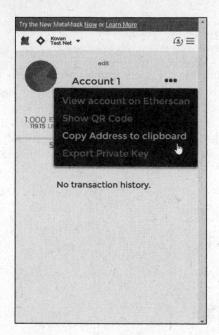

FIGURE 11-6:
MetaMask Copy
Address to
Clipboard option.

FIGURE 11-7:
Kovan account
balance in
MetaMask.

Compiling your code

Although the deployment process will ensure that all of your code is compiled, it's always a good idea to make sure that everything compiles before trying to deploy. Truffle makes compiling easy. Simply type the following command at a Windows command prompt or Windows PowerShell in the desired project root folder:

```
truffle compile
```

This command will compile all contracts in the current project that have changed since the last compile. If you want to compile all contracts, even if they haven't changed, type the following command:

```
truffle compile --all
```

You can also specify the target network when you compile. Truffle will save compile artifacts to the specified network. You should always include the target network option after you define multiple networks in truffle-config.js. Type the following command to compile all contracts and store compile artifacts to the development network:

```
truffle compile --all --network development
```

After you're ready to compile for the live network, type the following command to compile all contracts and store compile artifacts to the live network:

```
truffle compile --all --network live
```

All of your code must compile cleanly (and be thoroughly tested) before moving to the next step of deployment.

Deploying your code

Truffle makes the process of deploying your contracts to a network easy too. You've already accomplished the hard work of setting up your account, acquiring ether, and configuring Truffle to interact with your desired networks. Now all you have to do is tell Truffle what network you want to use when you deploy your code.

In Truffle, the process of creating a transaction to write your contract to the blockchain is called both *migration* and *deployment*. That's why the `migrate` and `deploy` commands do the same thing. You can use either one. Regardless of the keyword you use, Truffle looks in the migrations folder under your project's root folder to find out what contracts to deploy (or migrate) to the network. Truffle runs the JavaScript files it finds in the migrations folder in alphabetical order.

When you're ready to deploy your contracts, type one of the following commands to deploy your code to the development network (your Ganache local blockchain).

```
truffle migrate --network development
```

or

```
truffle deploy --network development
```

Figure 11-8 shows the output from deploying the SupplyChain project contracts to the local development network.

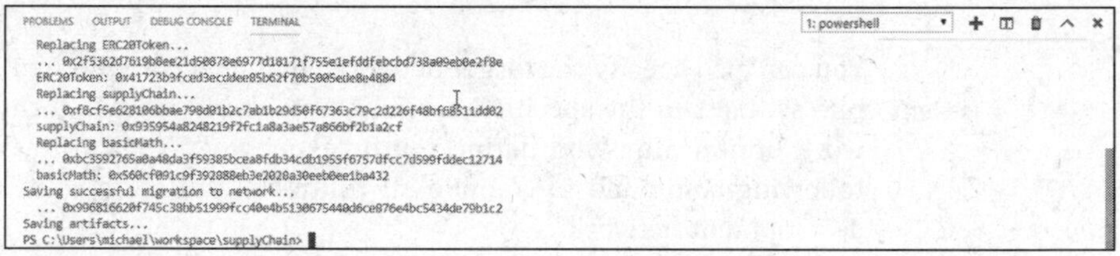

FIGURE 11-8:
The result of the
Truffle deploy
command.

Note that Truffle found existing versions of each contract, replaced each one, and reported the new address for each contract. The last line of output tells you that Truffle is saving the artifacts of the deployment operation on the blockchain. You've already seen how you can query the artifacts and find the current addresses of smart contracts. That's how blockchain users find the contracts they want to interact with.

After you have successfully deployed your fully tested smart contracts, your application is available to anyone else to examine and run. Your blockchain app is now part of Ethereum blockchain history.

Chapter **12**

Integrating Non-Blockchain Apps with Ethereum

Although you can build entirely blockchain-based applications, it is far more likely that your applications will be a combination of traditional and blockchain components. You learn in Chapter 3 that some use cases lend themselves well to blockchain apps but others do not. In this book, we chose to highlight one use case, supply chain, because blockchain offers clear advantages over traditional methods. However, even a comprehensive supply chain application will likely run partially as a traditional application and partially on the blockchain.

Many emerging blockchain apps consist of core components that operate as smart contracts and other components that operate as traditional applications that interact with users and provide supporting functionality. This hybrid approach to application development requires the capability to integrate the two different development models. In other words, to develop hybrid applications that run partially on the blockchain, you need to know how to design them to talk with each other and operate seamlessly.

Distributed application design and development isn't new. In fact, some of the difficulties with distributed applications led to the need for technologies like blockchain. Remember that blockchain technology doesn't solve all application problems, but it does have its place. Now that you know how to develop dApps for the Ethereum blockchain, in this chapter you learn how to integrate your smart contracts with applications that do not include blockchain technology. The capability to integrate blockchain and non-blockchain applications makes it possible to develop applications that use the right technology for a wide range of needs.

Comparing Blockchain and Database Storage

In Chapter 2, you learn about some of the differences between storing data in a blockchain and a database. Both technologies can store data, but clear differences exist between the two. One of the first obstacles you might encounter when asked to integrate blockchain with an existing application is determining what data you should migrate to the blockchain.

Traditional applications store most of their data in a database. Databases provide fast access to shared data. Blockchains can also provide access to shared data, but they may not be as fast as a database. As you learn in Chapter 2, there are other differences as well. It is important that you understand the relative strengths of each data storage technique to make good design decisions for integrating blockchain into your organization.

When you begin the design process for integrating new blockchain apps with existing non-blockchain apps, determine the best home for each type of data based on how you plan to use it. For example, it doesn't make sense to store on the blockchain low-importance data that you update regularly. However, if it is important that you maintain a historical record of all changes to that data, the blockchain might be a good place for it. Always remember that a cost is associated with writing to the blockchain.

The rest of this section lists the most important features that highlight the differences between databases and blockchains. Understanding the effect of each difference will help you to design hybrid integrated applications that meet your organization's goals.

Locating control

Databases are central repositories of data that are shared by a collection of local and remote clients. The database administrator controls access to the database and manages changes to the database's content and format. Although clients external to the database owner's organization may be permitted to access and update the data, a central authority controls the database and its content.

Blockchains are ledgers of data shared among many nodes. There is no central copy of the blockchain data. All copies are the same. The blockchain technology guarantees that each node verifies the integrity of the blockchain data and can easily detect unauthorized changes. With public blockchains, any node, and its users, can access the blockchain data without requiring specific permission do to so. Permissioned, or private, blockchains impose access restrictions and a more traditional central access control model.

Imposing data format

Databases (at least relational databases) are collections of tables that each contain data in similar formats. Each row of data in a relational database has the same data format. Likewise, each column of a table contains a list of items of the same data type. A database's *schema* describes the format of the tables in that database. The database administrator maintains the database schema and controls any changes to it. Database applications can count on the fact that when they read data from the database, it conforms to the current database schema.

Blockchain does not enforce any data format for data stored in its blocks. Smart contracts may define formats for the data each one stores, but any block on the blockchain may contain transaction data created by many different smart contracts.

Updating data

Traditional databases support the classic CRUD operations: Create, Read, Update, and Delete. Databases depend on the capability of each client, based on granted permissions, to be able to create and manage data in the database. Part of the data management process includes the capability to update and delete data. The current state of the database stores only the latest version of any table row's data. The capability to overwrite data reduces redundancy and confusion over multiple data versions.

Blockchain technology supports only two operations: verifying a transaction and writing data to the blockchain. After you write data to the blockchain, it is immutable. Blockchain technology does not support update and delete operations. The only way you can update data is to add new data to the blockchain that supersedes the previous data version.

Optimizing performance

Database vendors include new performance features with every new release. The goal is to provide the fastest access to data stored in the database. Database application developers routinely analyze their database queries to ensure that they are optimizing their code for the fastest data access. In most cases, slow queries are viewed as defects and become candidates for modification.

Blockchain technology is not generally focused on performance. In fact, blockchain has sometimes been referred to as a slow database. Although this comparison is incomplete and unfair, it is generally accurate in that blockchain data access is slower than equivalent database access. The distributed nature of blockchain data, along with its integrity guarantees, mean that blockchain data storage will continue to be slower than database storage for the foreseeable future.

Protecting confidentiality

Traditional databases benefit from their central control. The database administrator can restrict access to any data to only authorized individuals. Most database management systems provide built-in table and row-based permissions, and some include column-based permissions as well. And most current database management systems provide mechanisms to encrypt part or all of the data in a database. These features can make it easy to enforce confidentiality.

A public (permissionless) blockchain does not enforce access controls for its data. Any user who has access to a blockchain network node can view the data the blockchain stores. Some blockchain apps use encryption to enforce confidentiality, but managing keys in a distributed, trustless environment is challenging. These challenges have minimized widespread adoption of data encryption for blockchain data. Private, or permissioned, blockchains can provide a general level of confidentiality. Users must have blockchain access granted to them to access the private blockchain. However, after a user gains access to the Ethereum blockchain, that user can access all blocks, just like in a public Ethereum blockchain.

Paying for storage

Many people view traditional database storages as free and blockchain storage as costing cryptocurrency. This view is only partly correct. Although it is true that every database operation does not have a direct cost associated with it, the infrastructure on which the database operates is not free. Setting up and running a database server requires a substantial investment. Hardware, software licensing, software development, and personnel costs can be high.

Blockchain apps have software development costs but generally far lower infrastructure requirements. To compensate nodes for contributing to the infrastructure and mining operations, each transaction costs a small amount of cryptocurrency. In the case of costs, both technologies require investment.

Providing integrity and transparency

Traditional databases do not provide data integrity or transparency by default. Multiple users can modify data, and even overwrite each other's changes. Further, most database management systems do not log all data changes by default. These problems are well-known and have resulted in extensions to database access languages and database management system to support integrity and transparency. Database transactions can help define scope of work to maintain a steady database state. For granular integrity, database administrators can enforce strict rules on who can modify data, and concurrent control mechanisms such as locking can help avoid data write collisions. To provide more transparency, many database management systems provide the capability to log selected data modifications in separate tables, providing audit trails for later inspection.

The fundamental design of blockchain technology provides integrity and transparency by default. The consensus mechanism provides sanctioned integrity for every write to the blockchain. And because the blockchain is immutable, it automatically keeps every version of every data item written to any block.

Protecting resilience

A central database is the core data repository of many organizations. Although a central database is convenient, it provides a Single Point of Failure (SPoF). Failure of the database means no user can get the data he or she need and the application stops working. For some organizations, that situation would be catastrophic. Many organizations invest heavily in hardware, software, and personnel to maintain current separate copies of their data for disaster purposes. Creating an information ecosystem that is resilient to failures of its primary data repository is expensive.

Blockchain technology depends on the distribution of a ledger across many nodes. Because the network nodes trust each copy of the ledger, that data is accessible through any node on the network. If any node fails, all of the other nodes can continue to operate and the data is still available. The design of blockchain technology provides resilience by default.

Table 12-1 summarizes the differences between storing data in a database and on a blockchain.

TABLE 12-1 Database Storage versus Blockchain Storage

Feature	Traditional Database	Blockchain
Locating control	Centralized control; one central database copy	Decentralized control; complete copy of the blockchain on each node
Imposing data format	Data schema defines data format	No schema; each smart contract decides how to store its data
Updating data	Create, Read, Update, Delete (CRUD)	Read, Write
Optimizing performance	Optimized for short response time and high-throughput	Not optimized for performance
Protecting confidentiality	Centrally managed permissions	No default confidentiality for pubic blockchains
Paying for storage	Up-front infrastructure costs	Per-transaction costs
Providing integrity and transparency	Dependent on DBMS and application	Consensus and immutability provide integrity
Providing resilience	Possible with substantial investment	Complete copy of the blockchain stored on each node

Contrasting Execution and Flow in Blockchain dApps and Traditional Applications

A big difference doesn't exist between traditional distributed applications and blockchain dApps. With traditional applications and distributed dApps, the software sets up an initial state, waits for user input, and responds to that input. The main difference is in where the application code operates and what component handles validation.

Traditional applications mostly operate on a small number of computers. Although some programs operate entirely on a single computer, it is more common for functionality to be split up among at least two computers. In this architecture, some parts of the application, such as the code that interacts with the user, runs on the client computer, while other code, such as code that interacts with a database, runs on a server computer. This client–server architecture is an older but still common architecture for software applications.

Over the last two decades, reliance on the Internet and its resources has grown fast — and that growth is constantly accelerating. Internet resources were once primarily endpoints or information sources, but now a growing number of resources are computational components. Today, you can write applications that mostly call functions that run on other servers. That changes the overall flow of today's applications. Instead of just executing a series of steps on a client or server, tasks may run on many remote computers or devices.

Blockchain dApps are really extensions of the distributed application model, with one important difference: Smart contract code runs not on one node but on all nodes. And any transaction that you create for the blockchain has to wait until a miner selects it and successfully completes the requirements of the blockchain to write that block to the blockchain.

The response time for any blockchain can be far longer than writing data to any other storage location. Although this longer write cycle may not change the flow of your application, it can affect how users perceive and use the application. You have to be aware of how blockchain operates to anticipate slower writes to the blockchain.

Whenever possible, avoid making users wait for blockchain operations to complete before moving on. You might have to redesign your user interface to allow users to carry out some tasks, but inform them that other tasks take longer. Perhaps you can allow users to submit data for the blockchain, and then allow them to do other things within the application while you're waiting for the blockchain return status. After your application receives a blockchain return status, it can alert the user and provide a way for the user to view the status and choose to move to another step in the application.

When integrating distributed application components, one of the most important factors is considering how new components will affect users. A large part of your design activities should involve developing a design that best meets the needs of your users.

Designing Goals for Incorporating Blockchain into an Existing Application

The first item to consider when planning to integrate multiple applications is to define your goals for the integration. You have to be able to clearly explain why you're integrating the applications in the first place. If you can't explain your reasons for starting an integration project, you'll likely encounter problems.

Although blockchain technology is one of the most talked about innovations of the last decade, that fact isn't a good enough reason to embrace it. You learn in Chapter 3 about different use cases for blockchain technology. They aren't the only ones, but they are examples of where blockchain can fit well.

No mandatory goals exist for integrating blockchain technology into another application, but a few high-level objectives should be part of any integration project. The following list is a collection of goals you should resolve for every migration project, especially those that involve integrating blockchain components. You can use this list as an initial checklist when planning to integrate blockchain technology with your existing applications:

>> **Address application shortcomings.** Integrating any non-blockchain application with blockchain technology should solve one or more ongoing problems with the existing application. If your traditional application doesn't have any unresolved problems, integrating a new technology may have little value. New technology should always be a way to solve existing problems.

>> **Introduce previously unavailable features.** Your application may be fine as it is but unable to provide new functionality that your users want. For example, integrating a blockchain supply chain application could allow your users to see where their products are along the supply chain and trace purchased products back to their origin. Providing functionality that was previous unavailable is a potential reason to integrate blockchain technology.

>> **Enhance the user experience.** Integrating any new technology should enhance the overall user experience, not harm it. You could argue that the previous supply chain example fits this category too. Giving users more visibility into the supply chain path provides a more complete picture of product status and enhances the user experience. This goal is also a warning that blockchain integration should avoid creating obstacles for users that reduce the application's usefulness.

>> **Reduce operational costs.** One of the main features of blockchain technology is its capability to offer *disintermediation,* which is the reduction of the reliance on intermediaries to control and manage transfers of items of value from one party to another. Blockchain technology should be able to offer ways to eliminate at least some of the middlemen in business transactions. With fewer middlemen charging service fees, overall operational costs of blockchain applications should be lower. Your design specifications should include statements of how much operational cost the integrated blockchain app components should reduce.

>> **Enhance auditability and compliance.** One of the most obvious advantages of blockchain technology is in the context of auditing. The process of auditing organizations for compliance to various standards or regulatory requirements

includes examining audit trails that represent organizational activities. You learn in Chapter 1 that blockchains are immutable, and all data ever written to it is maintained in its original state. Therefore, the data you move to a blockchain will automatically create its own audit trail. You can easily trace all of the data that any account has changed.

The most important goal when designing a blockchain integration solution is to articulate clear reasons why blockchain is better than what you have today. What does a blockchain solution offer that is superior to what you use today? If you can't clearly explain the specific reasons why blockchain is better, it probably isn't any better. As cool as blockchain is, it must solve a problem before it has value in any organization.

After you decide what you want the blockchain integration to provide, the next step is to decide how the integrated applications will work together to provide the features you want. Designing your integration has two starting points: You have existing smart contracts that provide the functionality that you want, or you must develop new smart contracts from scratch. Each approach has its own challenges.

Using existing smart contracts

It's a good idea to design the integration as if you were designing your smart contracts from scratch. If you already have smart contracts that provide the functionality you want, you will already have a map of the data you need to provide and the functionality you can access. Even if you have existing smart contracts in place (perhaps you purchased code from a software vendor or acquired open-source code), you may still have the ability to modify and extend your smart contract code.

If you can change any existing smart contract code, start with the existing smart contract functions and data items, and add data and functionality as needed. If you can't modify the smart contract code you'll use, you must modify your existing application to conform to the smart contract requirements.

Developing your own smart contracts

Another approach to developing an integrated blockchain solution is to start with the existing traditional application and no smart contract code. This requires more design effort but gives you the most flexibility. If you choose this approach, carefully consider what you want to move to the blockchain. Remember that you have to pay for transactions in a blockchain environment, and those transactions will complete more slowly than in a traditional database application environment.

For example, if you plan to migrate your core supply chain functionality to an Ethereum public blockchain to provide transparency, define the minimum data and functionality you'll need to accomplish that task. Don't put more in the blockchain environment than you really need. If you aren't careful in what you put on the blockchain, you could increase operational costs, slow down your users, and leak more information than you intended. Always start with simple, streamlined features that you deploy to the blockchain, and build from there.

Identifying Interface Data and Transaction Requirements

You start developing a blockchain interface by examining your existing environment and the goals of your project. You learned in the previous section that the degree of flexibility in your design depends on whether you have smart contract code to start with, and whether you can modify it. Once you know your starting point and what abilities you have to modify code in each environment, you can design the data and functional requirements for your interface.

An interface definition basically answers three questions:

>> What do you want the interface to do?

>> What data must you provide to the interface?

>> What data will the interface return to you?

You answer the first question by defining smart contract functions. If your first requirement is to create a new product, you'll probably need a function named createProduct(). It's a good idea to name your functions as verbs, because they carry out actions. In most cases, your functions will create items, get items (that is, fetch and return data), or change the state of some items. (Of course, changing the state of any data really means adding some new data to the blockchain.) You should define all of the actions your new integrated blockchain dApp must carry out and define a function for each one.

After you define each of your new functions, you can answer the second question by defining the input parameters each function needs to carry out its intended purpose. As you design your interface, validate that all required data is either already available in the traditional application, can be generated by the traditional application, or is available by some other means in the blockchain environment. Don't add data into your design unless you can provide that data.

Finally, you must specify what data each function returns to the traditional application. You must identify what data your traditional application needs to maintain integrity with the blockchain data. In this case, some redundancy is required, as in the case of unique identification tokens, and other redundancy may be desired. For example, you may decide to keep copies of supply chain registrations in your local database to support fast lookups for your application's users. Remember that if you do store any redundant data, you have to takes steps to ensure that it stays current and correct. You should only store redundant blockchain data if you can identify specific value in doing so.

After you define all functions, input requirements, and output requirements, you will be ready to write or modify the code to create your integrated blockchain application solution.

Creating or Modifying Contracts to Provide Data Interface

The process of writing smart contract code should be a smooth one, as long as you invested in the design process. A well-designed application is far easier to write than one that lacks a detailed design specification. The output of the design phase should include detailed function definitions, along with input and output requirements, and specifications of what each function does and the state and local data each one needs to operate.

You'll find that coding smart contracts with a detailed specification is little more than translating requirements into another language, Solidity. The design process is more than a simple translation exercise, but it is important that the design phase addresses as many of the development requirements as possible. A good design document leaves few questions for developers to answer. Comprehensive design documents give developers the ability to focus on the most efficient and effective ways to implement the required functionality.

Testing Integrated dApps

Proper testing of integrated applications is an extension of individual testing of each participant application. In other words, you still have to test each individual application first. You should completely test all functionality of your traditional application, and then completely test your blockchain dApp. The testing requirements for integrated dApps depend on properly working components as a foundation.

After you've completed the testing each application component, you can move to integration testing. *Integration testing* is much like full dApp testing. You have to develop tests that run in the context of your existing application. Your integration tests should generate calls to each function you defined as part of the blockchain interface. Your tests should create normal calls, invalid calls, and calls that pass boundary data. Invalid calls include the following:

>> Wrong function name

>> Wrong number or format of input parameters

>> Out of range or bad input data

>> Input data containing boundary values

>> Wrong expected output parameters

>> Attempt to call a function that isn't visible

>> Smart contract function properly completed with return codes

>> Set a timeout for a function call that is too short

>> Reverse a transaction

Your calling application and smart contract code should properly handle each of these situations without generating failures or crashes. Your tests should ensure that all errors are handled in a manner that does not interrupt the normal flow of the application.

Deploying Integrated dApps

Finally, after you are through the testing phase and ready to move your new integrated application to production, it's time to deploy to a live blockchain. The deployment steps for the blockchain dApp are the same as the ones you used when you deployed your supply chain dApp. Truffle makes the deployment process easy. The difference is in the synchronization between the application components.

Because your traditional application will call functions in the blockchain dApp, you can't update your traditional application until the dApp is deployed.

TECHNICAL STUFF

Technically, you can deploy the traditional application before deploying the dApp, as long as your updated traditional application has some configuration control that disables any interaction with the dApp. After you deploy the dApp, you change the configuration to allow the traditional application to communicate with the new dApp.

Here are the three simple steps to deploying all of the components of an integrated blockchain app:

1. **Deploy your fully tested dApp.**
2. **Deploy your fully tested updated traditional application.**
3. **Run any maintenance utilities required to synchronize initial data.**

After both sides are up and running, you can (and should) run real-time tests to ensure that everything works in the live environment. The deployment process should be the easiest step in the process. As long as you start with a solid design, integrating traditional applications with blockchain dApps is an effective way to take advantage of blockchain's many benefits.

5

The Part of Tens

IN THIS CHAPTER

» Examining top free Ethereum frameworks

» Exploring free Ethereum IDEs

» Interacting with the Ethereum blockchain for free

» Keeping your dApps secure for free

» Highlighting great free resources to learn Ethereum

Chapter **13**

Ten Free Ethereum Resources

Many free resources are available to help you develop advanced Ethereum dApps. In Chapter 4 you learn about different tools in four categories: blockchain client, test blockchain, testing framework, and IDE. You don't have to search very hard to find lots of free resources in nearly every category. In Chapter 6 you learn about different options for establishing your Ethereum wallet, some of which are free. The options in those chapters are worth exploring. In Chapters 5 and 6 you install five free tools to help you develop and manage Ethereum dApps. Because you've already learned about five effective free tools in Chapters 5 and 6, I won't cover them again in this chapter.

In *Dummies* Part of Tens fashion, in this chapter you learn about ten more free tools to help you create your own Ethereum blockchain dApps. Some of the resources in this chapter are alternatives to the tools you used in the book's examples, and other complement the tools you're already using. Each of the resources in this chapter has unique features and should be on your list of interesting research ideas. They're all free and they're all worthwhile additions to your Ethereum development toolbox.

Exploring Alternative Ethereum Development Frameworks

You use the Truffle framework for the examples in this book. Although Truffle is the most common framework in use, it isn't the only one. Depending on your needs and preferences, you should look at a couple alternatives. At the end of the day, choose the development framework that fits most closely with your experience and makes developing dApps for Ethereum as frustration-free as possible.

Managing you development with Populus

The *Populus* framework provides many of the same features as Truffle. However, because Truffle focuses on the JavaScript environment, you have to write lots of JavaScript code to automate tasks, test, and maintain dApps using Truffle. That's fine if you have lots of experience with JavaScript and are comfortable in the environment. But if you don't know JavaScript or don't want to invest time to learn it, you may want to look at a framework based on something else.

Populus is a Python-based Ethereum development framework. If you have Python experience or just like working with Python, Populus may be worth looking into. You can get Populus by navigating to `https://populus.readthedocs.io/en/latest`. This web page includes a quick start guide, documentation, and instructions on installing and using Populus. If you like Python, try out Populus to see how it compares with Truffle.

TECHNICAL STUFF

Populus requires that you have Python already installed. Because the Python 2.7 End of Life (EOL) is scheduled for November 2020, you should install Python version 3. Go to `https://populus.readthedocs.io/en/latest` to find the most current Python version for your operating system.

Exploring Ethereum blockchain containers with Cliquebait

Cliquebait is another Ethereum development framework alternative to Truffle. Instead of running a blockchain environment natively on your computer's operating system, Cliquebait uses *Docker containers,* which are similar to a lightweight virtual machines. Docker allows you to launch multiple containers, all running as separate virtual machines (VMs), with far less overhead than running multiple standard VMs. Each standard VM that you launch runs a full copy of an operating system, along with virtual copies of the hardware that the VM's operating system needs to run. A container, such as a Docker container, runs only the operating system components and virtual hardware that the programs need. The result is virtualization with lower resource requirements.

Cliquebait provides a Docker image that provides a single-node Ethereum blockchain that you can use to develop and test your smart contracts. It also supports launching multiple Docker containers to simulate a multi-node blockchain, all running on your computer.

Docker must be installed before you can install and run Cliquebait. Go to `https://docs.docker.com/docker-for-windows/install` for instructions on downloading and installing Docker. After you have Docker installed, go to `https://github.com/f-o-a-m/cliquebait` for instructions in using Cliquebait.

Selecting a Free Integrated Development Environment

The IDE you choose to write code will be the most visible tool in your dApp development toolkit. You'll spend more time using (or fighting) your IDE, so finding the right one is crucial to being productive. The best IDE is in the eye of the beholder. You should try several IDEs and choose the one that is most comfortable to you.

Developing Solidity code with Atom

Atom, like the Visual Studio Code IDE you used in the book's examples, isn't strictly a blockchain-based IDE. It's a powerful general-purpose IDE with Solidity plug-ins. When you add the Etheratom plug-in, you get syntax highlighting, code completion, and the capability to call the Solidity compiler with a single keystroke.

Figure 13-1 is the main Atom interface. It looks and feels much like VS Code, with a character of its own. You can get the Atom IDE at `https://atom.io`. After installing Atom, go to `https://atom.io/packages/etheratom` for instructions on installing the Etheratom plug-in.

Going online with Remix

An alternative to installing an IDE on your own computer is to use a browser-based IDE. *Remix* is a popular IDE that you can access from any web browser. It enables you to write code in Solidity, and then deploy to a blockchain. With Remix, you can easily select a specific Solidity compiler version, along with many features and options you'll find helpful when developing dApps in Solidity.

To get started with Remix, navigate to `https://remix.ethereum.org`. You can add code from your local computer or you can write it right from the Remix editor. Figure 13-2 shows Remix with the SupplyChain.sol smart contract you created in Chapter 9.

Keeping it simple with EthFiddle

Another web-based Solidity IDE is *EthFiddle*. EthFiddle is a great choice for a straightforward web-based IDE for writing and compiling Solidity smart contracts. Unlike Remix, EthFiddle doesn't provide a way to deploy your code. Figure 13-3 shows the SupplyChain.sol smart contract you created in Chapter 9 in the EthFiddle IDE. Navigate to `https://ethfiddle.com` to get started in EthFiddle.

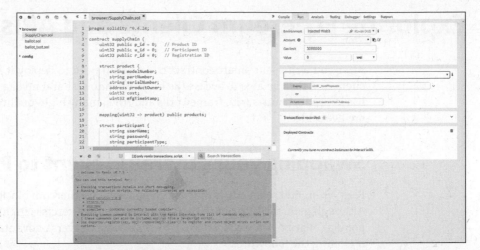

FIGURE 13-2:
Remix web-based IDE.

FIGURE 13-3:
EthFiddle web-based IDE.

Exploring Ethereum Clients and APIs

After you write your smart contract code, you'll need to deploy it to an Ethereum client and then be able to access the blockchain to test and invoke your code after it's in production. As with frameworks and IDEs, many high-quality free resources are available.

Swapping your Ethereum client to Parity

Parity is an Ethereum client that runs a node on an Ethereum blockchain network. Although geth, the Ethereum client you used for the exercises in this book, is more popular, Parity is a good alternative that boasts several advantages over geth, including the following:

» **Faster:** Syncs the full Ethereum blockchain in just hours and is built to reduce CPU and network load.

» **Lower disk space use:** Prunes the Ethereum blocks to use less local disk space.

» **Web-based GUI:** Provides easy-to-access features through a user-friendly web-browser interface.

Navigate to `https://www.parity.io/ethereum` to get started with Parity. If you want to use the Parity UI, navigate to `https://github.com/Parity-JS/shell/releases` to find the latest release. Figure 13-4 shows a newly installed Parity UI. Note that the first time you run the Parity UI, it runs Parity and starts the sync process with the live Ethereum network.

Interacting with Ethereum by using Web3.js

In Chapter 10 you discover how to interact with your smart contracts. Although the techniques you learn make it possible to access blockchain data and run your functions, they aren't elegant. By far the most common way to interact with Ethereum smart contracts is through a collection of libraries written in JavaScript named *Web3.js.* You can write code in JavaScript or any language that supports JavaScript calls. From there, Web3.js makes it easy to interact with Ethereum data and functions.

Navigate to `https://github.com/ethereum/web3.js` to get the latest version of Web3.js, and go to `https://web3js.readthedocs.io` for the latest Web3.js documentation.

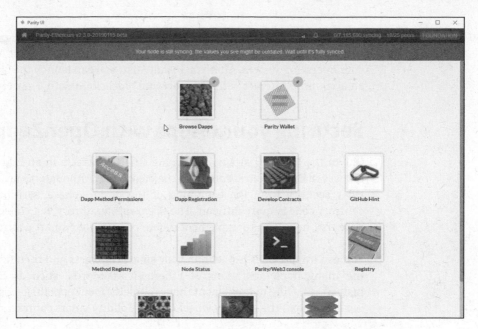

FIGURE 13-4:
Parity UI.

TECHNICAL STUFF

If you're looking for a good Web3.js tutorial, go to www.dappuniversity.com/articles/web3-js-intro and check out Dapp Tutorial's introduction.

Focusing on Wallets and Security

Security is always a concern when developing Ethereum dApps. The nature of blockchain technology makes the deliberate focus on security a required design goal. Building security into dApps depends on having the right building blocks and a solid method to maintain security after deployment. Two free resources that help you write and maintain secure dApps are the Mist wallet and the OpenZeppelin security library.

Protecting your crypto-assets in Mist

Mist is both an Ethereum wallet and an Ethereum browser. Mist is the official wallet for Ethereum, developed by the Ethereum Foundation. It also provides access to dApps, similar to the way popular web browsers give you access to websites around the Internet. Mist does more than just browse blockchain apps; it provides a suite of tools for interacting with the Ethereum network. With Mist, you can generate smart contracts, pool cryptocurrency, and share information among participants who don't trust one another. Mist attempts to make Ethereum blockchain access as easy as possible.

To get started with Mist, use a traditional web browser to navigate to `https://github.com/ethereum/mist/releases` and download the latest Mist release for your operating system. After you install Mist, you can launch the browser to create an account or interact with the Ethereum blockchain with a variety of tools.

Securing your dApps with OpenZeppelin

One of the hardest parts of developing smart contracts in an Ethereum environment is making them secure from the beginning. Although it may be easy to consider security from the beginning of the design phase, writing secure smart contract code is more difficult. The *OpenZeppelin* library is a collection of Solidity code that helps you to implement secure code in your smart contracts.

You can import OpenZeppelin in your smart contracts and then take advantage of the many implementations of Ethereum standards, such as ERC-20 tokens, instead of having to implement them yourself. OpenZeppelin keeps you from having to reinvent the security wheel in your Solidity smart contract code.

To get started with OpenZeppelin, navigate to `https://openzeppelin.org` for instructions on installing and using this valuable library.

Learning More About Developing Ethereum dApps

You learned a lot about Solidity and developing dApps for the Ethereum blockchain in this book. If you want to learn more about Ethereum development and have a lot of fun in the process, check out CryptoZombies. *CryptoZombies* is a step-by-step Solidity tutorial in which you develop a blockchain-based game involving a zombie army you create. As you gain experience, your zombies level up and gain new skills. Navigate to `https://cryptozombies.io` to get started building your own Ethereum game — and zombie army.

Chapter **14**

Ten Design Principles for Distributed Blockchain Apps

Blockchain technology is a disruptive, transformative approach to the way we manage data. It promises to radically change how we carry out tasks that handle sensitive information in shared environments. Critical operations on sensitive data historically required a strong central authority to convince data owners to trust the environment enough to allow it to manage their data.

One of the more difficult obstacles that every blockchain dApp must overcome is building trust. Users have to trust that the software running on the blockchain includes solid measures to provide security and protect privacy before they'll supply sensitive personal and business data. You can go a long way toward building this trust by adhering to several basic design guidelines. If you follow the ten design goals for blockchain applications presented in this chapter, you'll help encourage your users to trust your application enough to use it and rely on it.

Designing for Trust

One of the primary reasons most organizations move toward blockchain solutions is its capability to share data among nodes that do not trust one another. If you think about it, that really sets a high bar for dApp developers. To develop a successful dApp, you have to convince your users to trust your software with their data as you send it to a large number of other nodes that you don't trust (and they don't trust, either).

Trust is normally (but not always) transitive. (Yes, I'm taking you back to math class. If A = B, and B = C, then A = C. You're welcome.) This is the most common way we, as humans, deal with trust. If I trust Mary, and Joe trusts me, then Joe is probably fine with trusting Mary. Let's assume I'm a food critic. Joe trusts that I recommend good food. If I post that I really like Mary's peach pie, then Joe will be more likely to try her peach pie since Joe trusts my taste in food. But that doesn't track with a trustless environment. In the case of blockchain dApps, your users trust you, but you don't trust others in your own blockchain network.

Your first design goal is a high-level objective that you have to keep as a top-of-mind motivator for all decisions. Many of the subsequent design goals support this one: Design your dApps for trust. That goal means you want to consider what your users wan, and what makes them feel that they can trust your dApp.

Users have to know that you'll take care of their data. Your dApp should not hide anything and should make it easy to check up on what's happening. It should clearly communicate good and bad information and provide an overall sense of well-being. Although that's a tall order for software, it's necessary to build trust.

The most important aspect of designing for trust is understanding who your users are and what makes them feel comfortable. In short, know your users. Know what they want and how you can convince them that you aren't going to waste their time or take advantage of their trust in you.

Enforcing Consistency

One of the easiest ways to avoid confusion is to limit the options and conflicting experiences in your dApps. Microsoft learned long ago the power in consistency. They developed standards for how to interact with users, and explored and defined every aspect of creating a user interface. That's why Microsoft applications feel similar to one another. If you've used one Microsoft application, you'll recognize at least the general user interface in other Microsoft applications. (And if you've used Microsoft products for a while, you'll remember the huge disruption Microsoft caused when they converted to a tile-based user interface — largely because everyone was so comfortable with the legacy Microsoft interface.)

For example, if you want to find the current version of a Windows program you're running, you can almost always click or tap Help, then click or tap the About menu item on the Help menu. Figure 14-1 shows the About menu item in VS Code. The About menu item exists in pretty much every Windows application and shows basic information, including the version number, of the program you're running. That simple example of user interface consistency makes it easy for anyone to find application information without having to hunt for it.

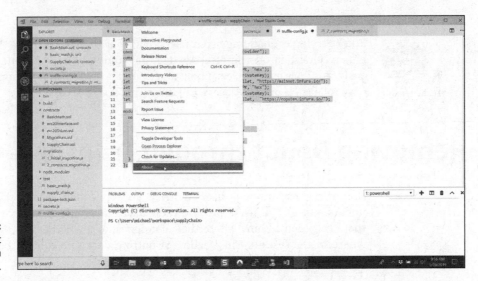

FIGURE 14-1:
Help ➪ About
menu item
in VS Code.

Figure 14-2 shows the About dialog box in VS Code. You'll find release information for most Windows applications by clicking or tapping Help➪About. That's the power of consistency.

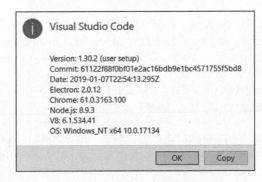

FIGURE 14-2:
VS Code About
dialog box.

Your dApps should define clear standards for every user interaction. When you ask your users to provide input, do it in the same way throughout your dApp. When a user enters a product ID in multiple places, the input field should look the same in each location. Use the same colors, fonts, and input method to give your dApp a consistent look and feel. Another area in which you'll find consistency in GUI apps is keyboard shortcuts. You can almost always use Ctrl-C to copy highlighted text and Ctrl-V to paste that text in a new location. Consistent keyboard shortcuts make it even easier to learn and use new software.

In the same way, standardize all output. Error messages and alerts are prime areas for standardization. When possible, use common input and output layers, so that all input and output uses the same set of functions. The entire dApp will look more consistent.

REMEMBER

You're trying to encourage your users to keep using your dApp. A dApp that presents a consistent user interface is one the builds trust. Consistency also makes it easier for your users to learn how to use your software, and an application that is easy to learn is one that users will likely prefer and accept.

Removing Doubt through Transparency

One of the reasons why users distrust an application is that they don't really understand it. The users provide their data but aren't sure what happens after that. They don't know where their data goes, and whether it's even still somewhere in the system. This feeling of putting data into a black box can be even stronger with blockchain dApps.

As blockchain technology becomes more popular, overall awareness of its features is increasing. That means many of your users will know that your dApp sends their data to many other computers, potentially all over the world. One of the hurdles you will have to overcome is convincing your users that you are protecting their sensitive data.

Clearly communicate what data your dApp needs, why it needs each type of data, and what you do with it. You won't need to convey this information every time you prompt for data, but it should be available the first time you interact with a new user and on demand thereafter. You should also make it easy for users to see what they have done (and what your dApp has done with their data.) Providing transparency at each step gives users a sense of confidence.

Make it easy for your users to drill down and get verification of actions. This level of transparency gives users the confidence that your dApp is doing what it claims to do, and can reduce the concern that your dApp is hiding something. Depending on the level of user concern and your own design guidelines, you can build transparency into each workflow or into on demand functions to allow power users to drill down at will.

Providing Feedback, Guidance, and Setting Expectations

The next design goal is providing feedback and guidance and setting expectations. This goal is a logical extension of transparency. Whereas transparency makes transaction and workflow details readily available to users, feedback, guidance, and expectation setting puts transparency into the normal workflow. Instead of just allowing users to see what happened, you should present them with informative feedback at every significant workflow step.

For example, if you are a manufacturer and have just transferred the ownership of a new tractor to a shipper, your new supply chain dApp may give you a message "You just transferred tractor with serial number ABC-12345 to Unified Shipping — Transaction number 456778." Of course, you'd probably get more details for a capital item transfer, but you get the idea. The dApp provided feedback that essentially says "Hey, good job. Here's what you did." Informative feedback is the first step in convincing users to trust your dApp. The feedback gives them the assurance that they're using the software correctly.

You can extend the feedback example to inform users of the next step as well. In the tractor example, your feedback message could also include a "Do you want to release the title now?" message with the option to click or tap a button to go to the next step. End-of-task prompts like this help to ensure that users understand the proper workflow and give them the impression that the software is helping them do their jobs correctly. When software makes users more effective, it goes a long way toward building trust. Everyone loves software that makes them look good!

Handling Mistakes with Class

Face it, errors happen. And sometimes those errors are big ones. I hope you found all the big errors in your software during testing. (You did test exhaustively, right?) If you did, most of the errors you encounter in production will be user errors.

TIP

When you handle user errors, try to avoid any notifications that subtly say "You messed up!" Focus on resolving the situation, not placing blame.

You probably remember using your first GPS device in a car. In the early days of GPS, if you deviated from the suggested route, you heard a fairly stern "Rerouting" message. The voice might as well have said "You're not going where I told you. Hang on, I'll tell you how to get back to what I told you in the first place." Error messages should inform users as to what has happened but focus on what to do next. Yes, the GPS did that, but it was generally after a subtle scolding. Don't scold your users.

On the other hand, don't spend too much time focusing on errors. Overly verbose error messages can be confusing and take too long to read. Get to the point. Always design error handling from the user perspective. Give users everything they need to respond quickly and decisively to errors, and nothing more.

TECHNICAL STUFF

Error messages help end users understand what is happening, and also help support personnel when they're troubleshooting. Design your error messaging system so that it provides necessary user messages as well as more verbose messages on demand for troubleshooting and investigations.

Remember that the blockchain is immutable, so any errors that make it into a block will always be there. Your dApp should resolve user issues with data before storing that data to the blockchain. The trick to handling errors is to guide users to the right solution without slowing them down. That requires attention to who your users are, how they use your dApp, and what they need to resolve a problem. One of your design goals should be to provide error handling that meets your users' needs in all cases.

Designing Functions that Focus on User Actions, Not Data

Functions provide the actions of your smart contracts. One way to look at smart contracts is that they are made up of data (nouns) and actions (verbs). Framing smart contracts in this way makes it easier to describe and design them, and generally results in an application that flows well from a user perspective.

Because all applications exist to meet some users' requirements, it makes sense to design software in light of the user. At the highest level, if a user wants to create a new order, your should start with a function named `createNewOrder()`. You might change things as you refine your design, but starting with a user perspective helps to maintain authenticity with the software's goals. Designing technical components that fulfill user goals also helps to avoid deviating too far from high-level functional goals.

Many of today's software development organizations depend on methods that start with user stories. As a developer, you'll be asked to produce software that fulfils a requirement that looks like "As a user, I want to _____." Starting your smart contract with a function that matches what users want to do (that is, the filled-in blank from the preceding statement), is a good design strategy for making user-friendly software.

Every function doesn't have to map directly to user actions, but your high-level functions should look like they satisfy user stories. You will always need lower-level task-oriented or data-oriented functions to carry out the technical steps of any task. It's okay if those functions don't map directly to user stories. But your lower-level functions should all play parts in the functions that users interact with. As a very general rule of thumb, your public functions should look a lot like user story responses.

Storing Data Based on User Actions, Not Data Structures

Users may not interact directly with data, but you should still attempt to organize data based on user requirements. This general goal is more a rule of thumb. Use this goal when initially designing your smart contract data requirements. You'll likely need to refine the design and change it, but starting with data mapped to user requests helps your software stay true to user requirements.

For instance, if you're designing software to create and maintain orders, start with a Solidity `struct` statement that defines an order the way a user sees it. An order can be a collection of fields that describe it, such as order number, order date, customer order, instructions, and a list of order lines. Order lines contain fields such as product number, price, and quantity. You can define this as a `struct` of variables and a list of order line `struct`s.

Regardless of the technical details of how you define data, the main purpose of this goal is to consider how users will use data, and try to present the data that way. If you make orders directly available to users to promote transparency in your software, you want to make the orders as easy to access as possible. You don't want to promote transparency and then make users work hard to figure out what your data means. Making data easy to access and understand will build even more trust.

Keeping It Simple

You have many things to consider when designing a dApp. Although focusing on users should help direct design decisions, the tendency is to attempt to meet every user need. If left unchecked, this desire to do it all will make your software overly complex and difficult to use. Giving users lots of choices sounds like a good goal at first, but an overwhelmed user is not going to like (or use) your software.

The general-purpose adage "keep it simple, stupid" is still relevant. It's a stern reminder that simplicity is far smarter than complexity. You may have heard that "a confused mind always says no," but you want your users to accept and use your dApp. You want them to find that your software makes them more effective and efficient. To achieve those goals, you have to make understanding and using your software easy and clear.

Simplicity starts with the user interface, but it doesn't stop there. Every aspect of your application's functional and data design must be as simple as possible. Don't try to do too much. Instead, determine what your users need and want most, and do that. Prioritize the functionality that will make your software stand out. Keeping it simple takes more work, but often results in a focused, consistent product that users will use.

Expecting Blockchain Access to Be Expensive

Another handy design goal that will help you avoid post-development rework is pretending from the beginning that storing data on the blockchain is expensive. Because in reality, it is. For many of us who started programming way back when Y2K was far in the future, storage is much cheaper today than it used to be. Most developers today don't have to worry about data size or where to store it. Blockchain is changing all that. Now, instead of having tons of cheap and fast storage available, you have to pay as you go.

Expensive storage isn't a new thing in blockchain, but it can be easy to forget. If you remind yourself that storage is expensive early on, you'll be more likely to think about storage options more thoroughly. For example, do you need to store the city and state where a product will be shipped? City and state are both dependent on zip code (or postal code in more generic settings.) You can store the zip code in the shipping address, and then just look up the corresponding city and state using an online API at runtime.

Separating data such as the zip code example may not make sense for your application, but you'll always benefit from thinking through your data storage options. The most expensive storage options are almost always the result of poor design planning. Don't design blockchain dApps the same way you design traditional database applications. They just aren't the same. Design with a different mindset and you'll end up with a better software product.

Staying Out of the User's Way

Earlier goals in this chapter focus on your users' needs. A good application meets the most important user needs in a way that helps them be more effective and efficient. However, your design should consider not only what your application does but also what it doesn't do.

Every application has constraints and limitations. This design goal focuses on another thing that your application doesn't do: It doesn't get in the user's way. Simply put, your application should help users, not slow them down. Your user interface should help users do their jobs, and the transitions between user interface elements should be intuitive and instructive when necessary.

Sometimes you'll have to take data from users, and then store it on the blockchain. (You remember that this is expensive, right?) Because you know that you're going to make users pay to store data on the blockchain, don't make them wait for it as well. Whenever possible, let your users do something productive while the function that handles their data operates in the background. This might be a good place in your code to use events.

Do everything you can to avoid becoming an obstacle to your users. Nobody likes to wait. Design with thought and your product will have a much better chance of meeting your users' needs.

IN THIS CHAPTER

» **Predicting future events**

» **Playing games and collecting cryptocollectibles**

» **Exchanging and paying with cryptocurrencies**

» **Identifying yourself and blockchain-tweeting about it**

» **Finding jobs and computing power**

Chapter **15**

Top Ten Ethereum Projects

Blockchain technology in general, and Ethereum in particular, is rapidly growing in popularity. Increasing numbers of organizations are embracing Ethereum for new projects. The variety of projects that use Ethereum as their foundation is almost limitless. A quick look at the State of the dApps website shows how many Ethereum projects exist in different categories and how popular they are. Navigate to www.stateofthedapps.com/ to explore a large number of popular dApps. This resource is a great way to stay current on trending dApps.

This chapter lists ten of the top Ethereum projects. Although these projects are just a small representative sample of what is out there, they will give you some exposure to what others are doing with Ethereum. I hope these projects give you some ideas for new and exciting ways that Ethereum can help transform your organization.

In spite of the diversity of functionality in each project in this chapter, they are all built on Ethereum. Each project uses smart contracts running on the EVM to carry out functionality and the Ethereum blockchain to store state data.

Predicting Future Events with Gnosis

Gnosis is one of the many innovative companies using Ethereum in interesting ways. Gnosis provides a platform for prediction markets. The Gnosis Olympia product is the alpha version of their platform. Using Olympia, participants get an initial balance of OLY tokens, pretend money they can use in Olympia, which they use to make predictions on a variety of topics. Participants can win GNO tokens for making successful predictions.

Participants who set up predictions associate the prediction with an oracle, for outcome validation. For example, the true value of a specific stock price at a specific date and time is easily validated by comparing the prediction with published stock prices. The stock price data source would be the oracle that the stock price prediction uses for validation.

Gnosis Olympia provides the platform for participants to determine the probability of some outcome. You can use Olympia to determine an expected value of some item of value. Knowing an item's value gives you more leverage in negotiations.

Another possible use case is with elections. Distributed prediction markets could emerge to provide better forecasts of upcoming elections. Political polling has undergone criticism for a lack of precision, and emerging products could help increase their accuracy.

You can find out more about Gnosis on their website at `https://blog.gnosis.pm`.

Crowdsourcing Event Predictions in Augur

Augur is another offering in the prediction market category. Like Gnosis, participants can record events and then provide a prediction on the outcome of the event. Augur rewards participants with REP tokens in exchange for providing accurate data related to the event and for voting with the majority.

Augur is based on crowdsourced data and gets more accurate with the inclusion of participant data. That's why submitting accurate data results in a reward. An oracle validates event data and outcome, but the emphasis is still on crowdsourced input.

Augur is completely decentralized and depends on smart contracts and the Ethereum blockchain to operate. Its goal is to provide a global portal that generates better forecasts about the outcome of any future event that enjoys widespread global interest.

To learn more about Augur navigate to their website at `www.augur.net`.

Managing Decentralized Organizations with Aragon

Aragon is a platform dedicated to helping manage decentralized organizations, which often suffer from a lack of infrastructure and functionality. Aragon participants purchase Aragon Network Tokens (ANT) from one of several popular cryptocurrency exchanges, and use ANT to pay for Aragon services.

Aragon facilitates distributed autonomous organization governance, fundraising, and accounting. For example, Aragon participants can pose questions to their organization for voting. The Aragon environment handles all of the details of managing the voting process, resulting in verified election outcomes. Voting is just one of the features of the platform.

The Aragon project has as its goals to empower decentralized organization participants by promoting participation and providing financial transparency. Aragon enables organizations to exist outside the traditional hierarchical, centralized model.

You can find out more about Aragon on their website at `https://aragon.org/`.

Breeding and Collecting Cryptokitties

Ethereum isn't just about cryptocurrency and business function. You can find some fun games in the Ethereum space as well. *Cryptokitties*, one of the first Ethereum-based games, is still popular. This revolutionary game introduced blockchain-based cryptocollectibles. That's right. Cryptokitties are collectable.

Each cryptokitty is unique. Technically, each cryptokitty is an ERC-721 token and has a unique set of cattributes (cryptokitty DNA) that come from each cryptokitty's parents. That's right, you don't create cryptokitties; you breed them. And just like in real life (well, kind of), you can either trust genetic luck to create a rare and valuable cryptokitty, or you can pay a siring fee to another cryptokitty for the capability to breed using their cryptokitties. Each cryptokitty has a different value, based on the rarity of its cattributes. In the past, some cryptokitties with rare cattributes (and a favorable ETH exchange rate) sold for over $100,000 USD.

Figure 15-1 shows the Cryptokitties website with examples of a few cryptokitties, each with its own unique cattributes. To learn more about cryptokitties, navigate to their website at www.cryptokitties.co.

FIGURE 15-1: Cryptokitties website.

Exchanging Tokens with IDEX

You learn how to create your own ERC-20 token in Chapter 9, but you don't learn much about how to buy tokens. Thousands of ERC-20 tokens are in use. Before you can use a token to pay for something, you have to acquire it. Some tokens are free, but others must be purchased. To purchase a token, you must exchange currency or cryptocurrency, so you need an organization that provides exchange services.

IDEX is a decentralized exchange (DEX) that specializes in trading between ETH and ERC-20 tokens. It confirms transactions in its smart contract, without waiting for Ethereum block mining. IDEX's capability to confirm transactions in real time allows traders to trade continuously. Orders are recorded on the Ethereum blockchain in the order in which they were received, but traders don't have to wait for their tokens. They receive them as soon as their order is approved by the smart contract.

Figure 15-2 shows the IDEX website with a list of the most active Ethereum ERC-20 tokens. To learn more about IDEX, navigate to their website at https:// idex.market.

FIGURE 15-2:
IDEX website.

Creating Your Digital Identity with uPort

The *uPort* dApp is an innovative initiative with a simple purpose: to provide a decentralized identity for everyone, stored on the Ethereum blockchain. Users register their identity through uPort. Once authenticated, users can use the uPort digital identity to sign digital contracts and interact with other services that require validated identities.

The uPort dApp has scores of potential uses. One of the most visible needs uPort could help address is in providing people who have lost physical identification items to still provide proof of identity when required. Survivors of catastrophic events often have no identification with them. Accessing an immutable digital identification could help alleviate this problem. Digital identities could help with immigration, voting, and other cases where identification is required.

To learn more about uPort, navigate to their website at www.uport.me.

Sharing Your Thoughts on the Blockchain with EtherTweet

As its name suggests, EtherTweet is a blockchain alternative to Twitter. The main difference is that EtherTweet is censorship free because all messages are stored on the Ethereum blockchain. You can post up to 160 characters.

Although prices change based on the current value of ether, creating an Ether-Tweet account costs about 2 cents and each tweet costs about one third of a cent. Figure 15-3 shows the EtherTweet website with instructions on using their web interface to post and read tweets. To learn more about EtherTweet, navigate to their website at `http://ethertweet.net`.

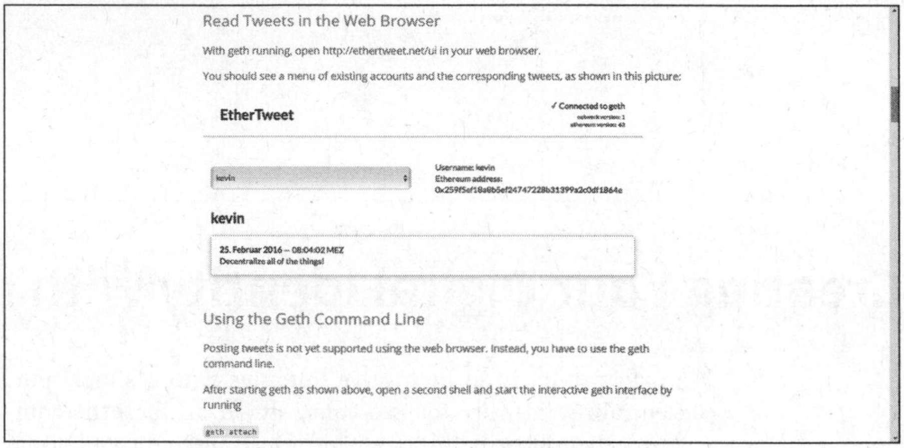

FIGURE 15-3: EtherTweet web interface.

Searching for Jobs with EthLance

EthLance is a distributed platform for freelancers and employers to find each other, engage in jobs, and transfer payment in ether. EthLance is part of the district0x network, which is a collective of decentralized marketplaces and communities. One of EthLance's outstanding features is that it does not collect any fees.

Membership in EthLance is free, and both freelancers and employers can use the network to match personnel with open jobs. Once work is complete, employers can pay freelancers directly using ether. The entire EthLance platform runs in Ethereum. The transparent nature of EthLance and its zero fees model make it a great resource for self-employed individuals.

Figure 15-4 shows the EthLance website with their "how it works" graphic showing how freelances and employers can use the services. To learn more about EthLance, navigate to their website at `https://ethlance.com`.

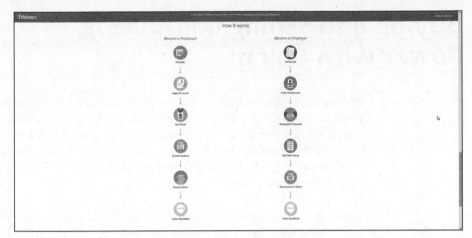

FIGURE 15-4:
EthLance website with participation description.

Using TenX to Pay with Cryptocurrency

TenX allows customers to use ether and other cryptocurrencies at retailers to pay for purchases around the world. Although most retailers don't directly support cryptocurrencies yet, TenX created their own line of crypto debit cards and credit cards that link up with its proprietary crypto wallet. The TenX cards provide the bridge between cryptocurrencies and traditional payment vehicles.

TenX records all payment transactions on the blockchain, and has plans for a larger network that will allow apps to communicate across multiple blockchains.

Figure 15-5 shows the TenX website with an image of their TenX debit card. To learn more about TenX, navigate to their website at `https://tenx.tech/en`.

FIGURE 15-5:
TenX debit card.

Buying and Selling Computing Power with Golem

The last innovative Ethereum project is Golem. *Golem* is a decentralized marketplace for buying and selling computing power. Whether you have excess computing power that you'd like to sell, or you need to temporarily rent more computing power to complete a project, Golem can help. You can use Golem supercomputers after paying in native GNT token, or you can earn GNT for letting others use your excess computing power.

Figure 15-6 shows the Golem website. To learn more about Golem, navigate to their website at `https://golem.network`.

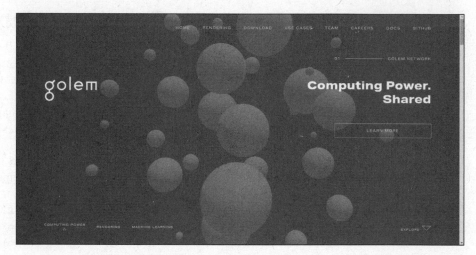

FIGURE 15-6:
Golem website.

Index

Symbols

^ (caret) symbol, Solidity smart
contracts, 134

A

access control, data storage, 207

access modifiers, Solidity

  `constant` access modifier,
143–144

  `pure` access modifier, 144

  `view` access modifier, 143

Accounts window, Ganache, 85

active chain, 35

address data type, 138

`allowance()` function

  ERC-20 tokens, 160

  payment token smart
contract, 150

`allowed` data item, payment
token smart contract, 150

ANT (Aragon Network
Tokens), 241

Apollo 11 moon landing, 22

applications

  coding/development phase,
development lifecycle,
73–74

  dApps, 18

    block structure, 60–64

    deploying, 191–204

    design principles, 229–237

    development tools, 69–73

    gas units, 68–69

    learning resources, 228

    overview, 59–60

    smart contracts, 64–65,
66–67

    traditional apps versus,
210–211

deploying code

  compiling code, 203

  ether, 199–202

  to Ganache test blockchain,
192–193

  integrated dApps, 216–217

  to live blockchain
environment, 195–196

  overview, 191–192

  preparing configuration for,
196–198

  to public test blockchains,
193–195

  smart contracts, 118–119,
120–122

  with Truffle, 203–204

digital identity management,
49–51

  device identities, 50

  ERC-725 standard, 51

  fraud and identity theft,
50–51

  overview, 49–50

financial services, 45–49

  banking, 46–48

  escrow, 48

  ICOs, 48–49

  overview, 45–46

governance, 54–56

  government spending, 55

  notary, 56

  policy development, 55

  tax payment, 54–55

  voting, 55, 240

industry, 51–54

  energy, 52–53

  healthcare, 52

  overview, 51

  supply chain, 53–54

overview, 43–45

testing

  command line testing,
181–185

  compilers and testing
frameworks, 72

  debugging, 190

  error handling, 188–189

  Ethereum, 17

  with Ganache, 178–181

  integration testing, 215–216

  with JavaScript, 185–187

  logging activity, 189–190

  overview, 175

  testing blockchain, 72, 83–86

  testing lifecycle, 177

  testing quality, 177–178

  writing tests from
beginning, 176

writing code

  Ganache test environment,
113–114

  gas units, 124

  smart contracts, 115–124

  Truffle project, 110–113

`approve()` function

  ERC-20 tokens, 160

  payment token smart
contract, 150

Aragon, 241

Aragon Network Tokens
(ANT), 241

`assert()` function, 146

Atom, 73, 223–224

Augur, 240

R

real estate applications, 47–48

Receipt root field, headers, 62

registration structure, supply chain smart contract, 151, 157

Remix, 72, 73, 224–225

Remote Method Invocation (RMI), 27

Remote Procedure Call (RPC), 27

remote processes
  communicating between, 25–26, 27–28
  launching, 26, 27–28

replication, blockchains, 41

`require()` function
  error handling, 146
  testing software, 189

resilience
  blockchain storage versus database storage, 209–210
  blockchains, 41

return values, testing for, 182

`revert()` function
  error handling, 146
  testing software, 189

Rinkeby test blockchain
  ether for, 200
  overview, 195

RMI (Remote Method Invocation), 27

Ropsten test blockchain
  ether for, 199
  overview, 194–195

RPC (Remote Procedure Call), 27

S

schema, database, 207

security
  Ethereum wallet, 227–228
  smart contracts, 170–171

semantics errors, 190

Serpent language, 66

Settings window, Ganache, 85, 112, 179

Signature field, transactions, 63

Single Point of Failure (SPoF), 209

single-line comments, Solidity smart contracts, 134

smart contracts
  access modifiers, 143–144
    `constant` access modifier, 143
    `pure` access modifier, 144
    `view` access modifier, 143
  coding, 116–117
  compiling code, 119–120
  creating new contracts, 151–157
    ERC-20 token interface, 153–154
    ERC-20 token smart contract, 154–155
    overview, 151–153
    supply chain smart contract, 155–157
  data storage, 136–140
  defined, 9
  deploying code, 118–119, 120–122
  designing, 115
  designing integration and, 213–214
  development lifecycle, 73–75
  Ethereum, 12–13
  events, 163–168
    defining, 165–166
    implementing, 163–165
    triggering, 166–168
  flow of execution statements, 144–145
  functions, 157–163
    ERC-20 token, 157–160
    supply chain, 160–163
  gas units, 140–142
  handling errors and exceptions, 145–146

invoking code, 122–124

minimal functionality, 171–172

modifying to provide data interface, 215

overview, 64–65, 125–126

ownership, 168–170

security, 170–171

Solidity, 66–67, 132–136
  comments section, 134–135
  contract section, 135–136
  import section, 135
  overview, 133
  `pragma` directive, 134

supply chain
  asset management, 130–132
  obstacles to implementing, 127–129
  overview, 126–127, 148–151
  payment services, 129–130
  payment token smart contract, 149–150
  supply chain smart contract, 150–151

Turing complete, 65

visibility modifiers, 142–144

smart meters, 52–53

software testing
  command line testing, 181–185
  compilers and testing frameworks, 72
    Embark, 72
    installing, 86–91
    Populus, 72
    Remix, 72
    Solidity compile, 72
    Solidity compiler, 72
    Truffle, 72
  debugging, 190
  error handling, 188–189
  Ethereum, 17
  with Ganache, 178–181
  integration testing, 215–216

T

tax payment applications, 54–55

TenX, 15, 245

test blockchains

deploying dApps to, 192–196

installing, 83–86

Kovan test blockchain

ether for, 200

overview, 195

Rinkeby test blockchain

ether for, 200

overview, 195

Ropsten test blockchain

ether for, 199

overview, 194–195

testing environment, installing, 86–91

testing phase, in development lifecycle, 73–74

testing software

command line testing, 181–185

compilers and testing frameworks, 72

Embark, 72

installing, 86–91

Populus, 72

Remix, 72

Solidity compile, 72

Solidity compiler, 72

Truffle, 72

debugging, 190

error handling, 188–189

Ethereum, 17

with Ganache, 178–181

integration testing, 215–216

with JavaScript, 185–187

logging activity, 189–190

overview, 175

testing blockchain

Cliquebait, 72

Ganache, 72

installing, 83–86

Local Ethereum Network, 72

Truffle, 72

testing lifecycle, 177

testing quality, 177–178

writing tests from beginning, 176

three-tier processing architecture, 23

Timestamp field, headers, 62

timestamp ordering, DBMS, 37

To field, transactions, 63

token exchange services, 242–243

tokens, Ethereum

defined, 130

ERC-20 tokens

functions, 157–160

interface, 153–154

smart contracts, 154–155

standard, 49, 130

`totalSupply` data item, payment token smart contract, 150

`totalSupply()` function

ERC-20 tokens, 160

payment token smart contract, 150

traceable data history, 45

Transaction root field, headers, 62

transactions, Ethereum

Data field, 64

fees, 141–142

To field, 63

Gas limit field, 63, 124

Gas price field, 63, 124

Nonce field, 63

Signature field, 63

Value field, 64

`transfer()` function

ERC-20 tokens, 158–159

payment token smart contract, 150

`transferFrom()` function

ERC-20 tokens, 159

payment token smart contract, 150

`transferToOwner()` function, supply chain smart contract, 162–163

transparency

blockchain storage versus database storage, 209

blockchains, 41

as dApp design goal, 232–233

Ethereum applications, 44–45

government spending applications, 55

supply chain applications, 53

Trezor wallet, 103

triggering events, 166–168

Truffle, 72

connecting to Ganache blockchain, 178–180

creating project, 110–111

deploying dApps with, 203–204

downloading and installing, 86–91

editing config file, 111–113

`try/catch` structure, testing software, 189

Turing complete smart contracts, 65

Twitter, blockchain alternative to, 243–244

U

`uint` data type, 138

uncle blocks, 60–61

underflows, testing for, 182

uPort dApp, 243

users, dApp design goals for

avoiding obstacles, 237

consistency, 230–232

data storage, 235–237

error handling, 233–234

expectation setting, 233

feedback, 233

functions with user focus, 234–235

guidance, 233

simplicity, 236

transparency, 232–233

trust, 229–230

V

Value field, transactions, 64

view access modifier, Solidity, 143

Vim Solidity, 73

Viper language, 66

visibility modifiers, Solidity, 142–143

external visibility modifier, 143

internal visibility modifier, 143

overview, 142–143

private visibility modifier, 143

public visibility modifier, 143

Visual Studio Code, 73, 92–94

voting applications, 55, 240

W

wallets

defined, 17

hardware wallets

handling, 99

KeepKey wallet, 103

Ledger Nano S wallet, 103

overview, 102

Trezor wallet, 103

MetaMask, 104–106

Mist, 101, 227–228

overview, 95–96

paper wallets

ETHAddress, 103

MyEtherWallet, 103

overview, 99–100

security and, 227–228

software wallets, 97–98

cold wallets, 97–98

desktop wallets, 98, 101

hot wallets, 97–98

mobile wallets, 98, 102

web wallets, 98, 100–101

web wallets

defined, 98

Guarda, 101

MyEtherWallet, 101

overview, 100

Web3.js, 226–227

While statement, smart contracts, 144

Wirex, 15

writing code

Ganache, 113–114

gas units, 124

smart contracts

coding, 116–117

compiling code, 119–120

deploying code, 118–119, 120–122

designing, 115

invoking code, 122–124

Truffle project, 110–113

creating, 110–111

editing config file, 111–113

About the Author

Michael G. Solomon, PhD, CISSP, PMP, CISM, PenTest+ is a security, privacy, blockchain, and data science author, consultant, and speaker who specializes in leading teams in achieving and maintaining secure and effective IT environments. As an IT professional and consultant since 1987, Dr. Solomon has led project teams for many Fortune 500 companies and has authored and contributed to more than 20 books and numerous training courses. From 1998 until 2001, he served a Computer Science instructor in the Kennesaw State University's Computer Science and Information Sciences (CSIS) department, is a Professor of Cyber Security and Global Business with Blockchain Technology at the University of the Cumberlands, and holds a PhD in Computer Science and Informatics from Emory University.

Dedication

I want to thank God for blessing me so richly with such a wonderful family, and I want to thank my family for their support throughout the years. My best friend and wife of over three decades, Stacey, is my biggest cheerleader and supporter through many professional and academic projects. I would not be who I am without her.

And both our sons have always been sources of support and inspiration. To Noah, who still challenges me, keeps me sharp, and tries to keep me relevant, and Isaac, who left us far too early. We miss you, son.

Author's Acknowledgments

All quality projects of any size are team efforts. I greatly appreciate and value the input from this book's project team, Specifically, my technical editor, G. Mark Hardy, provided valuable input to keep what you find in this book technically accurate, and the project manager, Susan Pink, did an astounding job throughout the project of keeping us all on track and making sure that I had what I needed to keep writing. Good PMs aren't as plentiful as you'd think.

Publisher's Acknowledgments

Executive Editor: Steve Hayes

Project Editor: Susan Pink

Copy Editor: Susan Pink

Technical Editor: G. Mark Hardy

Editorial Assistant: Matt Lowe

Sr. Editorial Assistant: Cherie Case

Production Editor: G. Vasanth Koilraj

Cover Image: © myella/iStock.com